WILD,
TAMED,
LOST,
REVIVED

———

WILD, TAMED, LOST, REVIVED

The Surprising Story of Apples in the South

Diane Flynt

FOREWORD BY **Sean Brock**

PHOTOGRAPHS BY **Angie Mosier**

A Ferris and Ferris Book

THE UNIVERSITY OF NORTH CAROLINA PRESS

Chapel Hill

This book was published under the

Marcie Cohen Ferris and William R. Ferris Imprint

of the University of North Carolina Press.

Designed and set in Miller, Sentinel, and Halis types by Kim Bryant

Manufactured in the United States of America

Cover art courtesy of Angie Mosier.

Endpaper, front: Sticks of scion wood for grafting from the Foggy Ridge Cider orchard.

Library of Congress Cataloging-in-Publication Data

Names: Flynt, Diane, author. | Mosier, Angie, photographer. | Brock, Sean,

writer of foreword.

Title: Wild, tamed, lost, revived : the surprising story of apples in the South /

Diane Flynt ; foreword by Sean Brock and photographs by Angie Mosier.

Description: Chapel Hill : The University of North Carolina Press, [2023] |

"A Ferris and Ferris book." | Includes bibliographical references and index.

Identifiers: LCCN 2023017145 | ISBN 9781469676944 (cloth ; alk. paper) |

ISBN 9781469676951 (ebook)

Subjects: LCSH: Apple industry—Southern States—History. | Apple industry—

Social aspects—Southern States. | Apples—Southern States—History. | Apples—Social

aspects—Southern States. | Apples—Varieties—Southern States. | Crop diversification—

Southern States. | Southern States—Social life and customs—History. | BISAC: HISTORY /

United States / State & Local / South (AL, AR, FL, GA, KY, LA, MS, NC, SC, TN, VA, WV) |

SOCIAL SCIENCE / Agriculture & Food (see also POLITICAL SCIENCE / Public Policy /

Agriculture & Food Policy)

Classification: LCC HD9259.A6 F596 2023 | DDC 634/.110975—dc23/eng/20230616

LC record available at https://lccn.loc.gov/2023017145

In memory of my father,

JAMES CLIFFORD HOGG

1918–92

CONTENTS

FOREWORD
Sean Brock

Whenever I crave the perfect apple butter or get a wild hair to make the most amazing apple cider vinegar that anyone has ever tasted, I know who to call. I count myself lucky that when I ask Diane about the possibility of making something unique, like a Hewe's Crab Apple Cider Vinegar (which *is* amazing, by the way), she's usually more excited than I am. She personally delivered the juice for this crazy idea, and I value that vinegar more than any bottle of Pappy Van Winkle I've ever had.

When my phone buzzes, *Chef, you have another package from Diane Flynt. Where would you like it?* I always say, *Put it somewhere safe with a big sign on it that says, "Do Not Touch."* That is how important Diane's apples are to my work. These boxes hold 300 years of the South's apple history, full of the most interesting varieties I've ever seen, each with their own note card explaining each apple's history, present, and future. I carefully place each piece of fruit on wooden trays with their respective note cards from Diane and photograph them. We taste them raw, and we taste them cooked; we take notes and file that wisdom away. The flavors and aromas range from hard apple candy to complex and earthy. They don't look perfect, uniform, or polished. People on our team always ask what is wrong with them, as they tend to appear rusty, dirty, and bruised before they get polished for the grocery store shelves. The answer is that there's nothing wrong with these apples at all.

Usually, we will judge an apple by the way it tastes raw, and I remember the first time Diane showed me the ropes she noticed that my eyes didn't light up like they normally do when a flavor sings to me. She explained with her winning smile that the character of an apple may not present itself until it's fermented and turned into a refined beverage. I bit into the apple again; it was great, really great, but still not extraordinary. My mind was spinning, and she handed me a glass. "Now taste this," she said. "It's an extremely elegant cider, and it's made from that exact apple."

Tasting that cider was a revelation. Knowing what can come of a single piece of fruit, knowing that it can tell us many stories, that is the kind of wisdom these old southern apples hold. That wisdom is a seed, of sorts, and seed-saving is a shared passion of both mine and Diane's. This book explains why. Why go through the effort to preserve or repatriate these old, ugly apples? *Wild, Tamed, Lost, Revived* lays it out in a way that shows how human desire can manifest itself in the form of an apple. These days, it seems like most consumers want only apples that are as hard as a rock and as sweet as a peach. Most people have never experienced the nuanced and complex flavors of these heirloom apples. Sure, there are plenty of shapes, sizes, and colors of apples at your grocery store, but, in terms of flavor, they're all pretty much the same.

I hope this book will expand the way you understand apples *and* the history of the agrarian South. I hope by reading it you will share in the admiration that I have always had for Diane's determination and grit. Diane grew up on a farm in Piedmont, Georgia, learning from her father about tending to plants and nature, just like his dad had taught him. Now Diane is teaching us all this invaluable wisdom that she has unlocked by starting her own orchard and by researching the history of apples for this book.

By studying how we used apples, from their discovery to how we grow and consume them now, we also witness how badly humans have been treated—and often still are. The complexity of southern history mirrors the complexity of the twisted apple trees and tells a story of discovery, mastery, loss, and, most importantly, resilience. This book will show you horrible choices that were made throughout the South's agrarian history. You will read about extraordinary varieties developed by enslaved people on orchards that they built and maintained, and yet, most of those apples ended up named after the enslavers.

We live in a complex world with a complex history, and the history of apples is no different. We're also taught to see apples as a symbol of well-being for the health of our bodies. Now I realize that they are also markers for our lives and the strength of our communities.

It takes a very specific personality to dive as deep into a single subject as Diane has done. We certainly need more people like her to make the story have a delicious ending. I'm looking forward to tasting the next box of wisdom and reveling in surprise after surprise. After reading this book, I have even more respect for apples, the people who came before us here in the South, and, of course, Diane.

PREFACE

They sit in bowls on kitchen islands and gather dust on hotel desks. In fall, they shine from split oak baskets on rural roadsides. All year they sprawl in yellow, red, and green mounds in grocery store bins: the ubiquitous apple, so inescapable we rarely *notice* them.

Outside the confines of grocery stores and roadside stands, it's hard *not* to find apples. Sliced into slimy wedges reeking of citric acid, they sneak into Happy Meals and linger on salad bars. Convenience stores display plastic-wrapped versions as a healthy snack. Well-worn names like Golden Delicious and Granny Smith crowd produce displays, sharing space with splashy modern varieties with stripper names like SugarBee and SweeTango. But these apples tell the same tired story. Every year the same colors, the tidy piles of groomed fruit that taste only sweet, juicy, and crisp. Today's apples tell a buffed and polished tale.

But what if I told you there was a deeper story here than yellow, red, green, and sweet? What if behind the corporate piles of groomed fruit lurks a scruffy, tangled narrative, one that is infinitely more interesting and flavorful than worn-out stories of presidential apple growers and backwoods brandy makers? The apple's family tree, the *Malus* genus, includes crazy aunts and drunk cousins. Behind each knobby brown orb, underneath every quirky apple name or sprightly flavor, lies a person, culture, and history. And nowhere is this history more interesting than in the South.

This book tells the story of the rise and fall of southern apples.

When we think about apples, most people conjure up Washington State, New England, and Michigan. Some may envision the mountain South or the Georgia foothills. We don't think about Pomaria, South Carolina. Or Washington, Mississippi. Coastal towns like Charleston and Norfolk usually don't come to mind.

Surprises fill every page of the southern apple tale.

For thousands of years, the tiny sour southern crabapple, *Malus angustifolia*, the most ancient apple species, flourished throughout the

South, providing hard green fruit for birds, mammals, and Indigenous people. *Malus domestica*, the sweet edible apple, arrived with Europeans and immediately ran wild, spread by mammals and humans.

Apples make themselves known on every page of the South's complex history.

In the early South, almost every real estate advertisement touted an orchard. Newspapers offered cider for sale as often as eggs. Farmers—and almost everyone was a farmer—swapped apple varieties with the enthusiasm of fantasy football. Agricultural writers extolled southern varieties. The South exported apples to England and northern states, as well as cider to the Caribbean. Nurseries from Virginia to Mississippi sold thousands of uniquely southern apple varieties in the region and throughout the country. The influence of southern apples traveled far from the tree.

Southerners ate fresh apples from June through May and chose specific varieties for drying, applesauce, apple butter, pies, vinegar, cider, and brandy. They harvested dense apple wood to make mallets, handsaws, the teeth for mills, and chair rockers.[1]

Southern apples were sweet, tart, and tannic. They were as tiny as shiny red golf balls and as big as a small melon. Southern apples smelled like pineapples, fermenting fruit on the orchard floor, wintergreen mint, ripe bananas, and peach skins. The deep, complex flavors of southern apples inspired names like Early Strawberry, Lady Sweet, and Magnum Bonum.

For 300 years, the southern fruit basket showcased uniquely southern apples, apples chosen by Black, white, and Indigenous people. This agricultural bounty was so ingrained in southern life that one of the most common apples grown in the South, the Horse apple, rarely appeared in nursery catalogs because every farmer, which meant almost every person, already had a Horse apple in the family orchard.

Then, in less than fifty years, this bounty vanished. Nurseries disappeared. Southern regions with vibrant orchards ceased growing apples. The number of commercially available varieties grown in the South shrank from almost 2,000 to less than a hundred. What had been a central character in southern farming, one entwined with the region's history and culture, faded to a bit player. Today, it's rare to find more than a handful of southern apple varieties planted in backyard gardens and commercial orchards.

———————

We'll begin our journey with the first section, "Wild," where I will show how seedling orchards spread through the region, entangled with the

South's legacy of land seizure and slavery. Black, white, and Indigenous southerners selected apples that met their needs, replicated them, and named this fruit. Their choices reflect culture and history and provide a deep-seated connection to the past. But many deeply mythologized apple stories reveal only partial truths. The desires of the people who did the work of growing apples and making cider, who grafted thousands of trees and replicated varieties we enjoy today, often do not have a voice in the South's early history.

The second section, "Tamed," reveals the ways apples flourished in the South and traveled far beyond regional borders—bearing not only their unique flavors but influence. The South's special soil and apple-friendly climates gave rise to apple legends like Albemarle Pippin and created regions like Apple Pie Ridge. You will hear stories of southerners who held on to family apples and hyperlocal apples longer than farmers in other parts of the country. The nineteenth-century "golden age of apples" created a flowering of hundreds of southern varieties, all reflecting a useful trait, a flavor, or an emotional connection to fruit. Here I profile two of the most prominent southern fruit nurseries and relate their divergent paths on the road to modern industrial agriculture. The United States Department of Agriculture codified apples, including many from the South, but USDA policies also put southern orchards at risk and disadvantaged African American, Indigenous, and women farmers.

In "Lost," we learn about the fallout that occurred when southerners left their farms and abandoned diverse agriculture. You might be surprised to hear that apples from the South traveled to the American West, helping to found an apple industry behemoth that threatened southern orchards. A stew of technology, transportation, tourism, government policies, and other forces of modernity segregated apples to a narrow band of the South—and the result was an astounding forfeiture of diversity and a palpable loss of some southern culture.

The southern apple story includes a cautious note of optimism. The final part of this journey, "Revived," shows the creative ways that multigenerational southern orchards are surviving in the twenty-first century. From organic apple production to agritourism, smart, nimble business owners are finding ways to keep southern apples alive. You will meet growers who utilize the latest science to grow fruit in a changing climate and will learn about preservation orchards in Georgia, Tennessee, and North Carolina that have resurrected forgotten apples that thrived for hundreds of years. We will take a tour of southern universities and research centers that are investigating cider fermentation and high-tech apple breeding. Cider apples, including old varieties, may represent a way forward for some southern orchards. Modern apples could be revived through genetic research into *Malus angustifolia*, the native southern crabapple.

Alongside the surprising story of apples in the South, I will tell you a bit about my own life, from planting the first twentieth-century cider apple orchard in the region to founding the first modern cidery south of Massachusetts. Each chapter begins with a scene from my path from a small-town Georgia childhood to a corporate career and then to a solid landing in rural Appalachia, a route that has much in common with the twisting history of southern apples.

Planting trees that will outlive me, noticing their growth, and tasting their fruit propelled me into a more proximate way of living, one central to the lines of my desire. This book reveals how I grappled with the complications of growing an agricultural ingredient and turning it into a beverage. My journey is a window into the southern fruit that has persisted.

I came to write this book because growing apples and making cider changed me. Apples rooted me deeply in place *and* took me to spaces I never imagined I would inhabit. My orchard pulled me into a web of connections with scientists and scholars, farmers and makers—people who have become central to my life.

Writing this book cemented my belief that planting something beautiful, unique, and in danger of being lost is a worthy pursuit, one that speaks of abundance, not scarcity. Our modern view of apples has narrowed from richness and flavor to a marketplace vision. I believe this narrow space is a poor place to live.

Reading this book will, I hope, transform the way you look at the South. Just as I scout my own orchards today, for over 300 years southerners paid attention to the fruit around them. Apples rose in the South entwined with the region's complex history, a history that demands a careful examination. Though we have lost much of the region's rich apple diversity, the desires that prompted southerners to replicate apples are larger than the fruit. Desires to notice names and flavors. To listen attentively to the past. To revive, if not a fruit, a deeper understanding of this corner of the world.

WILD,
TAMED,
LOST,
REVIVED

—

Wild

SEEDS

The apple's sweet flesh and bitter seeds bear a history of the South, but this fruit also holds my own story, equally rooted in the rural landscape and people.

On Saturdays in Troup County, Georgia, my eight-year-old view of the world was the passenger seat of my dad's dusty 1961 Ford Country Squire station wagon, my worn Keds, stained pink from red-clay river water, propped up on the dash, the side vent cranked open to stream air to my face. We rode together, mostly in comfortable silence, to the hardware store to get nails, to the icehouse to fill the cooler, or often just to ride. Dad, whose name was Cliff Hogg, turned down a country road because he liked the name or because he wanted to see "what the old Lewis place looks like now." I sat, lulled by the asphalt ribbon ahead of us or tossed by the bounce of the low-slung station wagon on washboard dirt roads. Dad sometimes talked about local politics, sometimes told stories about growing up on Granddaddy's farm. Red clouds of dust streamed behind the car and swirled in the open windows at every stop sign.

My grandparents' home near LaGrange, county seat for Troup County, was a typical small farm during the middle of the twentieth century, a remnant of the South's agricultural past. My grandfather William Newton Hogg owned a Texaco station and farmed as a sideline. He grew corn and ran cattle. He raised a few pigs to slaughter for the family and planted an enormous vegetable garden. He purchased his bull from the local textile magnate, Fuller Callaway, and named it Fuller Bull. Dovey, my grandmother, tended chickens and a milk cow. Her pride was a field of yellow and white daffodils on the bank along their steep driveway.

Dad grew up riding his piebald pony, Texaco, to the county elementary school, but, like me, he had an ambi-

3

tious spirit. He graduated from Gordon Military Academy and then finished his first engineering degree at Auburn University on an ROTC scholarship. Dad met my mother, Bonnie, when she attended LaGrange College. They married and lived in Brooklyn during World War II, where Dad trained British pilots to fly by instruments. Their move to Brooklyn was the first time Dad had been north of Augusta, Georgia. He often told a story about asking for "sweet milk" in the Sperry Gyroscope employee cafeteria—meaning not buttermilk—and receiving chocolate milk instead. After the war, my parents moved to Atlanta, where Dad earned another engineering degree at Georgia Tech. After I was born, he took a final step away from the farm into a textile career back in Troup County.

Dad's everlasting interest in the natural world, in growing and discovering, remained a thread throughout his life and an interest he passed on to me. He showed me how to divide a thick mass of lily roots and when to take a softwood cutting. His slender, freckled hands taught me the feel of a ripe seed head or to know when a plant's side limb was flexible enough to root in soft soil, knowledge I use today.

At some point on our drives, Dad would swerve to the shoulder of a back road and jump out with a roll of plastic flagging tape. He'd wade into tall grass to tie a tiny section of bright yellow tape around butterfly weed, his favorite wildflower. Or to mark a patch of lilies he admired. He'd say, "We'll come back when it goes to seed." Or sometimes, "We'll dig this up in the fall."

Dad scattered his yellow bows all over Troup County. Watching him pay close attention to every meadow and ditch, I learned about the magic and the practical work of harvesting and digging. The need to grow things infected me in that dusty station wagon. And an invisible cord stretched across the front seat and bound us as closely as if we were conjoined.

An old apple tree standing alone in a field with fruit hanging from every limb signals self-sufficiency. Apples sprout on their own along fence lines. They thrive in abandoned cemeteries and linger in subdivisions built on former orchard land. Untended, an apple tree can produce fruit for decades. At first glance, apple trees seem to be autonomous, independent of human intervention, a little more self-reliant than the rest of the plant world.

The truth is more complex. That lone apple tree standing in a field requires a vast network of helpers to produce fruit. For that tree to reproduce from seeds entails an even larger supporting cast. But to actually *replicate*, to create a genetically identical tree? That *requires* human help.

Dad taught me about flowers and vegetables; he schooled me in bulbs, rhizomes, and shrubs. But he was not a tree guy. When I chose apples as an agriculture venture, I needed to know this fruit as intimately as I knew roadside plants from my childhood in red-clay Piedmont Georgia.

I needed to learn about apple sex.

Like many plants, apple trees are hermaphrodites, meaning each apple flower contains both sexes. Before fruit can form, pollen must move from the male flower part, the stamen, to the female flower part, the pistil. Sounds pretty simple. But apples complicate the pollination process. To create fruit, most apples require *cross-pollination*. This means pollen must transfer from the male flower part of one apple variety to the female flower part of a different, genetically compatible, apple variety. That's why a home gardener must plant at least two different varieties of apples. A commercial orchardist plans and executes apple pollination with a geneticist's skills.

From an evolutionary standpoint, sexual reproduction is good. I had spent time with my dad kneeling in the dirt planting onion sets and potato tubers, so I already knew about asexual reproduction, which creates an identical plant or a clone. In sexual reproduction, cross-pollination creates *new* and sometimes better-quality fruit. But sexual reproduction also creates something called hybrid vigor, or *heterosis*. Mixing genetic material to obtain hybrid vigor can lead to greater adaptability for any plant. Since almost all apple varieties require cross-pollination, apples have a strong natural bent toward producing hybrid vigor. The fact that in North America apples grow from south Alabama to Canada is one by-product of their hybrid vigor—or, in other words, their ability to survive in multiple climates.

When I first began trying on the idea of growing tree fruit, the permanence and self-sufficiency of apples appealed to me. But the more I learned about apples, the more I realized their life depends on a troupe of supporting actors.

Pollinators are the first members of the cast. Apple pollen is too heavy to be transferred by wind, so apples need active agents such as bees and insects to move pollen from the male to the female flower parts. That lone apple tree full of fruit must entice a community of pollinators to visit its flowers.

Apple orchards explode in pink and creamy white blooms each spring. Carmine-striped petals fly through the air like a late snow, and

the sweet-spicy aroma of apple blossoms fills the air. But high drama plays out beneath this sylvan scene.

Apple flowers produce abundant nectar and pollen, more than most fruit trees. They are ready for apple sex. Apple flower clusters, each containing about six flowers, remain open for several days but are most receptive to pollination soon after the buds unfurl. An individual apple variety will remain in bloom for about nine days, longer in cool weather and shorter with warm, dry days. This nine-day window, give or take, is all the time an apple has to sexually reproduce, or it's a long wait until next spring.

The primary or "king" bud opens first, and this bud usually produces the largest apple in that cluster of blooms. At this point, the drama begins—pollinators must transfer pollen from one variety, say a Parmar apple, to another apple variety blooming at the *same time*, such as Grimes Golden. Bees, the most common pollinators in my region, are shy in cold weather, so this critical activity must occur on a warm day without too much wind.

Plant sex happens every day, but picture all that must align to make an apple: to reproduce, an apple needs nine days or so of bloom, with another apple variety blooming at the same time on a warm, still day with plenty of pollinators around.

Bees have a lot of work to do in a short flowering season, but they're up to the task.

Honeybees arrived in Virginia in the early 1620s, brought by European colonizers for honey production.[1] While domestic honeybees (*Apis mellifera*) can visit up to 5,000 flowers a day, honeybees are not the most efficient pollinators. Solitary bees, bumblebees, gnats, flower beetles, and even hoverflies all pollinate apples. Bees in the *Osmia* genus, which includes the blue orchard bee, visit more blossoms per day than honeybees and transfer pollen more effectively.[2] Most orchardists today create habitat for wild solitary bees and also rely on managed honeybee hives to pollinate orchards.

After pollination, the fleshy part of the apple, the sweet flesh we eat called the pome, grows from the base of the fertilized flower. Inside the pome, around the stiff core, three to five carpels, or interior seed containers, develop. Each carpel usually holds two glossy seeds. Because apples reproduce sexually, these seeds contain a combination of DNA both from the tree that bore the blossom and from the variety that provided the pollen.

What amazed me most about apple reproduction, and the characteristic that has led to so many tens of thousands of cultivated apple varieties, is that each seed in an apple is *a new apple variety*. Each of the ten

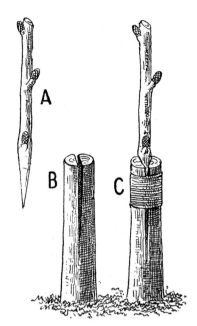

Grafting by inserting scion wood into rootstock.

seeds in every apple, on every tree, if planted, will result in an entirely new apple variety.

Germinating apple seeds requires another cast of characters.

The carpels that hold the apple seeds contain a growth inhibitor, so apple seeds can germinate only if the seeds separate from the core of the apple. Apple seeds, like many seeds of temperate woody plants, need a period of at or near freezing temperatures, called "chill days," before they will germinate.

Apples also need to be dispersed away from the base of their parent apple tree to find enough light and soil moisture to thrive. This is where animals enter the supporting team. Birds perform poorly as what scientists call "dispersal agents" because when they eat the apple flesh they don't fully remove seeds from the flesh and core of the apple. For millennia, fruit-loving mammals have played a big role in spreading apple seeds in a way that supports germination. In the early South, hogs and cattle roamed unfenced and were among the chief dispersal agents, spreading apples and peaches throughout the region.

Apple seeds plus hogs plus a few freezing nights added up to a welcoming home for apples in the South.

But each of those dispersed seeds made a brand-new apple. How did apples *replicate*? How did we end up with acres of Golden Delicious or Granny Smith, each tree identical to its neighbor? This is where humans have the starring role in the apple drama.

People *replicate* apples through *tissue propagation*. The wood or tissue of a tree contains the DNA of what's charmingly called the "mother tree." Farmers in the South often pulled up suckers growing from the roots of their favorite trees as a simple way to duplicate or clone a desired apple. They also practiced grafting. Grafting consists of connecting the growing tissue of one plant, the desired apple, to the growing tissue of another. Modern grafters connect a twig of the desired apple variety to a similarly sized growing shoot from a specialized rootstock. Early southerners were more likely to graft tissue or twigs onto a small wild apple seedling or to cultivate crabapple seedlings as receptors for grafts of favorite trees. Humans have been grafting plants for at least 2,500 years.[3]

Sexual reproduction means that each apple seed is a new combination of apple DNA. But apples take their strong tendency to genetic diversity one step further. Apples are what pomologists—apple scientists—call "extreme heterozygotes." Human children often resemble one or both parents, sometimes strongly, but apple offspring almost always bear little resemblance to their pollinating parents. If you plant seeds from a big green Granny Smith apple, you might end up with trees full of tiny apples with brown skin, or red apples so sour they make your mouth pucker. Apples grown from seeds are called *seedling apples*, and each seed creates a dramatically different new fruit.

In early southern seedling orchards, apples threw their extreme genetic diversity out into the world, and people noticed. The people who noticed first were intimately connected to growing and tending the trees—the dirt-under-the-fingernails farmers, women seeking food that would last the winter, and enslaved men and women who grew hundreds of trees on many southern plantations. Indigenous people who scoured their own seedling orchards for valuable fruit understood the payoff of genetic diversity, as did early European immigrant farmers who knew how to pull up root suckers and graft twig to branch. All those who grew seedling trees *chose* apples that met their desires, and they replicated those trees through grafting.

Of course, there were countless wild apples that humans never tended, fruit full of random DNA from all sorts of errant, untamed apples. But every apple in the history of the world that has ever held *a name* required a person who noticed that specific apple and replicated it. By learning the stories behind apples, by noticing the paths and detours those stories take, we also learn about people and how human desires manifest in fruit.

BLOOMS

My own stories begin in the summer of 1965, when I was twelve years old and had never been north of Atlanta, never higher than Pine Mountain's puny thousand-foot elevation. My mother and her best friend, Jessie Summers, took me on a trip to visit Jessie's friend who owned a summer house on Lake Burton. One of the Georgia Power Company lakes that tamed the Tallulah River, Lake Burton nestles deep into the thick forests of the southern Appalachians.

The first thing I noticed was the breeze on my skin. The light wind off the lake felt foreign; it was a cool breeze, not the sticky, moist air that hung heavy in my hometown of West Point. I remember sitting on the dock, my legs in blue-green water so clear I could see my toes. Though I had traveled only 200 miles northeast, I felt transported to another world.

I've come to believe that we carry inside us a landscape that is fundamental to who we are. Landscape is another form of language, a way of communicating, and at some point we find the one that fits our story best. That weekend it was love at first sight for me and the southern mountains. I talked to trees and flowers. I communed with trout in the lake. I saw the southern sky with new eyes, and I discovered my new language, one that felt as familiar as my own soft Georgia drawl.

All my life I'd played in red-clay creeks but had never walked beside a rushing stream filled with smooth, tumbled stones. Jessie's friend loaned me a *Peterson Field Guide to Wildflowers* and pointed out a few of her favorite spring blooms. I ate wild asparagus and saw my first trillium. I used my Girl Scout camp skills to paddle an old canoe around the sparkling lake and didn't see a single water moccasin, creatures I regularly encountered in the red-tinged waters at home. I read my pocket-size copy of *The Adventures of Sherlock Holmes* by lantern light on a porch with no screens.

That summer, I knew I had discovered my landscape, the land I carried in my heart. It took decades to find my way back.

During college in Laurinburg, North Carolina, I spent as much time outside as my full course load and a twenty-hours-a-week job allowed. I rode my horse along the edges of sandy cotton fields and hiked through pine forests. On rainy days, local farmers gathered at the mobile milling warehouse where I answered the phone and paid bills in my part-time job. We drank Cokes in glass bottles, and I soaked up farmer-talk about hogs, corn, and cattle. When I graduated with an English degree in the midst of a recession, I couldn't see a path to farming. Instead, I ended up in a bank training program.

My corporate work at a large North Carolina bank immersed me in a world far from red-clay dirt roads. For half a decade I commuted to Charlotte from a rented farmhouse in Davidson, where I attempted to keep a toe in the soil. My banking colleagues benefited from my enormous vegetable garden. The heavy, sweet melons I carted to work in summer perfumed our offices. But a long commute did not fit the demands of my accelerating career. I eventually moved to Charlotte, bought my first home, and shrank my farming dream to fit flower beds and herb pots.

I was thirty-nine years old when I met Chuck, and my yearning to plant and grow still burned. When we decided to get married, I made a big confession. "Chuck, you are the love of my life, but I can't give up this dream of living a rural existence. Can you join me?" Chuck had grown up spending time on his grandparents' North Carolina tobacco farm. He knew all about farming and had spent his life running away from it. Today we laugh and say it was good we were still in the lust phase of love, because he said, "Yes."

In June 1995, Chuck and I stood under a new moon at the bottom of a steep pasture—*our* pasture. After years of searching, we had finally found a farm that worked for us: land close enough to our jobs that we could begin a farm venture while continuing our business careers. Far enough from city sprawl that we didn't risk our land soon becoming an agricultural zoo, surrounded by gated communities and faux farms.

Just a few weeks back we had bumped into an old friend, a talented landscape architect, who suggested we look at land near his home in Laurel Fork, Virginia.

"You are going to love this place," Chip said. "It's beautiful; anything will grow there. And there are apple orchards everywhere!" When the realtor showed us the old Spence place, we knew—this was the landscape that had lived in my heart for decades.

Fireflies covered the hill, flickering like hundreds of candles held up at a rock concert, each life a brilliant spark. That early fall night, our concert was crickets and tree frogs. The deep bell voice of a bullfrog bellowed below in Rock House Creek, a stream that jumped out of the ground just a few yards from us. I'd soon discover spring-fed creeks all over our hills, but that night I just grinned under the stars, scattered like more fireflies across the sky.

Standing with Chuck on our new land, brimming with hope and anticipation, I felt myself settle into a new chapter. All the earnest searching, the years of researching farming ventures. All the angst of falling in love with land only to conclude it was too far from an airport to manage my job, or too close to a college town to remain farmland much longer—all this fell away. I knew that everything I'd lived up to this point would forever be the "before." This was the end of Book 1 of my life. I was ready to turn the page, ready to begin a second story, one rooted in the landscape and language of my heart.

By the time we moved to the high Blue Ridge Plateau in southwest Virginia, I had settled on apples. Or, rather, as ubiquitous neighbors, *they* had settled on *me*.

Scraggly apple trees lined all the dirt roads surrounding our farm. Nearby Cana, Virginia, sheltered multigenerational commercial orchards in the folds of the Appalachian foothills. Thirty miles north at our same 3,000-foot elevation, Bent Mountain orchards produced stunningly delicious Albemarle Pippin apples. A little research taught me that our new home in the southern Appalachians held the greatest remaining apple diversity in the country.[1] The landscape of my heart turned out to be apple territory.

With my dad's early tutelage, I learned how to grow vegetables, bulbs, and wildflowers. Over the last twenty years I had left behind elaborate perennial gardens in every home I had owned. Yet growing vegetables for the local farmers' market or starting a perennial nursery didn't strike a chord with me. Trees seemed more significant than decorative flowers, more enduring than vegetables. With trees I could grow something that would produce and outlive me, a fruitful legacy.

In the late 1990s, Virginia's wineries were beginning to garner a reputation for producing surprisingly good wines. Agriculture and forestry was the largest segment of the state economy, and a forward-thinking Virginia Department of Agriculture offered programs to support farm wineries. I thought, "Why not a Virginia cidery?" I could grow trees and create a business selling a value-added product, alcoholic cider.

For most of my business career I had been the "first" or the "only" woman at the table. I had always held creative jobs, positions that often placed me in the role of trailblazer. Doing hard things that had never been done before fueled me. I thought, "Could I become a cider pioneer on our Virginia farm?"

Over the next few years, with support from Virginia Tech pomologists and enologists, I launched an audacious plan to plant the first twentieth-century cider apple orchard in the South and to build the first modern southern cidery. My childhood dream of living a rural life surrounded by a heartfelt landscape finally melded with a business venture. I had landed on territory that felt like home, a home that included apples.

Even with new orchards and what I hoped would be a vibrant local business, I knew that life in our small mountain community would offer complications. Having grown up in a rural Georgia county full of kin, I knew how outsiders such as Chuck and myself would be viewed—we'd never be *from* here. Our insistence on a gravel driveway when we could afford asphalt would brand our class and wealth. We planned to build our house on a hill, not by the road, no less. I knew no matter how many trees I planted or how much cider I bottled, this farm I hoped to inhabit for the rest of my life would forever be known as the "old Spence place."

But countless immigrants, both plants and people, inhabit the landscape that feels like home to my neighbors, including the southern apples lining mountain roads around our farm.

My neighbors look at the landscape that has been their home for generations and see a familiar natural world. Many don't realize that the South they see today is a much-altered version of the landscape that greeted colonizers. Everyone knows about kudzu, the invasive Japanese import that can cover a mobile home in a summer. Ditto for honeysuckle, the scent of my childhood. Ancient boxwoods, some over twenty feet tall gracing old homesites all over the South, are immigrants. As are the crape myrtles around the Walmart parking lot. Same for Queen Anne's lace and orange daylilies, summer staples on every southern roadside. From the Basque cod fishermen who left apple seeds in Newfoundland to the peaches that accompanied Jesuits to Florida as early as 1565,[2] plants we consider from here are really from somewhere else.

But our continent has always been fruit-filled. Before Europeans arrived with their colonizing plants, Indigenous people used more than 200 species of trees, shrubs, and small fruits for food and medicine.[3] The Seneca in New York planted plums around their settlements, and

all across the South, Native people used persimmons, cherries, mulberries, and crabapples.

Apples belong to the genus *Malus*. North America claims four *Malus* species: the Oregon crabapple (*M. fusca*); the prairie crabapple (*M. ioensis*); *M. coronaria*, or the sweet crabapple; and the southern crabapple, *M. angustifolia*. These apples are "strikingly astringent,"[4] more likely to cause a grimace than a smile. But while these hard, bitter fruits are not edible fresh, once dried, the sugars concentrate. Indigenous people dried crabapples and occasionally roasted this tree fruit.

Malus domestica, the sweet apple lining southern roadsides, is an immigrant, just like the honeybee that pollinates it.

A few years after I had settled in the southern Appalachians, I began pressing apples each fall in my newly constructed cidery. Crushed apples spilled off the loading dock on press days, and each spring, like magic, apple seedlings sprouted in the gravel parking lot.

Spring was always a fraught time for my young business, with cider bottling in full swing and blooming apple trees to fret over. While I rushed from the farm truck to a cider house packed to the ceiling with empty bottles destined for the bottling line, those hopeful green shoots in the dry gravel always grabbed my attention. Apple seeds that have traveled through a grinder and press—or a horse or pig's guts—and were then ground into soil, or even gravel, grow into trees. My cidery's parking lot reflected the story of just how apples that were not from here came to be thoroughly southern.

———————

Before cider, there were apples, and the story of how domestic apples came to the South includes unexpected characters and circuitous routes.

Flowering plants, called angiosperms, originated in the fossil record at least 120 million years ago, and possibly as early as 170 million years ago. Around 100 million years ago, plants appeared that are today classified in the Rosaceae family, the family that includes the genus *Malus*, or apples. Around 10 million years ago, changing climate in Central Asia isolated the Tian Shan mountains and trapped an early form of apples on a fertile mountain range that was never glaciated. The precursor to today's southern apples evolved on this mountain island to attract large animals, creatures like bears, that could disperse seeds widely. And in doing so, apples became bigger and sweeter.

Fast forward to the Silk Road, which began not with silk but as a migratory grazing path for wild horses, donkeys, and camels around 13,000 years ago. When humans domesticated horses around 7,000 years ago, communities began trading along this migratory path through the Tian

◄
(Clockwise from left) Half-inch green, late pink and bloom, bloom and petal fall, and early fruit set.

Shan mountains. Unlike camels, whose teeth and digestive tract destroy apple seeds, horses dispersed without damaging the seeds. Apples began to roam.

From their original home in Central Asia, apples traveled through the Persian Empire into Greece, Rome, and Europe. Though a few native apple species existed in Europe, Romans reproduced the sweeter apples that originated in Asia and even perfected grafting techniques. Romans brought their complete package of apple skills—cultivation, grafting, storing, and likely cidermaking—to northwest Europe and Britain. And from England, the now solidly domesticated apple we today call *Malus domestica* sailed to Virginia.

But Virginia was not the apple's first landing spot in America.

Scandinavian fishermen left *Malus domestica* seeds on islands off the Maine coast as early as 1550. Spanish missionaries and explorers brought citrus and peach seeds to Florida and likely also dispersed apple seeds in the lower South. Orchards surrounded the Spanish fort established in Memphis, Tennessee. Traveling the South in 1702, the naturalist William Bartram found old orchards planted by the French in Alabama. By 1615, orchards grew in Jamestown, Virginia, 300 miles east of our farm, the cultivated apple's first significant toehold in the South.[5]

There, many apples ended up in the cider mill, and the apple pomace, the leftover ground flesh, contained apple seeds. Each seed promised a brand-new tree.

Seedling trees, like the seedlings that sprouted in the Foggy Ridge parking lot, were the norm for early southern orchards. Colonists, enslaved men and women, and Indigenous people planted apple seeds—thousands and thousands of seeds. Once these seeds hit the ground, they germinated and grew more vigorously than in their British homes. Apple genetic diversity became greater in America than in Europe due to "spectacular germination."[6]

Early southerners planted seeds and created seedling orchards, some as large as 10,000 trees.[7] But animals spread apples even more widely. Farm animals roamed largely unfenced. Robert Beverley wrote that on early Virginia farms, "hogs swarm like Vermine upon the Earth."[8] Apple seeds passed through the digestive tracts of hogs, horses, and deer without damage, and their sharp hooves drove seeds into the soil. Free-range livestock did their part in spreading apple diversity in the South.

In these early southern orchards, every apple seed created a new apple, but few seedling apples tasted sweet. In a search for sweetness and utility, humans began to impose their desires on this wild fruit. People began to select and replicate the apples they most valued through grafting or pulling up root suckers. Plantation owners grew nursery stock of carefully selected and grafted apples for their own use. The skilled labor of grafting and tending large orchards was performed by indentured servants and later by enslaved men and women. Small farm owners swapped grafting wood from their favorite trees. By the mid-eighteenth century, commercial nurseries sold named southern apple varieties in Charleston, South Carolina, and across Virginia.

Southern farmers began domesticating wild apples.

By the 1750s, in Virginia alone, nurseries sold over a dozen varieties originating from seedling apples, including Virginia White Apple, Hewe's Crab, Taliaferro, Gloucester White, Carthouse, Rall's Genet, today called Ralls Janet, Pryor's Red, Limbertwig, Father Abraham, Lowry, Winesap, Milam, Pilot, and Royal Pearmain.[9] By 1815, the Fruit Tree Association in central Virginia, an organization founded by multiple former United States presidents and farming dignitaries, all apple growers, ordered $1,000 worth of fifty-eight fruit tree varieties from the famous Prince Nursery in New York. They ordered no apples. In less than 200 years after *Malus domestica* landed in the South, these experienced farmers believed the South had its own apples.

———

The connection between apples and people runs deeper than propagation. As southerners domesticated apples, the apples acquired names and stories. Some southern apple names are as literal as Beauty Shop Road, an aptly named road near our farm. Names like Carolina Red June alert us to three facts about this popular southern apple, the early-season apple of choice in the South for over 200 years. Many southern apples take place names, names that often obscure the fruit's origin. Nickajack is named for a North Carolina creek but was likely cultivated by Cherokees and introduced to nursery trade by a white slave owner, Silas McDowell.[10]

Today people purchase apples with glossy names like Cosmic Crisp every month of the year. North Carolina Keeper, Sour June, Camack's Sweet, July Delicious . . . these southern apples reveal qualities people valued. They give us a glimpse into the lives of those who replicated them.

Wherever apples migrated, humans welcomed this fruit into all aspects of their lives. Unlike most mammals, humans are unable to generate vitamin C and must gain this important building block from food sources. Apples, even when dried, are an excellent source of vitamin C. Apples preserved on strings were discovered in the Tomb of Puabi, a 4,500-year-old royal burial site at Ur, near modern Iraq. They are one of the most easily consumed foods—they can be eaten fresh, and many improve with age. Trading ships carried long-storing apples to prevent scurvy. Beyond nourishment, apples also seep into human consciousness, our language, and our culture.

When apples arrive in a culture, they enter in full force. In *The Extraordinary Story of the Apple*, Barrie Juniper and David Mabberley write, "Into every country in which it was brought and unlike almost every other food source . . . the apple almost immediately entered the realms of the names of villages and private residences, and later, surnames, such as the topographic 'Appleyard,' given to someone associated with orchards."[11] Apples turn up in literature, song, and art. And as they are tamed, they acquire names.

Southern apple names trick us with gauzy back stories, like the Mattamuskeet apple from coastal North Carolina said to have been found in the gullet of a wild goose by members of the Mattamuskeet tribe. We know that Caleb Ralls grew the Ralls Janet apple in Amherst County, Virginia, in the 1790s. It obtained an aristocratic veneer with the oft-repeated and highly unlikely story of a Frenchman named M. Genet delivering this apple from France to Secretary of State Thomas Jefferson.

More tantalizing for me are the partial stories, the left-out narratives. North Carolinians in Rowan, Stanley, and Cabarrus Counties grew the Toby apple and thought it "unsurpassed" for applesauce, apple butter, and drying. This apple carries parallel and opaque narratives: Is Toby named for a wounded Confederate soldier who planted a seed from an apple he ate on the way home from Gettysburg? Or did an enslaved man named Toby replicate a seedling tree that he believed bore valuable fruit? Who chose and grafted this tree, what it meant to the families who grew it . . . this apple story is deeply mythologized in a way that obscures history.

Though my immigration to a southern Appalachian farm was the result of a serendipitous conversation with a friend, I intended to sink roots in my loamy clay soil as deeply as a tree. Even if my neighbors would forever consider me not from here, I was as determined as an apple tree to plant my dreams deep.

For my long-held dream of an agriculture venture, I wanted to create something that would outlive me.

ROOTS

In a southern Appalachian fall, dusk comes early and cold. By four-thirty on a November day in 1997, pale light spilled down Tony Goad's cow pasture, clipped the top of the big oak tree, and cast long shadows through my orchard site. The Spence family grew cabbage in the 1940s on this steep slope as a cash crop for their family of nine children. For decades, only thick orchard grass, blackberry brambles, and a few locust trees had grown in the spot I planned to cover in cider apple trees.

In the years Chuck and I spent searching for a farm, I explored a handful of business ideas for a farm venture but never strayed far from trees. I wanted a *real* business, one that offered an opportunity for success. But even more, I dreamed of creating something that would outlast me. Apple trees can live fifty years or more, rooted to one spot. I kept circling back to these twin thoughts—place and permanence.

In the late 1990s, the Virginia Department of Agriculture was bullish on farm-based beverages. One of the most respected pomologists in the country taught at Virginia Tech, less than an hour from our farm. My research into growing cider apples and fermenting cider convinced me that the combination of technical and intuitive skills fit my inclinations.

After years of searching and planning, I was ready to plant trees.

That afternoon, pink plumber's string stretched like plastic pickup sticks over the grassy hillside, marking rows north to south and planting spots east to west. A total of 250 apple trees lay under tarps on the back of the farm truck, protected from dry wind by moist sawdust. I had set aside five days to plant my precious trees. I hoped this orchard of varieties like Parmar, Harrison, and Hewe's Crabapple would yield cider that spoke of apples and this place.

The four-foot-tall feathered whips, pencil-sized trees with a few scrawny side limbs, represented two years of detective work and arm-twisting. In the mid-1990s you couldn't buy a cider apple tree at the corner nursery. These bundles of spindly sticks began as eight-inch sections of dormant wood called scions or grafting wood. I scoured heirloom apple nurseries from California to North Carolina for old-fashioned apples that might make the deeply flavored cider I hoped to create. I begged sections of wood from cidermakers in New Hampshire and Oregon. A friend carried a few illicit sticks of wood from a Somerset cider apple in his luggage from England. I eventually chose thirty apple varieties, praying they would grow in Virginia apple country *and* result in delicious cider.

My plan was to plant this orchard, this experiment in cider ingredients, by myself. By hand. With a pick and shovel. I'd planted trees all my life; I was forty-four years old and in great shape. And after all, the Spence family never owned a tractor when they farmed this site.

I'm also a quick learner. Three hours and six holes later, I knew that the piles of milky quartz, the "flint stone" common to our corner of Carroll County, Virginia, would better me.

Fortunately, Tracy Blevens, the fence builder, was on the farm finishing the last of the deer fencing. Using Tracy's posthole auger and our Kubota tractor, we dug 250 holes, spaced fifteen feet apart in the squiggly rows I'd plotted on my steep site. Tracy ran the tractor while I placed the auger and levered out larger rocks with a five-foot-tall metal tamper we christened the "Man Maker."

That day Tracy and I made good time digging holes. But as the auger twisted through the loamy clay and threw dirt into the orchard grass, I had a sinking feeling that my plan was deeply flawed. The next weekend, ice rimmed each hole and hard clay crusted the sides. The good soil that spun out with the powerful auger had disappeared in thick grass. I knew there was no way young trees would thrive with this beginning.

For two days I tried to repair the damage. I broke up the sides of the augered holes to create loose soil so young roots could grow outward. I cracked ice, pulled out more flint rock, and backfilled the holes with rich topsoil from the edge of the woods. During my thirty-minute lunch breaks, I took four Advil and lay on the kitchen floor.

At an elevation of 3,000 feet in the Blue Ridge Mountains, November is a cruel month. I worked alone, bundled in lined Carhartt and a down vest. At five o'clock, the setting sun cast long shadows over my new deer fence. I stood in light sleet at the edge of a frozen hole, having planted thirty trees in two days, and thought, "I need reinforcements."

———————

Reinforcements arrived in the form of K. C. Murphy, a local nursery owner and prodigious worker. Powered by Red Bull and Marlboros, K. C. swung a pick and turned slick-sided holes into receptive homes for young trees. I followed her down the meandering rows with my favorite old shovel inherited from my father, levering white flint stone from each hole. I carefully spread the young tree roots, tamped down soil, and gave each a benediction: "This is your home for life. Send your roots deep."

K. C. and I finished planting the orchard in one long day, a day full of satisfying labor that sparked my curiosity about how early southerners planted their orchards. I had a tractor-powered auger, sharp shovels, and a Gator to haul tools, plus a Wonder Woman. Who planted early southern orchards? And what did this labor look like?

In my search for the origin of the southern apple story, I found as many twists and turns as the tangled limbs of an ancient fruit tree. William Fitzhugh's seventeenth-century orchard planted on sandy soil in Virginia's Northern Neck has long been celebrated as the first significant southern apple orchard. But I found that this "large Orchard of about 2,500 Apple trees, most grafted, well fenced with a Locust fence,"[1] was not the first, nor was it wholly southern.

———————

Sometime in 1670 or 1671, nineteen-year-old William Fitzhugh from Bedford, England, alighted in Jamestown, Virginia, packed with aspirations. As the youngest son of a wool merchant, Fitzhugh had a modest estate, a legal education, and a currency this southern colony needed most—labor in the form of indentured servants.

Fitzhugh settled in the Northern Neck, the northernmost peninsula in Virginia that pushes like the prow of a ship into the Chesapeake Bay. Bordered by the Potomac River to the north and the Rappahannock River to the south, Indigenous people, including the Powhatans, had long occupied this fertile region. When Fitzhugh joined the small settlement of white colonizers in Westmoreland County, the Northern Neck was still a rough frontier with few roads. White colonizers were engaged in armed conflict to seize land from Native people.

He pursued land and status and found the path to both when, on May 1, 1674, with fruit trees blooming across the South, twenty-three-year-old William Fitzhugh married eleven-year-old Sarah Tucker, the daughter of Rose Tucker, a legal client.

Through this fortuitous marriage he gained connections to the most prominent Virginia and Maryland families. He received a wedding gift from Rose Tucker of an enslaved man and woman.[2] Two years later, Fitzhugh was elected to the Virginia House of Burgesses. Sarah, who moved to England after the wedding to complete her education, gave birth four years later at age fifteen to the first of six children. Powered by servants, the labor of enslaved people, inherited wealth, and an advantageous marriage, Fitzhugh launched a Virginia dynasty. He also planted apple orchards.

Fitzhugh was not the first southern apple orchardist, or even the first person to cultivate fruit in the region. Since 1300, the Indigenous people who lived around the Potomac River cultivated crops,[3] including the practice of protecting native fruit trees, such as mulberries, from competitors and predators.

Most apple texts report that Reverend Blaxton planted the first American orchard in 1625 in Boston. But a decade earlier, Ralph Hamor wrote about Sir Thomas Gates's garden in Jamestown where "many forward apple & pear trees come up, of the kernels set there the yeere before."[4] In 1622 the Loudon Company sent grafting wood, called scions, to the Virginia colony.[5] George Menefie planted apples in 1623 at his Littleton home, south of Jamestown. Governor Berkeley planted a cider orchard of 1,500 trees at his Green Spring estate. By the time William Fitzhugh arrived in the Northern Neck and married well, every southern farm had an orchard of apple and peach trees, many planted and tended by enslaved people.

We know about his significant southern orchards because he wrote hundreds of letters that documented his ambitions and his apple trees.

Fitzhugh's letters burn with dreams. If tobacco was wealth for early southerners, land was the means to wealth, and Fitzhugh pursued land with a passion. Stafford County was newly formed in 1674 when Fitzhugh purchased his first tract on what was the edge of European colonization. Throughout his life he sought larger and larger land purchases, at one point proposing to purchase his neighbor's almost 22,000 acres and house French Huguenots as tenants.[6] Everywhere he planted apples.

Virgin forests blanketed Virginia: oak, walnut, hickory, chestnut, chinquapin, and cypress more than eighteen feet in diameter and rising so straight that shipbuilders harvested the trunks for masts. The indentured servants and enslaved men and women who planted Fitzhugh's orchards cut giant trees with axes and mattocks. They burned brush and

sawed lumber that Fitzhugh traded as pipe staves and walnut plank. Plows were useless in soil thick with tree roots, so laborers planted apples and other crops among the cut stumps.

Fitzhugh's orchard was not the first in the South, nor was it wholly southern. Like many immigrants in this era, Fitzhugh considered England "home" and longed to return. And like an English orchardist, he planted "mains, pippins, russentens, costards, marigolds, kings, magitens and bachelors,"[7] apples common to his Bedfordshire home. "Mains," or Pearmains, are apples shaped loosely like pears, like the White Winter Pearmain and Cannon Pearmain apples in my mountain orchard. Even today, old-timers in the rural South call a brown, rough-skinned apple, like Fitzhugh's "russentens," a Rusty Coat apple. "Costards" are large, ribbed, densely fleshed apples, similar to the Horse apple grown throughout the South. In Fitzhugh's time, orchards in the South were more advanced than in the North, with grafted trees far more common in southern orchards.[8] Fitzhugh's orchards overflowed with the diversity of named English varieties and wild seedling fruit.

But it was the wild fruit, the southern-spawned apples, that founded the southern apple dynasty. And these apples accomplished this through drink.

Fitzhugh planted apples for "plentiful house keeping"[9] but also, like me, for cider. Southerners drank cider more than any other beverage. Cider was used for rent and as payment for indentured servants and enslaved people. Planters and farmers distilled cider into apple brandy, called a "Virginia dram," which was sold at the same rate as English spirits.[10] Every orchard in the early South was first and foremost a cider orchard, full mostly of wild fruit producing unnamed apples.

Like other Virginia plantation owners, Fitzhugh exported cider to the Caribbean, likely made by enslaved labor. He bragged in a 1686 letter that his orchard "ought in a few years to bring in an annual sum of fifteen thousand pounds of tobacco."[11] He thought well enough of his own cider to send some in 1696 to George Mason in Bristol, England, saying, "I had not the vanity to think that we could outdo, much less equal your Herfordshire red streake. . . . I only thought because of the place from where it came, it might be acceptable, and give you an opportunity in the drinking of it to discover what future advantages this country may be capable of."[12] Fitzhugh's apples came alive when he wrote about them as a beverage.

Fitzhugh's apple trees, planted and tended with indentured and enslaved labor, sent roots deep into the Northern Neck sandy soil. They grew over forty feet tall, with sprawling, unpruned limbs. Their strong branches housed birds; their apple blossoms fed bees. The orchard floor sprouted Indian grass, field thistle, pale leaf sunflowers, and scores of other grasses and flowers native to America. Field mice, moles, and voles made homes in the soil. I once surprised a red fox eating apples in my fenced orchard, so even with its fence of "locust palings," wild animals fed on apple drops and scattered seeds into the surrounding fields, with each seed a genetically new apple. Fitzhugh's orchards were a utilitarian venture, but one bursting with life, complete with scents and flavors—and new southern fruit.

Fitzhugh put a European stamp on his orchards, but his southern-born seedling apples found a home in Virginia.

———————

In present-day Virginia, as a novice orchardist I quickly learned that critters were my enemy. Groundhogs might be cute, but they marked their territory by raking young bark with sharp claws. Rabbits browsed the bark of young trees, especially after a heavy snow. But deer caused the worst damage. A nine-foot fence with electricity on the bottom wires dissuaded deer and kept my orchards safe.

William Fitzhugh's orchards were as safe and carefully tended as any in this era. In his eighteenth-century treatise *The History and Present State of Virginia*, Robert Beverley criticized planters who failed to care for their land or protect their crops. "The orchards, numerous as they were, were generally neglected, the plentifulness of the yield rather than the quality being most valued. Many persons who had gone to heavy expense to establish very large collections of fruit trees were not sufficiently interested in their preservation to protect them from the depredations of the animals."[13]

Fitzhugh's 2,500 trees, on the other hand, were fenced, with locust rails as "durable as most brick walls."[14] His trees were mostly grafted, the sign of a sophisticated orchard. Always the striving businessman, Fitzhugh wrote that his trees bore fruit in six or seven years and produced enough fruit for him to export cider.

While his orchard sent deep roots into southern soil, William Fitzhugh always hoped to return to England. In April 1686 he wrote several letters to British friends proposing to exchange his Virginia estate for property in England. He expressed frustration about his plantation life, the lack of education for his children, and mercurial tobacco prices. Through a fortuitous marriage, inherited wealth, business acumen, and the labor of enslaved people, Fitzhugh gained land and social position in Virginia that he could not have obtained in England. But late in life he longed for home.

Apples, on the other hand, found their ideal home in the South. In orchards like Fitzhugh's, apples jumped the locust fence and, as seedling trees, began the giant breeding experiment that gave rise to southern apples.

People also played a role in apple genetics in the early South. On the Fitzhugh estates, it is likely that the indentured servants and enslaved people who labored in the orchards observed which apples tasted best, stored longest, or dried without rotting. Experienced laborers would have grafted and reproduced these apples. Though their history is obscured, the skills and desires of these unnamed farmers shaped the future of southern tree fruit. Apples grew in the South entwined with the power of privilege, the violence of land seizure, and the legacy of enslavement.

By the time William Fitzhugh died in 1701, southern-spawned apples appeared on American nursery lists. As local apples acquired names and uses, English apples became less common in southern orchards. Apples were as opportunistic as Fitzhugh, but, unlike him, they were happy in their southern home.

A generation after Fitzhugh, George Washington, St. George Tucker, and other aristocratic southern farmers wrote detailed accounts of apples' keeping qualities. They eschewed English apples and described superb cider blends and the subtle scent and flavors of their favorite southern varieties.

In the life span of a tree, apples became a ubiquitous southern fruit.

Though my trees are 300 miles southwest of the Chesapeake, the scents and sounds at Foggy Ridge would be familiar to a Northern Neck grower. On a spring day, orchards roar with life. Pollinators crowd blossoms and swarm over clover and cress. Brilliant white Hewe's Crab blooms smell like lemon and lime citrus. I sink my face into Parmar's carmine-striped blossoms and inhale the aroma of sweet orange candy. My White Winter Pearmains growing on a mountain slope sport pale pink blooms with a spicy fragrance, much like Fitzhugh's "mains" in his flat orchard to the east, an orchard that tells a tale of the beginning of southern fruit.

LIMBS

At 9:00 p.m. one chilly Sunday night in late April,
Dan Vest's pickup truck wound up my gravel drive, right
on time. The truck's headlights bounced and swayed as he
made his way to the orchard gate. I jogged out to meet my
latest recruit and his team of workers, hopeful that Dan
and his bees would improve my apple harvest.

Several years after that first cold day planting young
trees, my first orchard had begun to produce fruit, but
not enough. I grew strips of wildflowers to encourage
native bees and left nearby fields unmowed to provide
year-round food for pollinators. But my first harvests
showed signs of poor pollination. It was time to call in the
experts.

Honeybees are not the most efficient individual pollinators, but they are hive dwellers. This means they live in
houses that people can move around. I had sweet-talked
Dan, head of the local beekeepers society, into driving
over from Floyd, Virginia, to deposit a couple of his hives
with me during apple bloom.

Dan donned his bee hat and fired up his smoker. I wore
coveralls, gloves, and a borrowed bee hat. By the time we
backed his pickup into the orchard it was pitch black,
and the headlights were no help for our task. Dan's day
job was working at a nearby manufacturer that produced
military equipment. When he pulled out military-grade
night vision goggles, I knew we'd have no trouble placing
the two hives in just the right spot.

After we settled the bees in their new home, we sat on
the tailgate, talking apples and bees. I sheepishly asked if
I could try his goggles, and he said, "I need to get home. . . .
You just keep them until I come back for the bees."

Dan didn't know he had just changed my life.

That cloudy night with not a star in the sky, I sat on
the back patio, Dan's goggles glued to my face and a new

world all around me. Huge white moths hovered over the blooming clematis. Bats dove out of crevices in the chimneys. The air around me was thick with flying insects of all shapes and sizes. When I looked at the edge of the woods, I saw eyes. I had no idea there were so many possums and raccoons close by. And those taller eyes . . . I wasn't sure I wanted to know their provenance. Vibrant night life surrounded me as I saw with new eyes the world that lived right outside my door.

In the four weeks I kept Dan's goggles, I became a night walker. I saw owls killing field mice in the orchard. One night I caught the swish of a gray fox tail slipping under the orchard gate. I watched moths visit apple blooms and thought of all the nights I had walked through the orchards after dark, practically breathing the moths and insects but never seeing them.

The orchards I thought I knew so well came alive in new ways. Dan's goggles humbled me. What I had thought was my world had been only a partial view—there was an exquisite nighttime universe all around me, one I had barely noticed.

Dan's bees improved pollination, and the next fall we had the best crop ever. But the box of ripe apples I delivered to Dan were less in thanks for his bees than for my new eyes.

———————

When people ask me, "Why apples?" I'm tempted to tell the truth—I fell in love with apple names. It wasn't flavor, at least at first, or the thrill of planting a tree that will outlive me. It was names like Magnum Bonum, called "Maggie Bowman" on my home turf. Or Sheepnose, which makes perfect sense once you see the pointed end of this apple.

The names quickly led me to stories, often constructed to romanticize what might be a grittier tale.

Books about old apples tell the tale of the Junaluska apple (also called Junaluskee), said to be Cherokee warrior and leader Junaluska's favorite apple. Junaluska so admired this apple, he forced the federal government that seized his land during the removal crisis of the 1830s to compensate him an additional fifty dollars for his tree. While this story emphasizes the tree and Junaluska's determination, it fails to engage the physical, emotional, and cultural violence experienced by the Cherokee people when the US government drove them from land they had occupied for thousands of years. It also fails to highlight Junaluska's persistence in returning to North Carolina after being forcibly evicted.

My vision for making cider at Foggy Ridge was to be as proximate as possible, to live close to my fruit and inhabit my cider as intimately as I

could. I wanted the reality, not the myth. Nowhere was the apple myth more buffed and fabricated than for "Indian fruit."

———————

North America is a natural orchard. When Europeans arrived in the sixteenth century, plums, several species of crabapples, and cherries grew across the Eastern Seaboard. Mulberries populated much of the South, leading early colonizers to briefly flirt with a silk industry.[1] Persimmons grew as tall as eighty feet. But the native North American landscape was not the uncultivated, virgin space many imagine. As early as AD 1500, Indigenous people practiced complex forms of agriculture in the South. When white colonizers arrived, Native people commonly used more than 200 species of trees, fruits, and vines. Indigenous southerners were "ambitious disturbers and manipulators of the landscape."[2]

Native Americans were experienced in coaxing food and useful products from trees. They cultivated trees by protecting them from competition and encouraged productive growth through activities like thinning or pruning. Ethnographers have found evidence in north Georgia and western North Carolina of "the husbandry of large, and woody plants."[3] When *Malus domestica* arrived, Indigenous people were primed to embrace this useful fruit.

In *Nature and History in the Potomac Country*, James Rice imagines an Algonquian settlement in the 1650s, when Indigenous people still outnumbered Europeans in the region around Virginia's Potomac River, close to the site of Fitzhugh's orchard with its grafted English trees: "While the tobacco leaves were curing, workers . . . harvested and stored the corn. They harvested fruit, dried some of it, and made cider from the late apples. (October was referred to as 'cyder time.') This was also an opportune time to plant new fruit trees."[4]

By the eighteenth century, "this fruit was commonly grown by all Indian tillers of the soil."[5] White southerners pushing into Indigenous territories found apple orchards around Creek, Cherokee, and Choctaw settlements in North and South Carolina, Georgia, and Alabama.

During the Cherokee War of 1776, General Griffith Rutherford's troops raided Cherokee homes in western North Carolina and destroyed "great apple trees." In 1801, Thomas Jefferson directed Indian agents to send apple seeds to southern tribal groups "to encourage them to become more agricultural and less warlike."[6]

Apples also functioned as a tool of terrorism. In New York, Seneca villages and extensive orchards "were as powerful symbols of a settled and civilized lifestyle as existed in eighteenth century America."[7] On September 3, 1779, just as apples were ripening, the American army, on

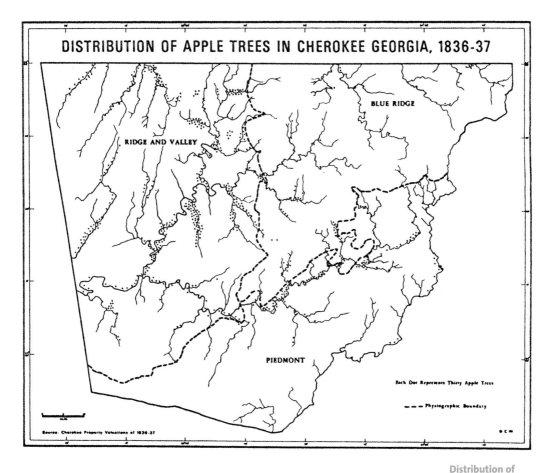

DISTRIBUTION OF APPLE TREES IN CHEROKEE GEORGIA, 1836-37

BLUE RIDGE

RIDGE AND VALLEY

PIEDMONT

Each Dot Represents Thirty Apple Trees

— — — Physiographic Boundary

Source: Cherokee Property Valuations of 1836-37

D C W

Distribution of Apple Trees in Cherokee Georgia, 1836–37. Museum of the Cherokee Indian, Cherokee, NC.

orders from General George Washington, destroyed Seneca orchards by girdling, or cutting the bark of, the trees and burning fruit stores. In the South we see similar destruction of "settled and civilized" lives and the orchards that grounded them.

In North Carolina and Georgia, the Cherokee people cultivated *Malus domestica* at least since the early 1700s. They dried apples and stored fruit in pit cellars in front of hearths where the heat prevented freezing.[8] Cherokee distillers, such as Ned Christie, John Smith, and Jesse Raper, likely used apples as well as peaches for brandy.[9]

In the South, the rich Native American apple experiment ended with the Indian Removal Act of 1830 and the expulsion of 123,000 Native Americans from their homelands in several waves of violent removals.[10] At the time of Native expulsion, federal valuators estimated Cherokee homes, crops, possessions, and land at $1.68 million. The details of this valuation paint a picture of rich Cherokee orchard practices. Over half of Cherokee households had mature orchards.[11] Smaller farms like Robert Brown's had "sixty-four peach trees, twenty-one apple trees, a cherry tree, and a Chickasaw plum tree."[12] Major Ridge's substantial orchards held "1,141 peach trees, 418 apples, 21 cherries, 11 quince, and several plum trees."[13] Federal agents who documented Cherokee property in North Carolina recorded over 3,000 apple trees on 309 farms in that state.[14]

In the early nineteenth century, Georgia had the most significant remaining Indigenous population in America. Over 10,000 Cherokee and Creek people owned a quarter of the present-day state, about 15,000 square miles.[15] That ownership changed forever on May 26, 1838, when 7,000 federal troops and Georgia militia expelled the Cherokee people from land they had occupied for centuries—just thirty-seven years after Jefferson had sent apple seeds to inspire Native people to become less warlike. They were driven from their land with brutal precision, "leaving no time for the dispossessed to collect their belongings or even gather their children. At night, they roused families from their homes, placed them under guard, and then slept in their still-warm beds."[16] State and federal troops marched Cherokee men, women, and children to military sites where they waited there for the disastrous trek to internment camps.

By mid-June, Gen. Winfield Scott announced, "Georgia has been entirely cleared of red population."[17] Though almost all the Cherokee people were expelled, some refused to leave their land or took shelter in the mountains. Others attempted to return to their home by escaping from the internment camps where they were temporarily housed. All the Native orchards remained.

Native Americans were some of the best farmers in the world. They grew seedling orchards in the most fruitful apple-growing region in the South. They lived close to their fruit; they selected and replicated apples that suited their desires and needs. And they still do today.

In 1843, Junaluska walked over 800 miles from Oklahoma back to his home in North Carolina. He eventually regained ownership of a portion of his land, including, according to some sources, his favorite apple tree. Today, tribal members of the Eastern Band of the Cherokee, descendants of the Cherokee people who resisted removal, escaped deportation, or who returned to the East from Oklahoma, grow apples with deep roots in Cherokee history.

Yet despite revitalization efforts, this Native apple narrative is a whisper. Like the many southern rivers and places that carry Native names, apples bear their origin in Indigenous culture, but the people and histories remain too often concealed.

JUICE

Nail-polish remover is not the best aroma for a beverage, but that was the scent coming off a five-gallon carboy full of my latest batch of cider. After several years of home cidermaking, I had created a few drinkable blends, many highly flawed gallons, and not a single drop I would choose to serve friends.

My test orchard was producing fruit, and I hoped to soon make cider commercially. But first I had to make cider worth drinking.

Compared to most home cidermakers, I was well equipped with know-how. I used a pH meter. I fermented in glass carboys that I cleaned and sanitized meticulously. I used an airlock and carefully added fermentation nutrients. But my tasting notebook was full of descriptors like "rotten eggs," "burnt rubber," "airplane glue," and "Band-aids." This was not the cider I had in mind.

I wanted to make cider that could be described, like Thomas Jefferson's, as "silky Champaigne."[1] I hoped for cider as rich and flavorful as the Normandy ciders I'd enjoyed in France. I would be happy with a smooth sipping cider like the local kegged ciders I sampled in British pubs.

I am someone who detests confusion. Give me a challenge and a path to a solution, and I'm all in. I'll bear down and work as hard as anyone. But wandering around, not knowing where to go or what to do . . . not my strength.

That day I sat on the basement floor and cried over my nail-polish cider. I had a serious pity party about all the money I had spent trying to learn how to make cider and all the time I had spent acquiring the best apples I could find, pressing them with my little home press and fermenting the juice. I had read every book about cidermaking I could get my hands on. I had taken short courses on wine fermentation at Virginia Tech and attended sensory training at a California wine lab. In spite of years of effort, delicious cider still eluded me. I cried over the dreams that felt more out of reach than ever before.

I picked up the heavy carboy and poured the whole batch down the drain. As I poured, I made a bet with myself: "In the next year, I will do everything I possibly can to learn how to make flavorful cider. If I still can't make cider I want to drink after one more year, then I'll give up this dream."

That five gallons of stinky cider started me on my real cider journey.

———————

Apples sneaked into America in a glass of cider. Colonists from South Carolina to New England grew seedling orchards "almost wholly for cider."[2] Seed-grown apples were mostly bitter or sour, but few sought apples for the table. In the South and elsewhere, cider was the most important beverage, "a staple for all classes of Americans and a form of currency for goods and services."[3]

In history books, New England owns the cider chapter, but the South's cider narrative is a barrel full of rich stories. After all, orcharding by English colonizers began in a coastal Virginia town with an elevation of just three feet above sea level. In 1629 Captain John Smith painted a rosy picture of Jamestown fruit: "Peaches in abundance; also Apples, Pears, Apricocks, Vines, Figges and other Fruits . . . prospering exceedingly."[4] This was in sharp contrast to the "starving time" twenty years earlier, when two of every three colonizers at James Fort perished. Even if we discount Smith's upbeat portrayal, descriptions of southern orchards fill the pages of farm journals and letters from this period.

And southern apples meant southern cider. "From the founding of Jamestown to the time of George Washington and Thomas Jefferson, on down to that of Robert E. Lee, every plantation owner made cider, drank cider, and bragged about his cider."[5]

Though not expertly plotted, the trees in my first orchard marched in loosely organized rows, north to south. Early southern cider orchards looked like haphazard collections, with trees planted in irregular rows among the stumps of newly cut virgin timber. Farmers sowed apple seeds in a nursery plot and then transplanted the seedlings into orchards of about fifty trees per acre.[6] Or they grafted cuttings, gained by pulling shoots from the base of trees, onto native crabapple roots. Pigs, sheep, and cattle grazed in most orchards, so tree limbs were pruned high. Every farm had an orchard of several acres. Plantations powered by the labor of indentured servants and enslaved people grew thousands of trees.

If they were not consumed by hogs, apples were most likely turned into cider. Lots of cider. Richard Bennett, a seventeenth-century York County, Virginia, apple grower, stored twenty butts of cider each year, about 2,600 gallons, enough to supply a family with thirty-six wine-sized bottles of cider a day.[7] Each fall, George Washington's Mount Vernon plantation produced an astonishing 120 gallons of cider or brandy a day.[8]

In an early southern economy based on exchanging one agricultural product, primarily tobacco, for manufactured goods, fruit trees provided cash income through cider. As early as 1697, Mrs. Mary Naylor, of Elizabeth City County, Virginia, received ten pounds sterling as lease for her cider orchard.[9] Cider was bequeathed in wills[10] and featured in real estate advertisements. In the seventeenth and early eighteenth centuries, southern cider commanded two shillings and six pence a gallon, higher than the price of cider in England.[11] Cider and brandy were in every southern market, and by the late eighteenth century, both were exported to the far South and the West Indies.[12]

Southern cider flowed freely: Hugh Jones, chaplain to the Virginia House of Burgesses, wrote in 1724, "Apple-trees are raised from seeds . . . and make . . . with good management, an Excellent Cyder, not much inferior to that of Herfordshire, when kept to a good Age; which is rarely done, the Planters being good Companions and Guests whilst the Cyder lasts."[13] The "morning draught" was seen as a "protection against the miasmatic exhalations of the marshes."[14] Southerners drank cider morning, noon, and night—and even at funerals. "So intemperate was the indulgence at funerals, more especially in cider and rum that some testators left instructions in their wills that no liquors were to be distributed on the occasion of their burials."[15]

While cider was freely drunk, it was often little respected. In his 1807 essay "On Cider," Reverend John B. Johnson describes at length the most common way of making cider, a process he condemns as "the art, not of making, but of spoiling cider." Fruit selection was more about volume than quality. And according to the reverend, little attention was given to careful fermentation: "Apples of all tastes, sweet, tart, sour—of all sorts, from the aromatic spitzenberg to the acrid crab—of every condition, unripe, mature, mellow, sound, knotted, rotten, depending from the branch or mouldering on the ground, are all gathered together; and, as though they had not already contracted impurity enough . . . they are heaped into one mass, to ferment and rot, for a period of time which conveniency, or perhaps chance, may prescribe."[16]

For my orchard and future cidery, I planned to employ temperature-controlled stainless steel tanks and a hydraulic apple press. But until apple presses arrived after the American Revolution, southern cider-makers transformed apples into juice by pounding apples in a trough with wooden mallets. In South Carolina, John Lawson reported the work that began a summer cider: "We beat the first of our Codlin cider" from June 10 to June 25, 1709.[17] In March 1760, when his Mount Vernon fields would have been striped with yellow cress, George Washington recorded bottling "91 dozn of Cyder."[18] Later he noted, "Began to beat Cyder at Doeg Run Muddy Hole, & in the Neck," referring to the first primitive step in making a new batch of cider at three of his properties.[19] Cider aged or "mellowed" in hogsheads or smaller rundlets, wooden barrels ranging from about twenty to sixty gallons. Cidermakers often topped off these barrels with a gallon or two of apple brandy to prevent spoilage.

English gardening books were the only agricultural guides for early southerners, and they all included advice for growing apples and making cider. J. S. Buel's 1869 *The Cider Maker's Manual*, which would have been available to well-read southern orchardists, detailed the steps to ferment, clarify, age, and bottle cider. In his 1872 book on southern fruit culture, James Fitz recommended pressing apples in haircloth rather than in bands of straw to achieve a "cooling, pleasant and wholesome liquor."[20] Newspapers as far south as the *Yazoo Democrat* published instructions on how to make cider.[21] I studied these early cider guides as carefully as I took the enology courses I attended at Virginia Tech, searching for clues about southern cider.

Early cidermaking was far from the scientific model I had in mind. Reverend Johnson's "On Cider" scolded American apple growers, "The art of making Cider is, in our country, little attended to; and, I am persuaded, little understood."[22] Johnson specified when to harvest apples for the best cider, how to mature them before pressing, the proper way to press apples in a mill, and how to clean the fermentation vessels. When he arrived at the actual task of making cider, his essay took on the tenor of a modern thriller—"Having now filled the casks with the new must, as it ran from the press, you approach the very crisis, the most difficult part of the whole process, that is, the fermentation."[23] Johnson knew that flavor can be made, and lost, as apple juice ferments into cider.

———

Early southern cidermakers knew that while cider is easy to make, it is hard to make well. First there is the labor: grafting and planting trees,

◄ Photograph by Tony Greatorex.

fencing to protect orchards from livestock and wildlife. These are the same tasks in the twenty-first century as they were in the seventeenth. For early southerners, after harvest came the brute work of pounding apples, pressing in a handpress, and then transferring heavy pails of juice into fermentation barrels. Even with my modern mechanical grinder and hydraulic apple press, I always needed a handful of ibuprofen at bedtime on press days.

But much more than muscle power goes into cider. Apple varieties contribute complex flavor to cider, and terroir bestows distinct characteristics. The cidermaker's know-how is just as important as the quality of the raw materials.

Farming is all about noticing—observing when and under what conditions a specific seed sprouts. Discerning the most useful fruits. Safeguarding young seedlings with all the vigilance of a parent watching over a toddler. Murdo Laird, one of my early cider mentors, stressed the connection between farming and fermenting by preaching, "When you ferment cider, you are farming yeast." Like a good farmer, I checked my ferments daily, sometimes several times a day, measuring acid and sugar levels, tasting for flavor. In early southern orchards, those closest to the tree and the fruit—the farmers who dug holes for trees and climbed high to pick apples, the ones with apple pomace under their fingernails—were best equipped to notice.

So who were the yeast farmers of southern cider?

The world of southern fruit has always been diverse, populated with skilled grafters from Italy and Scotland and enriched by the farming traditions of French Huguenots and Belgians. Southern apples were founded to a great extent on fruit cultivated by Native Americans. But the people who *did* the work and *owned* the knowledge and craft of growing apples and fermenting cider were often enslaved Black men and women.

Enslaved people ate apples, consumed cider, and practiced some of the most sophisticated cidermaking in the early South. In *Letters from Alabama* from 1859, Philip Henry Gosse lamented the paltry food rations provided to enslaved people and added, "In the fruit season, the orchard affords them a considerable help."[24] Gilbert Imlay's account of farms and gardens in Tennessee and Kentucky in the 1790s described orchards that fed appetites for cider and brandy.[25] In *The Edible South*, Marcie Ferris records a common eighteenth-century food consumed by enslaved people: corn mush with cider, hog's-lard, or molasses.[26] Myths about southern cidermaking feature some version of a white farmer pressing apples on a mountain farm or of an aristocratic landowner swigging cider at breakfast. The most skilled apple growers and cidermakers were often Black southerners, those who did the daily work of growing fruit and farming yeast.

Ferris writes eloquently about "slavery's rigid control of people and food . . . where racial power established a divided and contradictory southern cuisine of privilege, utility, and deprivation."[27] Enslaved men and women worked on the front line of agriculture. In doing the labor of clearing and planting, tending and harvesting, they were best positioned to notice. Just as culinary and management skills were closeted in kitchens, orchards cloaked the considerable skill required to make fine cider.

Cultivating cider fruit and making cider occupied significant time and labor at Thomas Jefferson's Monticello plantation: the labor and time of enslaved men and women. In *The Fruits and Fruit Trees of Monticello*, Peter Hatch points out that Jefferson's north orchard, which was devoted to cider apples and peaches, held about 265 trees, consisting of just a few cider varieties. Taliaferro and Hewe's Crab garnered the most praise in Jefferson's journals and letters, with the now-lost Taliaferro cider described as "the finest cyder we have ever known, and more like wine than any other liquor I have ever tasted which was not wine."[28]

Even with a dedicated cider apple orchard tended by skilled labor, Jefferson's household drank more cider than it produced. The large quantities of cider produced at Monticello were not sufficient—a note on household consumption listed 460 bottles of Taliaferro and 72 bottles of red Hughes bottled in March 1810. Jefferson regularly purchased cider from his neighbors Charles Massie and Fanny Brand.[29]

In an 1802 letter to Thomas Newton asking for assistance in purchasing cider from Norfolk, Jefferson acknowledged the skill required for correctly bottling cider and lamented what were likely common cider flaws of the time—"a great inequality in the bottles, from some being better or worse corked, and an inequality in the casked from their not understanding the true state of the liquor for bottling."[30]

Jefferson sent specific instructions on how to harvest fruit for cider, when and how to press, and how to handle bottling, as in this 1817 letter to overseer Edmund Bacon: "We have saved red Hughes enough from the North orchard to make a smart cask of cyder. they are now mellowing & beginning to rot. I pray you therefore to have them made into cyder immediately. Let them be made clean one by one, and all the rotten ones thrown away or the rot cut out. Nothing else can ensure fine cyder."[31] Making quality cider fit for a plantation owner's household clearly required skill.

Many of Jefferson's cider guidelines were enacted by an enslaved man named Jupiter, whose last name was likely Evans. Born in the same year as Jefferson, Jupiter was an enslaved personal servant to Jefferson for much of his life, as well as a coachman and skilled stonecutter.[32] Along with other household members, he was charged with many of the steps in crafting Monticello's cider. When Jupiter died, Jefferson wrote to his son-in-law Thomas Mann Randolph: "He leaves a void in my domestic administration which I cannot fill up—I must get Martha or yourself to give orders for bottling the cyder in the proper season in March. There is nobody but Ursula who unites trust & skill to do it. She may take anybody she pleases to aid her."[33] Ursula Granger, an enslaved woman known for her culinary and management skills, directed aspects of cidermaking at Monticello, along with her husband, George, an overseer at Monticello.

Monticello's cider, the "silky Champaigne" that twenty-first-century cidermakers aspire to make, was made by enslaved men and women, skilled beverage crafters who provided the labor and the know-how for one of the South's most storied beverages.

The high praise conferred on Jefferson's cider, the widespread popularity of Hewe's Crab and the Taliaferro apple—much, likely most, of this praise was due to Ursula and George Granger, Jupiter Evans, and the enslaved men and women who did the physical labor of farming and the intellectual labor of overseeing trees, fruit, and fermentation. They were best positioned to make the daily decisions that led to delicious fruit and cider that tasted like champagne.

This was the cider I aimed to make. Cider made with precious, highly flavored cider apples, crafted with care and attention. Cider made by the person who grows the fruit and who does both the physical and intellectual labor. Cider made proximate.

FRUIT

The cider apple trees that K. C. Murphy and I planted on that cold November day swayed in a warm breeze. With a few years' growth, most were already taller than I was and showed distinct personalities. Hewe's Crab sprawled in the rows, sturdy limbs extending in all directions. Parmar's slim branches formed an elegant brow at the top of the orchard. I was beginning to know my young trees as well as I knew the lines on my face.

Many apple trees naturally grow upright, a trait called apical dominance. The dominant trunk, called the leader, shoots upward in an attempt to steal light. Side limbs also reach up, competing for light. Apple limbs that grow upright tend to produce more leaves than fruit, so one task for apple growers is to train and prune limbs to a more horizontal growth pattern, a practice called spreading. Harrison's strong limbs always reached straight upward, no matter what I did to discourage this trait.

After several years of growing trees, planning a cidery, and fermenting the first apples from my baby orchard, I had found a rhythm to my bifurcated life. Almost every Monday I drove two hours to the Greensboro airport to catch a flight to a consulting engagement, usually in New York. Thursday, if I was lucky, I made it back to the farm. Then three delicious days of farm work . . . with expense reports, study for the next week's projects, and conference calls woven among orchard duties. The branches of my life were as tangled as an apple tree's.

Moments like this June day, when I spread a row of Cannon Pearmain trees, made the thousands of air miles and late-night planning sessions worthwhile. Southerners have grown this apple since the late eighteenth century for cooking and cider. Like Albemarle Pippin's, Cannon Pearmain's flavor intensifies with a few months in storage, and I thought I might one day ferment a blend of these two storied southern apples.

Today, I wanted nothing more than to be in this place. I carefully bent young limbs to near horizontal and then spread them with plastic limb spreaders. I examined the tender green leaves for insects and disease, a practice called "scouting," one of my favorite orchard chores. These trees would likely outlive me, and I wanted them to begin life healthy and headed in the right direction.

On 6:00 a.m. flights to New York with my laptop open, the struggles of my days overwhelmed me. I was rushing through life, charging from farm to airport to cities, careening from one barrier to another. I felt trapped by the equation I had designed. My consulting work stimulated me, but the corporate world bent for no one—if work called, it didn't matter if it was time to harvest or prune. I needed income to start my cidery, but I also required time to learn all I needed to know to grow apples and make cider. A perfect week meant three days in farm clothes, but a perfect week was a rare one.

I needed a pause.

That June day I took a deep breath and attempted a reset. I told myself, "Your orchard is healthy. You are learning every day. You can take small steps." I heard bees working the red clover around my feet. The brilliant green orchard grass shone in the morning sun. My pulse slowed, and my long list of roadblocks receded.

Then I heard a sharp cry, like an alarm cry from a bird. I looked around, thinking I might be close to a nest. A fast-moving shape at the top of the orchard rows caught my eye. The biggest black snake I'd ever seen in my life was slithering down the orchard, its head raised and a full-grown rabbit in its mouth. The rabbit's high-pitched squeal had caught my attention.

The rabbit cried and squirmed, but the snake had a firm grip. I had time for a few breaths before I saw the third actor in this drama—just outside the orchard fence, a gray fox stared at the snake and the rabbit, as transfixed as I was. The fox lunged at the fence, but the electric lines kept him at bay. He paced the fence line, sides heaving, tongue lolling, his eyes never leaving the snake and the rabbit.

Just when I thought this play couldn't get more dramatic, the rabbit pulled free from the snake and streaked up the orchard. The snake followed, but heading uphill it couldn't catch the rabbit. The fox went crazy, jumping and diving at the fence.

When I took a step to move closer, the fox disappeared into the woods. I caught the snake on the end of a shovel and threw him over the fence. I searched the orchard but never found the rabbit, dead or alive.

I took a few more deep breaths and tried to slow my heartbeat. I returned to scouting and spreading apple trees. For the rest of the day, thoughts about consulting gigs or barriers to opening a cidery never crossed my mind. The image of the shiny black snake, as thick as my forearm, moving in powerful waves down the orchard with a rabbit held aloft has never left me. The fox's intent gaze, the rabbit's near-translucent pink ears, the drama of those few seconds . . . this orchard scene lifted me above all the obstacles I imagined.

That night I slept poorly. The day's images lingered, perhaps along with some adrenaline. The next day I put away my laptop and expense reports. I returned to the orchard, convinced that what stood between me and my apple dreams were not formidable barriers but the thinnest of eggshells. A divider that could be conquered by a rabbit's squeal and dispelled by a deep breath.

In winter I could spot apples from a fast-moving car on winding mountain roads. Even before I noticed the fat fruit buds, I saw their silhouettes on every hillside—dark, drooping limbs and a tangle of branches. Each spring, pale pink and creamy apple blossoms dotted fence lines. Regardless of the season, I unfailingly recognized fruit trees.

It takes an experienced eye to catch an apple tree in winter. But in the fall, everyone sees apples.

On an early fall day in the late eighteenth century, Major Richard Taliaferro saw an apple tree full of fruit "in a large old field near Williamsburg."[1] Something drew this colonial architect to this specific seedling tree standing in the middle of a roadside field. Perhaps, as one researcher has suggested, he wandered into the field from Doncaster's Ordinary, a tavern on the New Kent–Williamsburg Stage Road. Or maybe he smelled ripe apples as he rode by on his horse.[2] We don't know what prompted Major Taliaferro to gain permission from the landowner to gather these unnamed apples. But once he did, he made a cask of cider.

As it turned out, this wild fruit made excellent drink.

Richard Taliaferro liked his cider so much that he grafted trees from this lone seedling and planted an orchard, likely at Powhatan, his home outside Williamsburg. He named the apple "Robertson," after the man who owned the field. He later provided grafting wood to his son-in-law George Wythe, a law professor, who planted another orchard with the Robertson apple and who also made barrels of exceedingly good cider.

By the early 1800s, this apple from a wild tree growing in the South at an elevation of eighty feet less than thirty miles from the Atlantic Ocean had gained an outsize reputation. Jefferson said that the cider from this apple "comes nearer to the silky Champaigne than any other."[3] In 1814, Jefferson wrote that the Robertson apple "has more justly & generally been distinguished by the name of the Taliaferro apple, after him to whom we are indebted for the discovery of it's [*sic*] valuable properties."[4] In just a few years, Major Taliaferro's wild cider apple was tamed. It gained a new name and launched a southern legacy of cider apples.

———————

Seedling orchards full of tart, tannic apples supplied fruit for much of the cider drunk in the South. Some early southerners experimented with English cider apples, like the Redstreak apple from Herefordshire. But southerners soon recognized that specific apple varieties suited to the South produced the best-tasting cider.

The Virginia White Apple, the first named southern apple variety, appeared in York County records in 1716.[5] William Byrd wrote in 1732 about drinking "exceeding good cider" from the Virginia White Apple, "which made us talkative till ten o'clock."[6] Around the time Major Taliaferro grafted scions from the lone seedling tree he found in an eastern Virginia field, George Washington recorded grafting 43 "Maryland Red Strick" on March 21, 1763, at Mount Vernon. Washington reserved his River Farm cider orchard for 215 trees of this popular variety.[7] In 1796, Jefferson's north orchard housed three varieties of cider fruit: Hewe's Crab, Golden Wilding, and Clarke's Pearmain.[8]

Driven by colonists' thirst for cider, southern apples began acquiring names, reputations, and stories.

Farther west, Edward Cranford planted apple seeds in 1790 in what is now Brooks County, West Virginia.[9] One of his seedling trees became Grimes Golden, a popular cider apple sold throughout the South and known for making a highly alcoholic cider. In my mountain orchard, Grimes Golden fermented into cider with over 10 percent alcohol, higher than other varieties from the same orchard.

In 1771, Virginian John Ralls listed his farm for sale by describing his cider orchard: "The Plantation is in good order with a very fine apple orchard from which are made seven or eight thousand gallons of cider a

▶

(*Clockwise from left*) Cannon Pearmain from Mineral, WV, by Amanda A. Newton; Limbertwig from Wake, NC, by Amanda A. Newton; Grimes Golden from Washington, DC, by Deborah G. Passmore; Smith Cider from Arlington, VA, by Mary D. Arnold. US Department of Agriculture Pomological Watercolor Collection, Rare and Special Collections, National Agricultural Library, Beltsville, MD.

59977
Cannon Pearmain
L. A. Arnold,
Keyser,
W. Va.

A. A. Newton.
10-16-12
10-23-12

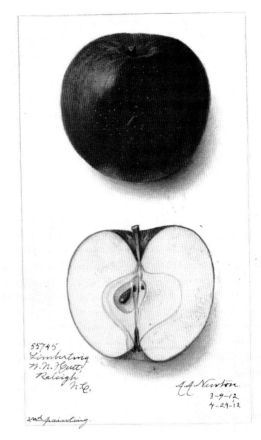

55745
Limbertwig
W. N. Hutt,
Raleigh
N. C.

A. A. Newton.
3-9-12
4-24-12

2nd painting.

Mary D. Arnold

34699
Grimes Golden
W. N. Irwin, Agr'l Dept.
D.C.

D. G. Passmore
9-13-'05
9-26-'05

year. (That quantity has been made on average ever since the year 1756.) There trees are of the best kind of fruit, and the cider as good as any on the continent."[10] Eight thousand gallons is equivalent to over 3,300 cases of cider per year or about 40,000 bottles. Even given the exaggeration that likely accompanied real estate listings, that's a lot of cider.

The *Farmer and Planter*, published in Pendleton, South Carolina, encouraged southerners to make cider from apples "which yield the richest juice" and promised that quality cider could garner "three to four dollars a barrel."[11]

The Hunge apple, famous for brandy, originated in Norfolk, Virginia, and flourished in the coastal South. Just six years after the Civil War ended, the American Pomological Society met in Richmond, Virginia, and tasted three southern cider apples: Gregory, Horse, and Smith Cider, extolled as "the rival of the Virginia crab."[12] Yates, known as a winter cider apple, came from Fayette County, Georgia, in the mid-nineteenth century. Cart-house, Parmar, the many versions of Limbertwig—the list of southern cider apples goes on, all apples noticed and selected by farmers from wild seedlings for the purpose of making their most common table drink. Southerners loved their cider and their cider apples, especially Taliaferro and Hewe's Crab.

Taliaferro's reputation as a superb cider apple spread beyond the South. William Coxe, a prominent pomologist, grew Taliaferro in New Jersey, where he called it Gloucester White. In 1809 he wrote, "I have the Gloucester Whites both in my nursery and Orchards sent to me by Colonel Mayo of Richmond as a most admired liquor fruit."[13] The Prince Nursery in Queens, New York, the largest nursery in America at the time, offered this apple in the 1840s as "a variety of the first rank for cider."[14]

As early as 1754, Hewe's Crab grew throughout central Virginia. This intensely flavored cider apple, splashed with brilliant red and yellow, makes a syrupy juice that ferments into richly flavored cider valued by contemporary cidermakers. Peter Hatch notes in *The Fruits and Fruit Trees of Monticello* that the *Virginia Gazette* property advertisements in the mid-eighteenth century mentioned the Hewe's Crab more often than any other apple.[15] A November 6, 1766, advertisement in this Williamsburg newspaper announced that the farm for sale contained "an extraordinary fine apple orchard, consisting of Hughe's crab, pearmains, latter russetings . . . from which this year has been made 4,000 gallons of Hughe's crabs cider."[16]

South Carolina's Pomaria Nurseries listed eight varieties of crabapples in its 1862 catalog and touted "Hughes" as "best cider . . . great bearer."[17] Farther south in Georgia, Fruitland Nurseries offered "Hewe's

Virginia Crab" in its 1868–69 *Descriptive Catalogue of Fruit and Ornamental Trees, Shrubs, Vines, Roses, Evergreens, Hedge Plants, Etc.*, stating that it is "the most popular apple for cider together with Waugh's Crab."[18]

Northern pomologists recognized the value of Hewe's Crab. Andrew Jackson Downing, one of America's most celebrated apple experts, wrote, "The Virginia Crab makes a very high flavored dry cider, which, by connoisseurs, is thought unsurpassed in flavor by any other, and retains its soundness for a long time."[19] William Coxe, known for his cider expertise, praised the Hewe's Virginia Crab as a cider apple with "sweet and highly flavored" juice that "runs through the finest flannel like spring water."[20]

By the late 1800s, southerners' preferences for cider fruit shaped orchards from Virginia to Mississippi. But southern cider apples suffered the same fate as cider fruit across America. Much has been written about the decline of cider in this country. Farms began to specialize as transportation improved, and farmers grew crops for distant markets rather than for local consumption. Immigrants brought brewing traditions along with a taste for far-easier-to-make beer. As orchard acreage grew, so did pests and disease, making it increasingly difficult to earn a profit from southern-grown apples. Even in the rural South, jobs began to shift from farms to towns. And between 1830 and 1840, alcohol consumption decreased by half due to the temperance movement.

In just a few decades, the South lost many of its most prominent cider apples.

Golden Wilding was last listed in a 1904 nursery catalog.[21] Virginia and North Carolina nursery catalogs sold the Gregory cider apple into the early 1900s, but this apple is now extinct.[22] The Prince Nursery listed Taliaferro in its 1835 catalog, the last listing for this storied apple. Carthouse (today often labeled Gilpin), Hunge, and Clarke's Pearmain can still be found in a few specialty nurseries. Thanks to its vigorous growth and cold hardiness, Virginia orchardists used Hewe's Crab as a rootstock for modern varieties, a practice that kept this valuable southern cider apple in production. The first orchard I planted included Horse, Parmar, Smith Cider, and Hewe's Crab.

But the Virginia White Apple is extinct, as is the much-lauded Taliaferro.

Because of rapturous accounts of cider made from this apple, Taliaferro is one of the most ardently sought lost apples in America. In 1997 I grafted a dozen trees from an old tree in Nelson County, Virginia, that several scholars believed to be of this long-lost variety. A half-dozen years later it was clear that I had devoted orchard space to a seedling apple that, fortunately for me, made excellent cider, but it was definitely not Taliaferro.

Taliaferro provides a tantalizing memory of the best expression of southern cider. Until recent scholarship from an Alabama district court judge with a talent for historical sleuthing, apple lovers have had only conflicting descriptions of this apple's appearance. Judge Susan Russ Walker has teased a credible picture of this storied apple from letters and unpublished manuscripts. She even posits where we might search for the missing Taliaferro. Apple rustlers interested in finding this missing cider link now have a reliable guide and a few clues.

Each fall, lifestyle journalists dust off the same tired article on cider in America. There is always a nod toward John Chapman, aka Johnny Appleseed. We invariably read the Benjamin Franklin quote on turning "all apples into cider." A handful of fall apple stories mention the many presidential cider drinkers, but they center the American cider story firmly in the North.

No one writes about the South's thorny cider history, one that knits the narratives of violent land seizure and enslavement with the strong thread of southern apples. No one talks about Taliaferro and the Virginia White Apple, the first American-born cider fruit. Each fall, cider boosters neglect to mourn the apples we have lost. And few mention the overflowing basket of southern cider apples that remain. Hewe's Crab, Parmar, Cannon Pearmain, Albemarle Pippin, the Limbertwig family, Keener Seedling, Mattamuskeet, Winter Jon, Yates, Kinnaird's Choice—it is a long list of southern fruit that still yields rich, syrupy juice each fall, full of pungent flavors and resonating with history.

LEAVES

"Should we wait to start pressing apples until Boss gets here?"

Murdo and his wife, Cindy, scurried around the tidy cidery, moving bins of bittersweet apples and shifting the grinder a few inches. Ever since a Virginia apple friend brokered an introduction to this West Coast cidermaker, Murdo Laird had been a generous long-distance mentor to my cider dreams. A few months after beginning our exchanges, I was able to tie a business trip to San Francisco with a detour to Murdo and Cindy's Napa Valley home to help with their first apple press of the season.

That's how it came to be that on September 1, 2001, I was standing on the concrete floor of a converted winery, nestled into a hillside off the Silverado Trail. Celebrated vineyards lined every inch of this valley—every inch, that is, other than the six steep acres of Murdo's cider apple orchard. I was in search of practical cidermaking skills from someone making cider in a style I envisioned for my southern orchard.

Murdo and I lived worlds apart, he in tony California wine country with a rustically elegant cidery, married to one of the country's most respected chefs, and I in Dugspur, Virginia, population 900, married to a beleaguered textile manufacturer and struggling to get my cider business off the ground. But through conversations and letters, Murdo and I had learned we were both pioneers, attempting to do a thing that seemed crazy to everybody else. Murdo was making eighteen-dollar-a-bottle cider on land that could yield eighty-dollar-a-bottle wine. I hoped to turn inedible apples into alcoholic cider in a dry, rural county populated by people who thought of cider as the brownish juice sold in roadside stands each fall.

We also learned that we both relished the fact that we didn't entirely know what we were doing.

That morning we began without Boss, who turned out to be not "Boss" but the musician Boz Scaggs, a friend from Murdo's filmmaking career who joined us later that morning for apple pressing. Murdo tutored me on cleaning and assembling the apple press, a hydraulic Squeezebox, named because it looks like a sideways accordion. Cindy manned the grinder and shoveled ground apples into the press. By our midday break we'd filled half of one of Murdo's stainless steel fermenters with rich, sweet juice.

Though we grew a few of the same varieties, Murdo's Napa Valley apples raised in stony volcanic soil with little rainfall had a much higher sugar content than apples from my 3,000-foot-elevation orchard. And they tasted very different from my Virginia-grown fruit. This was my first hands-on experience with the concept of terroir for apples, the idea that all the characteristics of a place—the soil, sunlight, rainfall, and even cultural practices—influence flavor.

Cindy served a Napa Valley lunch under live oaks with greens from her kitchen garden and grilled panini. I had a feeling that future lunch breaks in my Dugspur cider house would not be as chic.

As we talked and ate, my anxieties about being in this space with people I hardly knew began to recede. I desperately wanted to soak up the enthusiasm and creativity surrounding me, so I paid attention to everything. Cindy was all energy, a positive force and a strong wind at Murdo's back.

Like me, Murdo dove deep. He was full of knowledge, but like all great learners, he had questions too. He wanted to know, as did I, what kind of cider his apples would create and how best to coax flavor from his fruit. As I finished a glass of Murdo's cider, I began to understand that learning and problem-solving are fundamental to beverage making.

We talked about fermenting cider and how to achieve a balance between stressing yeast and giving yeast the chance for a healthy life. "Think of yourself as a yeast farmer. That's all wine- or cidermaking really is. . . . You are farming yeast."

Cindy gave me the best advice. "Just begin," she said. She was right. I needed to stop worrying over getting things perfect, over being perfectly prepared. I needed to *just begin.*

At the end of the day, Murdo guided me through tests to check pH. He helped me calculate the sulfite addition to kill off ambient yeast. The next morning we planned to "pitch yeast," wine-speak for adding a selected strain of yeast that Murdo chose to ferment his high-sugar apples at a low temperature. I was stunned by the joy of my first commercial apple pressing. The grace and hospitality of this couple moved me.

Ten days later I was in Washington, DC, leading a seminar at a bank near the White House when someone burst into the meeting room with news of the attack on the World Trade Center. We heard sirens and helicopters and saw smoke rising across the Potomac. The Pentagon had also been attacked. I crammed as many workshop participants into my rental car as possible and managed to make it back to our hotel in Chevy Chase.

Three days later I drove away from the city. I took the country route home rather than the interstate, angling southwest across Virginia down Highway 29. Golden ditch daisies and fields full of lime-green tobacco leaves lined the road. I listened to the service at the National Cathedral and stopped every twenty miles or so to lean on the steering wheel and sob.

Back at the farm I headed to the north field where our neighbor Wayne "Cornbread" Marshall was raking hay. Since Chuck and I moved to Virginia, Cornbread had pulled our truck out of ditches and repaired our tractor more than once. We talked about what just happened to our country. Goldenrod and Queen Anne's lace shone at the edge of the pasture, but I felt numb to the quiet farm rhythms that usually soothed me. The brilliant fall sky, usually full of air traffic, showed not a single contrail.

Cornbread said, "I ain't seen the sky so clear since I was a boy."

That night I dreamed I was in an art class. I chose to draw a simple still life, a bowl filled with fruit beside a vase of flowers. I'm sure my drawing was no good. I'm not an artist. But when I stepped back, I saw my rendering was very nice. My sister helped me place it in a wooden frame, and I realized my drawing was lovely.

When I woke, as was true for most of the following year, the first thing I thought of was the events of September 11. Then I remembered my dream.

I thought, "I can do this. Even though so much in the world is broken. Even though I'm not perfectly prepared, I can begin. I can begin making cider."

———————

In the fall of 1838, after militia evicted Cherokee people from their land, Jarvis Van Buren traveled from his home in Clarkesville, Georgia, deep into the Georgia and North Carolina mountains. The poplar trees were turning yellow as he rode on trails forged by Indigenous people and crossed rivers using ferries once operated by Cherokee ferrymen. That fall and for the next several years, Van Buren collected fruit and grafting wood from orchards that had been cultivated by Native Americans for over a century.

Apple hunting seemed an odd detour for this engineer and architect. Van Buren had recently moved from New York to manage the Stroop Iron Works.[1] His hometown of Kinderhook, founded in the early 1600s, was a thriving community thirty miles east of the Hudson River. Dutch and Huguenots, "the best farmers and gardeners in the American colonies," settled this region, bringing their rich agricultural traditions and skills.[2]

Native Americans had long farmed and cultivated seedling apple orchards in central New York and the Hudson River valley. Around 1715, a Tuscarora orchard in Oneida County was described as having several hundred trees.[3] Van Buren worked on the railroad connecting Schenectady to Albany and would likely have been familiar with Native American orchards.

Van Buren would have known of General John Sullivan's destruction of extensive Seneca orchards in New York's Finger Lakes region in 1779. He may have been aware that twenty years later, white farmers who occupied Indigenous orchards harvested fruit from the trees that sprouted from the roots of Seneca apples.[4]

Wealthy landowners cultivated apple orchards and sophisticated estate gardens around Kinderhook.[5] Fruit tree nurseries sold grafted English and American apple varieties, including Esopus Spitzenburg, discovered in New York in the early 1700s and one of Thomas Jefferson's favorite apples. By the time Van Buren immigrated to Georgia, fruit growers in his home region had access to scores of named apple varieties from established nurseries like the Prince Nursery on Long Island and David Thomas's Botanic Garden in Aurora, New York.[6]

In the early 1800s, on the eve of Van Buren's move south, the Hudson River valley was home to the largest apple orchards in America. Local horticultural societies and journals sparked the exchange of information and plants. Van Buren would likely have read the *Genesee Farmer*, a widely circulated agricultural journal founded in 1830 by Luther Tucker in Rochester, New York.

Van Buren grew up amid a rich horticultural tapestry woven with wild seedling orchards and cultivated fruit farms. He was aware of the apple-growing traditions of Indigenous people and may have known of harvests that white orchardists reaped from stolen Native orchards. He had read the best horticultural writing of his time. By the time Van Buren left New York, apples had ignited his imagination.

Van Buren moved to Clarkesville in 1838 to manage an ironworks but soon established himself as an architect and a contractor. He founded a sawmill and cabinet shop and built Greek Revival churches like Grace Episcopal, which still stands on the corner of Wilson and Green Streets. He designed picturesque Andrew Jackson Downing–inspired summer homes and built elegant furniture, patterning many after Downing's designs in books like *The Architecture of Country Homes*.[7] Informed by his horticultural background, Van Buren wrote articles in southern agricultural journals as well as in Downing's own publication, *The Horticulturist*. He became an influential advocate for diversified agriculture in the South.

By the mid-1830s, newly chartered Clarkesville in the northeast corner of Georgia offered a summer retreat for wealthy white southerners fleeing humidity and the threat of yellow fever. The Mountain View Hotel, an imposing structure with double porches and white painted columns, dominated the town square. Traffic bustled around the two-story brick Habersham County courthouse and along streets named for American presidents. Nearby Tallulah Falls, the "Niagara of the South," attracted day-trippers. By 1848 a family could travel from Savannah to Clarkesville by steamboat and stagecoach in a little over a week, and many did just that.

The Cherokee Unicoi Trail passed near Clarkesville, a trading path that traveled from the Chattahoochee River over the lowest mountain passes into Tennessee. By the early nineteenth century the Unicoi Turnpike was the closest thing to an interstate highway of the time. Running west from Toccoa, Georgia, into Tennessee, the turnpike was wide enough for coaches and wagons whose drivers found accommodations every twenty miles or so. This ancient road became a modern pathway into southern apple territory.

Between 1805 and 1833 the Georgia land lotteries distributed three-fourths of the land in the state, seizing Creek and Cherokee lands and conferring white ownership. Gold was discovered in Duke's Creek in 1828, and within a year 10,000 whites were illegally prospecting gold on Cherokee land.[8] The Georgia gold rush lasted only twenty years but solidified white ownership of north Georgia. The north Georgia mountains, abounding with Indigenous-grown apples, had become not just a passage west but a destination for well-to-do white southerners.

In 1840, Van Buren purchased ten acres and five enslaved people and founded Gloaming Nursery. There Van Buren integrated stolen Cherokee apples into mainstream southern agriculture, their wildness diluted, their Indigenous names disappeared, their history muted.

LEAVES

Named American apples exploded in the nineteenth century. In 1839 the William R. Prince Nursery on Long Island sold 173 apple varieties, including 98 American apples and 15 apples specifically for cider. This early list included apples that originated in the South like "Hughes" Virginia Crab and Carthouse, as well as apples widely grown in the South like Winesap.[9]

All over the South, southerners were taming wild apples. Seedling orchards endured longer in the South, creating greater genetic diversity and a natural testing ground for new varieties. As growers noticed and replicated their most useful fruit, named southern apples appeared in southern nurseries.

William Summer founded Pomaria Nurseries in South Carolina in 1840, and by 1860 it offered 500 apple varieties, including 300 varieties that originated in the South. Thomas Affleck opened Southern Nurseries in Washington, Mississippi, in 1848, which listed fruit trees "acclimated to the south" as well as varieties like Mississippi Sweeting and Vick Pippin from the Deep South.[10] By 1853 Lindley Nursery in Greensboro, North Carolina, offered 169 apple varieties. Agricultural reform was the farming topic of the day, and this movement emphasized tree fruit growing.[11] Nursery catalogs and advertisements in agricultural journals meant names for apples, and names required stories.

Jarvis Van Buren's Gloaming Nursery catalog for 1859 and 1860 listed 142 apple varieties, along with pears, peaches, nectarines, cherries, plums, apricots, grapes, and strawberries. He boldly advertised his stock as "southern" and seemed to dare his customers to order apples from outside the region: "Our collection of Southern Seedling Fruits is now beyond all competition as to numbers and excellence, and, at present prices, we trust all excuses for importations from other States are untenable."[12]

Van Buren found an excellent keeping apple in a Cherokee field in Habersham County and sold it as Mountain Belle.[13] In the early 1850s, he sold the Kittageskee apple, first grown by North Carolina Cherokees. Kittageskee was exported to Europe and grown commercially in France until World War II.[14]

The names from Gloaming Nursery's catalog evoke flavors, aromas, and places. They hint at the stories behind the fruit—Cane Creek Sweet, Mountain Sprout, Webb's Winter. In apples like Nantahalee, they echo the theft of Native land, language, and fruit, and mirror the erasure of Native presence.

North Carolina dominated Gloaming Nursery's early listing with fifty-nine varieties originating in this state. Alabama, South Carolina, and Virginia all contributed apples. Mississippi provided four apples, belying today's conventional wisdom that apples won't grow outside the mountain South. Van Buren included twenty-two apple varieties from Georgia, many appropriated from Indigenous orchards.

The 1859–60 catalog listed the origin, ripening month, and a brief description, often with tantalizing details. Tenderskin from Georgia was "red, small but very delicious," while Virginia's Autumn Wine was "large and exceedingly fine." Flavor descriptions got short shrift. When I read the Gloaming Nursery catalog I want to hear more about taste than "a sweet apple" or "very delicious." We learn that Chestatee from Georgia was "fine for cooking." But for the pre-refrigeration era, "a famous keeper" was high and frequent praise, meted out for twenty-three varieties in this catalog. "A good bearer" or "fine for livestock" or, like South Carolina's Maverick's Sweet, "hangs well on tree" betray nineteenth-century farmers' interest in sustenance.[15]

But aesthetics also appeared as part of this early southern apple picture. Cullawhee, from North Carolina, ripened in January and was "striped, a monster in size." Hoover from South Carolina was "spotted, large, good & very beautiful." North Carolina's Wonder was "striped, large, beautiful" but "a poor grower."[16]

Compared with the Stark Brothers' 1896 catalog, the first full-color American nursery catalog packed with elaborate marketing promises for perfect fruit, Van Buren's apple descriptions seem naively principled. Mountain Sprout was "good but decays soon." Santouchee was "second rate." Gloaming Nursery showcased old varieties grown for a century as well as apples new to the late 1800s, like Simmons' Winter, Robertson's Pearmain, Vandervere, and Curry's Winter.

By the end of the nineteenth century, southern apples had cast a wide, leafy canopy across the region.

———————————

Naming apples tamed them, but providing pictures of them conferred a life in commerce. Van Buren was an artist who had a gift for marketing southern fruit. Frances Tufts, a Van Buren descendant who lives in Clarkesville, said, "Jarvis was a renaissance man."[17] Her family owns many of the over fifty vivid portraits of apples, pears, and peaches painted by Van Buren.

The paintings range from unpolished, flat depictions to lively botanic illustrations, complete with realistic detail. His Junaluska portrait pictures an orange apple with russeted patches and irregular dots. His painting of Disharoon, likely an apple selected and grown by Georgia Cherokee orchardists, has deep charcoal shading and flat, dark green

leaves. An elaborate image of three apples with curled green foliage would be at home in any collection of formal botanic illustrations, with the dramatic Black Apple at its center. These paintings were central to Van Buren's promotion of Cherokee apples and his role in proselytizing others to the merits of southern fruit.

Throughout his life, Van Buren continued to build churches and homes in Clarkesville, but horticulture remained the center of his work. His entry in the *Dictionary of Georgia Biography* simply states that in 1840, Van Buren "purchased ten acres and a family of five slaves and began making his living principally through horticulture."[18]

This nursery owner entered southern agriculture at the cusp of the "golden age of apples," when white southern agriculturists aimed to create a commercial apple industry in the South. Family history states that Van Buren operated Gloaming Nursery on the ten-acre site of his home, Gloaming Cottage.[19] By 1850 his holdings had grown to four improved acres and sixty-five unimproved acres.[20] In this time he designed and built the Clarkesville Presbyterian Church; his own home, Gloaming Cottage; and a Gothic Revival home called Woodlands, along with pews, furniture, and bookcases inspired by the latest design trends. But alongside what today might be called his "day job," Van Buren promoted southern fruit.

In less than twenty years, Gloaming Nursery offered 142 apple varieties, 191 pears, 44 peaches, 16 cherries, and 13 plums, as well as apricots, nectarines, strawberries, and grapes. Apples sold for one dollar per hundred, with "new and rare kinds" selling for two dollars.[21] Using stolen Cherokee apples and stolen Black labor, Gloaming Nursery was one of the first southern nurseries to promote apples originating in the South.

Jarvis Van Buren collected and sold apples selected by generations of Native people, apples that reflected their desires and needs. He named these apples, erasing Native names they would have carried. He painted them, and promoted Cherokee fruit in agricultural journals and in horticultural exhibitions. In a few decades, Cherokee apples dominated nursery lists across the South and beyond, but absent their connection to Indigenous southerners.

Tamed

PLANTED

Rows of freshly cut hay lay coiled in the pasture like long green plaits. On this sunny September morning Wayne Marshall started mowing early, and by dusk the lime-green rows had dried to sage-colored strips. What began as an ocean of fat seed heads rippling in the wind now lay flat and still. The previous week I had seen a doe wade through the tall grass, her body hidden, her head swaying forward and back on a slender neck as elegant as Nefertiti's. Wayne would return tomorrow to tedder the dried rows, but that evening I had the view to myself.

I propped my feet on the low stone wall surrounding our porch and began scanning lists of potential names for the cidery I had finally committed to building. A big part of me knew that investing in a capital-intensive business venture at this juncture was not wise. The textile world, my husband's lifelong career, was crashing around us. Bank mergers with attendant cost cutting threatened my consulting work. I planned to fund the cidery from my consulting income while at the same time taking care of my young orchard. And—no small task—I still needed to figure out how to make cider that my future customers would want to drink.

But that night I pondered a name. And somehow the name for this venture of the heart lay tangled in dreams and worries as convoluted as the twisting rows of hay. I had polled friends and surveyed names of cideries across the country. I didn't want a vanity name. I desperately wanted a name that honored our farm, our specific place in the world.

My grandmother used to say, "That girl frets over things like a dog worries a bone." That night on the porch I worried like a dog with a bone: the wrong name might jinx my crazy plan to grow cider apples and make an orchard-centric cider, something no one was doing

▲ (*Overleaf*) Hewe's Crab in bloom in Foggy Ridge Cider orchards.

61

south of Massachusetts. An off-kilter name might mean my dream was flawed. Though every part of me knew this thought was wrongheaded, I felt the name for my cider venture had to fit like a well-worn glove. I sat, breathed in the smell of freshly cut hay, and listened to birds in the black gum tree.

On about my third breath I felt a presence, as if someone was standing right behind me, watching me. I slowly turned my head and saw a large gray fox trotting calmly across the stone patio a few feet behind my chair. Not ten feet away, he raised his leg and peed on a planter full of pink chrysanthemums. Then he sat on his haunches at the top of the steps leading to the pasture. I could see the brilliant red ruff circling his neck and his red cheeks. A black stripe ran down his back to the tip of his tail resting on the stone floor. Gray Fox stared at the newly mowed pasture. I watched him breathe while I didn't.

We sat together, as the birds settled in the black gum tree and the hay dried in the field. His tongue lolled over his black lips as he scanned the pasture for field mice. Then, I must have moved or drawn too deep a breath. Gray Fox bounded off the porch in one great leap. He touched the grass once then flew across the lawn, barely skimming the ground, his brilliant tail flying straight behind him.

The sun set and the air turned cold. I gathered my notes and whispered a word of thanks for the fox and for an evening of a few calm breaths overlooking my orchard.

That night the temperature dropped and the wind died. At six-thirty the next morning fog rolled up from Rock House Creek in pale gray clouds. It wove low through the orchard and spilled into the rows of hay like a silver waterfall. I stood on the spot where my wild neighbor had visited me. I had it. Foggy Ridge. Foggy Ridge Cider. The perfect name for my place in the world and my crazy, wild dream.

In early spring I could never resist moving. By March the rush of winter pruning was over, and cold, gray days dragged on and on. Apple buds swelled in April, but many mornings started with near-freezing temperatures. Still, I walked our land, checking for green tips and the earliest spring flowers. My route often took me up the tallest hill on the farm for a long-range vista of our Appalachian spring.

A spring hike to the top of Carrie's Hill never failed to startle me—I began by Rock House Creek in cool bottomland air. Midway up the thousand-foot climb I walked through warmth that felt like May. Cold air and a brisk wind always greeted me at the top. It was as if I moved through a thermal layer cake of cold air, then warm, and then cold again.

My early spring walks traversed a phenomenon first described in the mid-1800s by southern fruit growers: the southern thermal belt.

In 1810, fifteen-year-old Silas McDowell walked on similar ridges in North Carolina's Rutherford and Buncombe Counties. McDowell was an impressionable young man, drawn to the natural world. He later described his early experience of the thermal belt in a letter to the botanist Moses Ashely Curtis: "When I attained a certain hight [*sic*] on the mountain, which I would reach through a cold, damp air . . . a warm dry glow at that hight would reach my cheeks & produce a pleasant glowing sensation, & my whole body would soon feel the change."[1]

On my walks up Carrie's Hill, I felt the same change McDowell had described 200 years earlier. He gained a spot in the southern apple story by documenting this unusual temperature pattern, a common phenomenon in the southern Appalachians.

In most elevation changes, the temperature drops a little over five degrees Fahrenheit for every 1,000 feet of elevation rise. In a thermal belt, this paradigm changes. A thermal belt is just what it sounds like—a horizontal zone of warm air often found on south-facing slopes where the temperature stays warmer than the air above and the air below. This band of warm air creates a microclimate ideal for fruit trees, so ideal that many call it a "frost-free zone."

Bloom time is an anxious time in an orchard. The most vulnerable period in the life cycle of an apple occurs when trees begin to break dormancy. As they wake up in spring, apple buds progress through a reliable series of evocatively named stages: silver tip, green tip, half-inch green, tight cluster, first pink, full pink, and, finally, king bloom, when the first bud in a cluster opens.

In my first decade of growing trees I kept an alarming chart on my office wall illustrating critical temperatures for frost damage at each bloom stage. When apple buds are at full pink, thirty minutes at twenty-five degrees Fahrenheit kills 90 percent of blooms. Same for the king bloom stage. Since many apple varieties in southern orchards set buds before the last frost date, southern apple growers had a big incentive to find frost-free, or at least "frost-protected," planting sites.

Silas McDowell was not the only southerner to describe the phenomenon of thermal belts. Matthew Fontaine Maury, a Virginia scientist and oceanographer, observed that orchards in western Virginia could avoid the spring frost crop loss experienced by Tidewater growers. Maury wrote, "In Frederick County there is an elevated ridge of land on which apples are so generally safe, when all others in the neighborhood are killed by frost, that it has acquired the name of Apple Pie Ridge."[2] He recorded temperature readings at different elevations to show ideal locations for fruit trees in Albemarle, Amherst, and Frederick Counties, data that led to a shift in Virginia's apple production.[3]

Maury and McDowell were as intrigued by the effect of site, or *place*, on fruit as I was. Place is central to the concept of terroir, the idea that a specific geographic environment imparts unique flavor to grapes and wine. I had seen this in Murdo's Napa Valley orchard. I was convinced that place was just as important to apples and cider.

The South is full of thermal belts, unique *places* that create ideal environments for fruit growing.

North Carolina boasts more thermal belts than any area in the eastern United States—so many that Rutherford County has a Thermal City and Isothermal Community College.[4] This western North Carolina county has enthusiastically embraced the term "thermal" as a marketing message about mild weather in the region.

In 1907 orchardist Ralph Levering walked from Asheville, North Carolina, to Roanoke, Virginia—twice—before finding a slope on the side of the Blue Ridge Plateau near the border of the two states with a warm thermal belt, a beautiful view, and a nearby Quaker community. The slopes of Virginia's Shenandoah Valley offer microclimates for both apple and grape growing. Cherokee orchardists grew apples and peaches in north Georgia's thermal belts. And West Virginia's Berkeley County offers the protection of this thermal phenomenon, but it also has "Apple Pie Ridge soil."

As part of a growing cider community in Virginia, I knew that my cider colleagues a two-hour drive from me in Nelson County grew some of the same varieties I grew at Foggy Ridge Cider. And I knew from tasting and testing that our apples ripened with very different flavors and chemistry. I had always assumed this was due to their 600-foot elevation and my 3,000-foot mountain orchard. But when I had a chance to taste a nearby neighbor's Grimes Golden side-by-side with the same variety from my orchard, I was shocked. Same apple. Same harvesttime. Same elevation. Entirely different flavor. And when I checked each apple's chemistry, I found big differences in acidity and sugar. If site was so important for frost protection and the flavor development that comes with ripening, I wondered what other factors expressed terroir in southern fruit.

West Virginia's apple history began on March 18, 1774, when George Washington leased 125 acres of land to William Barlett in an area he called the "Barrens of Bullskin" in Berkeley County. Washington required that Barlett should "within seven years plant one hundred winter apple trees, forty feet apart each way, and one hundred peach trees and should keep them well pruned and fenced in from animals."[5] Bartlet planted in a frost-protected zone, but he also planted on limestone soil. Called "Hagerstown loam," this limestone soil occurs throughout the Shenandoah Valley and is especially suited for fruit growing. Berkeley County's limestone soil contains flakes of shale and soapstone, which keep the soil from cracking in hot weather.[6] This special "Apple Pie Ridge soil" drew orchardists like nectar draws bees.

George Washington may have prompted West Virginia fruit growing, but W. S. Miller jump-started commercial orcharding in this southern state. When he couldn't sell his nursery's apple trees in 1851, Miller planted the first commercial orchard in West Virginia. By 1905, this family orchard grew to one of the largest in the world, with 11,813 acres of orchard and 583,657 trees.[7] Apple Pie Ridge's limestone soil nurtured an "almost unbroken chain of trees" for over seventeen miles, from Berkeley County into Virginia's Frederick County.

Virginia orchardists growing Albemarle Pippin apples for export to England in the nineteenth century bragged about the fertile "Pippin soil" on the flanks of mountain ridges lining the Shenandoah Valley. Farther south and west, Rock Castle growers thought warm thermals and rich mountain soil contributed to high flavor in their summer-ripening "still-house apples," fruit destined for the area's famous apple brandy.[8] Soil and site were clearly pieces of the apple terroir puzzle.

Bond Brothers Apple Pie Ridge advertisement. Old Time Apple Growers Association Collection, Handley Regional Library, Winchester, VA.

By the mid-1970s, the Appalachian Fruit Belt stretching from West Virginia into Virginia and parts of North Carolina and Georgia produced more than a fourth of all apples consumed in the United States.[9]

When I began my southern apple education, I was surprised to learn that early southerners grew apples throughout the South. When he traveled to Alabama in 1775, William Bartram noticed apple trees growing around the intersection of the Coosa and Tallapoosa Rivers in central Alabama.[10] In the mid-1800s, Pomaria Nurseries, located at an elevation of 400 feet outside Columbia, South Carolina, was one of the most influential nurseries in the South. Around the same time, Thomas Affleck operated Southern Nurseries in Washington, outside of Natchez, Mississippi. After the Civil War, apple growing boomed in Tidewater Virginia, where orchardists shipped summer apple varieties like Early Harvest, Early Ripe, and Maiden Blush to markets in the North.[11] Georgia's epicenter for apple varieties was Augusta and Fruitland Nurseries.

If southern apples were widely adapted to different sites and soils, why do most people think of the mountain South when they think of apples?

In the early South almost all farms had orchards, with apples for home use and for local sale. Transportation was difficult, with few roads suited for cartloads of heavy fruit. In the late nineteenth century, as agriculture shifted to crops grown for wider commercial distribution rather than for home and local use, farmers chose to grow not just what could be grown on their land but what could be *most profitably* grown and distributed for sale. Farms increased in acreage and decreased in crop diversity. For much of the South, tobacco, cotton, rice, and cattle crowded out large orchards that had previously provided cider and apples for a multitude of uses.

Commerce was not the only reason for the nudging of southern orchards into mountain regions. The temperance movement had a dampening effect, especially on large seedling orchards. New pests and disease made their appearance. After over 200 years of acclimation to a wide range of terroir, southern orchards shrank to fit a smaller footprint.

And that footprint was the mountain South, with its prolific thermal belts, apple-friendly soil, and brandy stills.

Today if you search for information on thermal belts, you'll find a mix of tourist sites, like the Thermal Belt Trail near Asheville, and ReMax realtor listings promoting an "ideal mountain climate." You will read about Silas McDowell and M. F. Maury.

If you visit the mountain South's best-known apple-growing areas, you will hear about limestone-laced Hagerstown loam and rich Pippin soil. Appalachian apple growers believe their high-elevation fruit has a unique "twang," or acidic bite unique to mountain terroir.

Researchers from Cornell and Virginia Tech have investigated the role of terroir in apples and cider. Science confirms that high-elevation apples have more acidity and more concentrated flavor. My own experience shows that the loamy clay liberally sprinkled with white quartz that undergirds the Foggy Ridge orchards produces different flavors and chemistry than those found in nearby apples grown on different soil. Over twenty-five years of growing cider apples in the South have shown me that cultural practices, harvest protocols, and even the aesthetics of the grower all affect apple flavor. Terroir, apples, and cider? For me, that remains a fascinating and mercurial intersection of taste and place.

One fact remains indisputable: the South is a special place to grow apples.

TASTED

Picking apples at Foggy Ridge Cider was really all about *picking up* apples. For my first real harvest of apples that would end up in cider that I actually might be able to sell, I wanted to harvest tree-ripened fruit full of all the flavor possible for each apple variety. Since these apples would head to the press within a week of harvest, it only made sense to follow the lead of cidermakers from past centuries and gently shake my trees so that ripe fruit would fall onto soft orchard grass.

Sounds easy, right? On the cusp of making my first cider vintage, I was learning that scaling up to larger production was far more complicated than I imagined.

Labor, for example. For the few small harvests in previous years, I did all the picking . . . or picking up. I gathered ripe fruit, pressed it with my home press, and fermented carboys of juice all by my lonesome. I gave away excess fruit, some to other cidermakers and some to friends and family. And I stored the long-keeping apples in our cool basement for winter pies and my favorite apple cake.

I took meticulous notes on Brix (a measure of sugar) and acidity levels for each of the thirty varieties in the orchard. I recorded detailed tasting notes, my nascent attempts at describing apple flavor and aromas, records that I knew would serve me well when it came time to ferment. In the past, I had done all the work. But I had never harvested tons of apples. As in, actual tons.

Standing in the orchard with fruit hanging heavy on every tree, I knew that the name Foggy Ridge Cider expressed this particular place. By tasting thoughtfully crafted ciders from my new cider friends in Massachusetts, New York, and New Hampshire, I had gained a vision for what my fruit might one day produce. Expensive stainless steel tanks and equipment crowded my little concrete and metal cidery, ready for ripe fruit. I knew how to track flavor and ripeness. But I was pretty sure I would not be able to pick, or pick up, every single apple from my first *real* harvest.

Once again, I needed reinforcements.

I started with friends who over years of watching this dream hatch had said more than once, "I'll help pick apples!" Two friends came for four hours and left with almost as many apples as they harvested. I moved on to Facebook friends of Foggy Ridge Cider, potential customers and cider lovers who had expressed interest in this venture. Countless emails and phone messages followed. "I can't make it after all. Sorry!" Or, "It's a little cold outside. Can we do this another day?" Most of the handful who did show up were so winded by walking to the top of the orchard they had no energy left to pick apples. I cooked lunch for everybody and sent them home early.

For that first *real* harvest, I ended up with a scraggly crew of teenagers who wanted extra money to repair a truck or buy another gun. Wayne Marshall, Cornbread's grandson, and a high school student who mowed hay on our land, joined the crew on weekends. A few sturdy local women who had cut timber with their fathers and worked most of their lives in furniture plants were important members of the picking crew. Best of all, I discovered Nora Quesenberry Mabry. She had a southwest Virginia double-barrel name, "Quesenberry" and "Mabry" seen frequently on mailboxes in our corner of the county. Nora was one of fifteen children, and her extended family had experienced much tragedy: early deaths, alcohol abuse, and chronic illness. But despite it all, Nora brimmed with optimism and joy.

Nora rushed into every day, full of energy, bubbling over with news. She was seven years older than I was but could walk my legs off. A typical harvest day included about five miles of hilly hiking while carrying forty-pound bushels of fruit. Nora was the glue. She kept the crew laughing with tales about her goats and guinea hens. She dispensed gentle wisdom in every breath. By the end of the first day, the teenagers were helping Nora haul apple boxes, and she had convinced them this was a good seasonal gig.

I was still living a deeply bifurcated life—my consulting work often pulled me away from the orchard to join long conference calls. I rose early to write presentations. I spent almost as much time in airports as I did in the orchard. But in that first harvest I hauled my share of apples, and I shook trees. Each morning I stepped up into the young trees and swung my body weight back and forth. Ripe apples destined for my first cider blends hit the thick orchard grass with satisfying thumps.

Years on, the early challenges of funding and founding this cider venture seem quaint. In the moment, everything was new—technical skills, complex mechanics, keeping a crew of teenagers focused on the job. I needed resourcefulness at every turn.

In that first harvest we picked bushels of richly flavored apples, far more fruit than I could store on site until our first press day. After a few days of phone calls I found a local business that agreed to rent short-term cold storage space. The icehouse eight miles away in Meadows of Dan consisted of a series of rambling metal buildings connected by sliding freezer doors and thick vinyl strip curtains. The ice machines ran all day while the owner and his wife handled accounts from a dusty office in the loft. I thanked the owner for his flexibility, signed a lease, and pocketed my set of keys.

My first apple haul to cold storage was at the end of a long harvest day. When I drove away from the farm, the western sky glowed orange and pink. By the time I pulled up to the icehouse loading dock, the ram-shackle buildings were pitch-black. I fumbled with my keys and finally unlocked three deadbolts on the rusty metal door. What had been a mildly creepy icehouse in daylight veered toward horror show at night. The dust-covered overhead lights barely cast shadows on forklifts and conveyor belts. I pushed through grimy vinyl curtains with my heart in my throat. By the time I unloaded my three bins of fruit and rolled my apples into the cold room, I was sweating. I practically ran back to the truck and flipped the locks on all the doors.

I had to laugh. Here I was, a financial services consultant, a barely experienced apple grower, a fledgling cidermaker, sitting in a dark parking lot on a back road in Carroll County, Virginia, with my pulse racing. All because I had to find my way around a deserted old ice-house. I thought, "This cidermaking is a crazy job. I'm not sure if I have all that it takes to be successful. But for sure, I need courage."

———————

On my way to the orchard in harvest season, I always reached for two things: a pocketknife and a garlic press. I wanted apples with full-on flavor, apples that offered a juicy mouthful of complex taste that would lead to delicious cider. I needed to know when my over thirty apple va-rieties were not just ripe but full of as much flavor as they could possibly express.

Walking down the long rows, I took a bite from apples I judged to be close to ripeness. I chewed a few times to gauge the flavor, spit out the pulp, and jotted copious notes. Then, using my battered garlic press, I pressed a drop or two of apple juice from a wedge of each variety onto a handheld refractometer, a simple device that measures the sugar concentration in liquid—in my case, the degrees of Brix in apple juice. For the apple varieties I deemed ready for harvest, I later extracted juice in a juicer and tested pH.

The combination of a sensory appraisal and a few simple tests helped me shore up my knowledge about the "what" and "when" of apple flavor.

My friends who owned commercial orchards relied on their long experience with a few varieties to determine harvesttime. They picked fruit in large sections called blocks. They'd say, "On Tuesday we're picking Galas in the north block." And on Tuesday the orchard crew would pick every Gala in that block of trees, regardless of ripeness. These growers wanted pristine fruit that could be shipped to out-of-state markets and stored for months. Our goals were different—I was harvesting for flavor, flavor that would translate into a high-priced alcoholic beverage. I needed to identify exactly when flavor was at its peak.

On apple-picking days, I tasted and tested scores of apples. By the end of each day my mouth was dry from tannin and puckered from acid. I was never hungry at lunch break, but at the end of the day I longed for a hamburger or anything with fat to clear my palate.

I learned that apple flavor can be elusive, that ripeness in fruit is complex, and that deciding exactly when to pick an apple is an art I will never master.

Apples progress from hard, starchy balls to juicy, full-flavored sugar bombs in a process designed to entice people and animals at a specific moment in an apple's development. Unlike most vegetables, apples are inedible when immature. Bite into a Ralls Janet apple in midsummer and—well, you might not even be able to bite into it. Apples stay unattractive to mammals until the apple seeds are physiologically mature, meaning the stage when the seeds can germinate and reproduce. This makes sense—from an evolutionary standpoint there is no reason for fruit to move away from the tree until the seeds can reproduce.

If apples develop flavor in order to entice mammals to consume the fruit at the moment when the seeds are ripe, how do apples actually develop flavor? In my preharvest tasting marathons, why did I taste honey in each bite of Grimes Golden and tropical fruit flavors in Albemarle Pippins? Apple seeds reach physiological ripeness, meaning the seeds will germinate if dispersed, when they change from creamy white to dark brown or chestnut. But at this stage apples are not necessarily full of flavor. Flavor was one factor that tied southerners to southern apples. And as a modern cidermaker, I needed to understand where apple flavor originates and how to best move flavor from the orchard to a glass of cider.

Trees exist rooted to a single spot, often for a very long life. I often hear of apple trees on family farms near Foggy Ridge that were planted in the 1940s and 1950s, standing on the same spot for their entire existence; the apples on them construct tissue from water, minerals, and air. They attract pollinators to reproduce, and they entice mammals to transport their seeds to sites where the seeds have a chance to grow.

We have flavor because apples evolved to entice mammals to move seeds.

Harold McGee, food scientist and author, describes plants as "stationary chemical factories" that develop strong flavors and practice chemical alchemy to compensate for their immobility. McGee points out that fruits are "among the few things that we eat that we're meant to eat."[1]

Apples consist of an outer protective skin and a thick, juicy layer of flesh surrounding stiff seed-containing capsules called carpels. When we bite into an apple, the flesh we taste, the pome, is actually what botanists call a "false fruit." This tasty flesh is the swollen ovary and tissue surrounding the carpels.

Apple flesh is made up of cells, each surrounded by a membrane and filled with fluid and vacuoles, compartments full of enzymes, sugars, acids, and proteins. Flavor lives here, inside the vacuoles.

For centuries, southern apple growers waited until apple cells swelled and apple flesh turned white or cream-colored. Though they lacked the sugar-measuring refractometer I use in my orchard, they understood the complex process of ripening, what McGee calls the intense stage of life in which the fruit is "organizing itself into a feast for our eye and palate."[2] And they chose their fruit for flavor and use.

Other than reproduction through seeds, apples serve no function for the tree on which they hang. Think of a big greenish-yellow Horse apple as a storage vessel filled with flavor designed to appeal to people and animals.

As apples grow, storage cells expand rapidly. Bitter tannins and other defensive compounds gather in the vacuoles to deter an early harvest before seeds mature. Apples begin to ripen—the stage I sought in my orchard—when the fruit releases ethylene. Once harvested, apples continue to respire ethylene, which is why apples in a refrigerator cause other fruits and vegetables to quickly deteriorate. Fruit that continues to ripen after being removed from the plant is called climacteric. Apples are a classical climacteric fruit, with the rush of ethylene production that begins ripening followed by increased cell respiration.

▶

Albemarle Pippin
tree planted by
Ralph Levering
in the 1920s in
Levering Orchard,
Ararat, VA.

Ripening is really the first stage in deterioration, a last chance for an apple to appeal to a two- or four-legged transport vehicle and cast its genetic diversity into the world.

Harvest festivals can offer apple-bobbing contests because air constitutes 25 percent of an apple's volume, far more than other tree fruit. Apples float. And as apples ripen, the cells swell with liquid and compress air pockets. Biting an apple breaks the cell walls and releases a rush of juice, the source of the satisfying "crunch" that so many people enjoy in ripe fruit. At the same time that flavorful juice fills the mouth, compressed air from the broken cell walls releases chemicals called esters to the back of the throat and on to olfactory membranes in the nose.

Taste receptors in the mouth perceive flavor, but the most powerful human organ for detecting nuanced flavor is the nose. Human noses, while no competition for our canine pets, are packed with olfactory cells. The aroma-receiving tissue in human noses measures about one inch wide by two inches long. Flavor captured by these olfactory receptor cells has a short ride on nerve fibers to the olfactory bulb, the part of the human brain that processes aroma. The flavor we perceive when we bite into an apple, or sip from a glass of cider, is a chemical reaction, the combination of taste plus aroma that quickly travels from our mouth and nose to our brain.

Apples are chemically engineered to engage us from the first bite.

I believe I inherited a tiny part of my dad's engineer's brain, the part that drives me to keep meticulous records. From my first harvest I've recorded flavor-tasting notes along with sugar and acid levels for each variety I grew, every year. As soon as the seeds turned dark, signaling physiological ripeness, I tasted and tested that variety every few days. Some signs of apple ripeness are obvious: sugar increases and starch and acid levels decrease. Aroma increases as esters activate. The flesh softens and the skin color deepens—reds get more vibrant and yellows turn golden. A tree-ripened apple is a rare treat, and I relished the moment in mid-September when the apple called Mother was at its peak and at Thanksgiving when Ralls Janet, often called Neverfall for good reason, was finally ready for picking.

But the longer I worked with my fruit, the more complex apple flavor seemed to be. Sometimes a ripe apple pulled from a tree—or, in our case at Foggy Ridge, picked up from the ground—was not yet at its best.

Traditionally, cidermakers left apples lying around in heaps to soften and supposedly gain flavor, a process called "sweating." While early cidermakers needed softer apples for their more primitive presses, I found that while some apple varieties gained flavor off the tree, most

lost complexity and the acidic pop of freshly picked ripe fruit. I was a fan of freshly harvested tree-ripened fruit for my orchard-centric cider.

But one southern apple proved me wrong. This apple defined the benefits of being a climacteric fruit and in doing so traveled far beyond the South and made an international name for one Virginia county.

———

"Pippin" is a generic term for any seed-grown apple, and pippin names populate early nursery lists from New England to Mississippi. In its 1858 catalog, the Vineland Nursery outside Mobile, Alabama, listed eleven apples with the name pippin, including Walker's Yellow Pippin, Red Fall Pippin, and Spring Hill Pippin. But the Newtown Pippin, discovered by Gershom Moore in the late seventeenth or early eighteenth century as a chance seedling in Newtown, New York, is the most famous apple sporting the "pippin" moniker.

It's hard to imagine Queens, the New York City borough we know today, as once rich orchard land, but Moore's apple orchard stretched from the East River to what is now Fifty-Fourth Street in Elmhurst. Like all good farmers, Moore closely observed his orchard. One day he noticed a lopsided greenish-yellow apple with bumpy ridges and rusty shoulders growing in a swampy corner of the orchard, and he took a bite. That wild apple must have startled him with its complex tropical fruit flavors, sweet citrus, and a hint of pine. When they're stored for a few months, Newtown Pippins mellow, and the sweet fruit notes become even more pronounced. Moore shared his find with the Prince Nursery in Queens, New York, and the rest is history—a history as complex as this apple's flavor.

By 1755 the tamed and named Newtown Pippin had moved south to Virginia. Dr. Thomas Walker was likely the first southerner to grow Newtown Pippins using grafting wood that he brought from Philadelphia to his Castle Hill estate in Albemarle County near Monticello.[3] An advertisement in the September 26, 1755, *Virginia Gazette* from William Smith's Surry County Nursery offered this northern apple alongside southern favorites "Hugh's Crab" and Father Abraham. On March 21, 1763, George Washington recorded in his journals, "Grafted 10 of the New Town Pippin from Collo. Masons who had them from Jr. Presidt. Blair."[4] Newtown Pippin was one of the most widely planted apples in Monticello's south orchard, and Thomas Jefferson wrote from Paris that "they have no apples here to compare with our Newtown pippin."[5]

Some apples burst with flavor the minute they are pulled ripe from a tree. Others utilize the properties of being climacteric fruit and continue to improve with age. In the South, Newtown Pippins ripen in late fall, usually mid- to late October. Stored in a root cellar or a hearth pit, the rich tropical fruit flavors deepen, and aroma builds. Newtown Pippins were the quintessential winter apple, and southern growers quickly claimed this flavorful, long-storing fruit as their own.

In 1838, Andrew Stevenson, the American minister to the Court of St. James, longed for pippin apples from his home in Albemarle County, Virginia. He arranged for a few barrels to be shipped to him in London, where he presented Queen Victoria with a gift of Virginia-grown apples he called Albemarle Pippins.[6] Stevenson's fortuitous introduction prompted the queen to remove the tax on imported apples and launched an export business for Virginia-grown "pippin apples" that lasted until the end of World War I.[7]

The name "Albemarle Pippin" first appeared in print in the *Southern Planter* in 1843. The author complained that southerners should not purchase northern-grown apples when there was a northern apple grown across the South that tasted better when "grown southern."[8]

Within a few years, nurseries from Georgia to New York promoted Albemarle Pippins as a winter southern apple of "superb quality." The *Fruit Culturist* described Albemarle Pippins as "cultivated chiefly in Virginia, and in great abundance in Albemarle County, at the foot of the Blue Ridge."[9] Wm. C. Geraty's nursery in Young's Island, South Carolina, advertised Albemarle Pippin as "a truly superb variety . . . very large greenish yellow, of exquisite flavor, and a fine keeper and heavy bearer."[10] By the turn of the century, nurseries all over the South listed this northern apple under its southern name.

Splinter groups formed, with growers promoting hyperlocal "Loudin pippins" in Loudin County, Virginia, and the "Nelson pippin" in Nelson County.[11] But the name "Albemarle Pippin" stuck.

In September 1871, the American Pomological Society held its thirteenth annual meeting in Richmond, Virginia. Alongside growers from New York, Massachusetts, Iowa, and Kansas, southern orchardists exhibited southern apples. Franklin Davis, owner of Virginia Nursery and Wine Company in Richmond, who exhibited 195 varieties of apples, praised the southern-grown Albemarle Pippin: "No apple stands higher in the market than this, or brings as high a price. It succeeds finely in the red soil of the mountains and rich valleys of the Piedmont region, and in most parts of the Valley of Virginia."[12]

Growers from each state boasted about their favorite fruit. West Virginia claimed Grimes Golden, a parent of the widely planted Golden Delicious. Georgia's Shockley apple was grown throughout the South. Tennessee had Kinnaird's Choice. Flavor tied apples to southerners all across the region. But no apple captured and stored flavor quite like the Albemarle Pippin.

To my palate, modern apples with unidimensional sweetness and brutal crispness lack the nuance and complexity of an Albemarle Pippin two months off the tree. A few old pippin orchards still produce high-quality fruit for top-dollar sales. And a number of twenty-first century cidermakers have planted Albemarle Pippin apples for hard cider blends.

Perhaps flavor in southern apples isn't so elusive after all.

CULTIVATED

It was one thing to identify flavor on the tree. I also needed to learn how to meld flavors held in thousands of dollars' worth of stainless steel tanks into cider worth drinking. On the cusp of my first commercial cider-making, my countless home experiments and extensive tasting notes seemed romantic and whimsical. For this initial Foggy Ridge Cider vintage, my commitment was on the line. I was beyond intimidated.

Matt Dyar was the perfect guide for my first dive into making cider that I could actually sell to customers. Educated in the California wine world, Matt knew both theory and practice. He helped me choose equipment for my tiny cider house and then taught me how to set up the conveyor, grinder, and press. He buffed up the lab skills I had gained in wine-making courses at Virginia Tech. And he calmed me down on that devastating day when a judge in Virginia ruled it illegal for wineries and cideries to sell directly to restaurants and retail shops . . . the same day our contractor was pouring $80,000 worth of concrete for the cider house. Matt and his wife had moved to the area for Cindy's job as cheese maker at a nearby winery. I felt lucky to snag him for a part-time consulting gig. He was happy to add cidermaking to his resume.

Matt convinced me to buy an expensive Karcher diesel-powered pressure washer to clean the press equipment. I quickly bonded with my Karcher and used it to clean everything from the tank room walls to all the concrete surfaces I could find. Its arrival at the cidery attracted great attention. Our contractor and his crew gathered around to give the Karcher a test run. Corn-bread, his son, and the entire Marshall family stopped by, full of ideas for how it could help them clean their "kill room," the cinder block building they used for processing hogs and deer. If this cider gig didn't work out, I knew I had at least one piece of equipment I would have no trouble selling.

Most important, Matt helped me demystify flavor. Using my small handpress, we pressed sample batches of juice from our choice apples and then tasted and took notes. He began by tasting for the most simple flavor components, a practice I use today: What does the sweetness taste like? Are there savory flavors? And the acid—is it biting or elusive? What about the tannin? Is it soft or edgy? And the aromas—what do I sense at the beginning, middle, and end of an inhale?

The most assertive flavors in a beverage appear first and can hide subtle components. I began to understand how to combine my many apple varieties into a few ciders that blended the most discernible apple characteristics without hiding delicate flavors.

I still wasn't expert at estimating harvest quantities or the juice yield. But we made plans. We built spreadsheets. I thought we had enough Hewe's Crabs to ferment this variety in a single tank. The rest of our harvest of early apples would head to tanks labeled "first fruit."

I've never lived more fully than in the days between my first real apple harvest and my first round of commercial cidermaking. Matt kept me grounded; without him I would have floated into space. While I was navigating a foreign country with a language I didn't know, I had never felt more rooted to a place, more alive in a moment.

One September night just before our first pressing, I drove up to our house to grab sandwiches to fuel our last hour of work. From our steep driveway I could see the long, low cider house tucked below Tony Goad's cow pasture, lights blazing and the tractor idling by the loading dock. A tiny crescent moon rose in the deep purple sky above the orchard. Clouds of steam poured off the crush pad from the pressure washer and billowed in white clouds off the tail of my little building.

I got out of the truck and stood under the stars, feeling as if I was at the top of a swing, that moment when you rise to the top of the arc and are, for a moment, breathless. My cider house looked like a silver ship on a green sea, powered by steam-colored rolling waves. Despite all the paradoxes that had plagued me in this urgent moment, I felt at peace. Work was both numbingly difficult and full of joy. I was inexperienced and I was insightful. I was afraid and I was courageous. I was ready to sail my little ship.

In the early 2000s, a dog-eared copy of Lee Calhoun's book *Old Southern Apples* sat on my desk, open to entries describing southern cider apples. Lee was a frequent advisor who said, "I don't know much about cider, but you really ought to take a look at" and then went on to name a half-dozen old southern apples I'd never heard of that might just be good for cider.

One name jumped out to me. Lee explained that several nineteenth-century southern apples carry the name "Aunt," and possibly some of these apples were grown and selected by enslaved women or their female descendants. The Aunt Cora's Yard Apple and Aunt Cora's Field Apple originated in Bath County, Virginia, a growing region similar to that encompassing my orchards at Foggy Ridge. The apples carried what seemed like a romanticized history with only a passing glance of accuracy. I was curious about this apple, but even more eager to know the history of apples and enslaved people in the South.

It didn't take much digging to learn that much of the labor of early southern apples fell to enslaved men and women. But how did that labor involve choices about reproducing apples? Replicating a desired apple means grafting that tree or cloning an identical tree by pulling up root suckers. Aunt Cora or one of her relatives likely reproduced the apple that carries her name, but was it possible to learn more about the Cora in this story? What agency did she and her family employ with this fruit and its cultivation?

Apple growing across the South varied by region and farm size. The early southern orchard could consist of a few seedling trees on the steep slopes of a small Appalachian farm, or a few hundred trees in north Georgia or South Carolina. Large orchards from Mississippi to Virginia held thousands of trees. Enslaved men and women, Indigenous farmers, small landowners, and plantation owners grew seedling apples. From these wild seedling trees, people selected and passed along the apples they most desired.

At the beginning of the nineteenth century, 90 percent of the American population was engaged in farming. By 1860, farmers still accounted for 60 percent of the American labor force, with a higher percentage of farmers in the South.[1] Southern farms meant southern orchards. Until the mid-1800s, seedling orchards were common throughout the South, creating, as Lee Calhoun said, "one giant experiment station for apple breeding in the South."[2]

Southern farmers of all kinds noticed and selected valuable apples. They grafted and passed these apples along to family members and neighbors. Nurseries began selling the most popular apples. The number and variety of southern-born apples exploded and launched the nineteenth century's golden age of southern apples.

The boldface names attached to the South's early apple history were almost all slave owners.

William Fitzhugh's large orchard in Virginia's Northern Neck was fenced, tended, and harvested by indentured servants and, as planters shifted from servants to enslaved labor after 1680, by enslaved men and women.[3] His apple orchard contributed to his wealth and produced the equivalent of "15,000 pounds of tobacco annually."[4] At his death, Fitzhugh divided his fifty-one enslaved men, women, and children among his six children, passing on wealth in land, orchards, and people.[5]

The presidential orchardists grew apples and made cider with the labor of enslaved men and women. Details on harvesting apples and bottling cider fill Thomas Jefferson's farm books. A June 1811 entry chronicled bottling 532 bottles of cider made with Red Hughes and

Taliaferro apples,[6] labor likely performed by enslaved men and women, and a formidable task even with my automated four-spout filler. George Washington described the brute labor of enslaved men who "began to beat Cyder at Doeg Run,"[7] the eighteenth-century version of my stainless steel apple grinder.

John Hartwell Cocke, a Virginia orchardist, founder of the University of Virginia, and an abolitionist who also enslaved men and women, personally budded or grafted many of his extensive apple and peach orchards at his Bremo plantation on the James River but also used enslaved labor. In 1817, Cocke wrote that two enslaved men, Peter and Dick, planted three orchards containing fourteen southern apples.[8]

Jarvis Van Buren founded Gloaming Nursery in 1840 by "purchasing ten acres and five slaves,"[9] creating one of the first nurseries in Georgia. Beginning around 1840, William Summer operated Pomaria Nurseries near Columbia, South Carolina. He shipped fruit trees as far as Mississippi and Louisiana and exported trees to Belgium. The Summer family owned as many as forty enslaved people who worked on the diversified Summer plantation and likely the nursery.[10] Silas McDowell, who wrote about thermal belts in the South, inherited an enslaved man from his grandfather. He wrote that he did not immediately move to the farm he purchased in 1820: "As my business was managed by a faithful slave I did not live on the farm until the year 1830."[11]

In 1835, William Massie expanded the orchards on his Nelson County farm, Pharsalia, by planting apple, plum, and pear trees grafted by enslaved workers.[12] He preferred what he called his "home grafts" to trees purchased from the famous William R. Prince Nursery in Queens, New York.

The people doing the work of growing trees and replicating desired varieties accumulated apple experience and wisdom. Journals written by white owners describe the labor but omit the skill and selection that enslaved men and women exercised in early southern orchards. The people who were most intimately connected to growing, harvesting, and propagating fruit trees were best suited to choosing the most valuable apples, and these people were often enslaved men and women.

Although slaveholders denied or regulated the ability of enslaved people to sell the fruits and vegetables they grew, some trading did occur on farms and plantations.[13] In her household accounts from 1805 to 1808, Anne Cary Randolph, Thomas Jefferson's granddaughter, recorded hundreds of transactions detailing the purchase of fruits and vegetables from enslaved men and women at Monticello.[14] Though chicken and eggs dominate the exchanges, apples, both dried and fresh, were part of the agricultural transactions between white owners and enslaved men and women. On May 27, 1808, Randolph recorded paying "Johnny" sixpence for pippin apples, a testament to the productivity of his tree and his ability to store this long-lasting southern apple.[15]

After the Civil War, the orchard knowledge of enslaved people advanced southern apples. When Maria Massie restored the Albemarle Pippin orchards as a moneymaking operation on the Massies' Pharsalia estate, she relied on her husband's orchard books but also on the knowledge of former enslaved workers.[16]

I learned that in the South, orchard labor and slavery were as entwined as the limbs of a wild crabapple tree. And sometimes all we are left with is a name.

Lee Calhoun wrote that Aunt Cora's Yard Apple and Aunt Cora's Field Apple carry Cora Gibson's name. Lee heard her story from Dr. L. R. Littleton, an apple collector who found the apples in Mountain Grove, Virginia, and related a version of this apple history to Lee.

The term "Aunt" has been used as a racial epithet with connotations of "Uncle Tom." As Toni Tipton-Martin documents in her book *The Jemima Code: Two Centuries of African American Cooks*, this term has been used to mask the talent of centuries of African American women cooks who created sophisticated dishes. "Aunt" is included in the names of several southern apples, but only one comes with a story linking the apple to an African American fruit grower.

Dr. Littleton reported that Cora Gibson was born in 1878, lived to be ninety-seven, and worked as a midwife in Bath County. Her father, an enslaved man, grew the apples from seeds. Lee liked the red Aunt Cora's Field Apple best and noted its nutty flavor and balance of sugar and acid. He dismissed the yellow yard apple and offered no description or tasting notes.[17]

This brief, hazy account left me wondering. Did Cora Gibson's family continue growing her apples? Apple growers, even those with one or two fine trees in their backyard, are proud of their fruit. Wouldn't the Gibson family have shared Cora's namesake apples with their neighbors?

At the Bath County Historical Society, the plot thickened. According to the historical society, Cora Gilmore, not Gibson, was born in 1845 to parents enslaved to Samuel V. Gatewood in Mountain Grove, Virginia. Its version of the Aunt Cora apple story paints Gatewood as an angry, cruel man who got his comeuppance when he was shot in an argument with a stranger and died. The story winds back to Cora, who, in this version, outlived at least two husbands, had eleven children, and worked as a midwife in Bath County until she was in her eighties. This Cora Gilmore died at her home in Covington, Virginia, in 1926. The Bath County

Historical Society has a pitcher she used in her midwifery practice, but not an apple tree.

Between ferments and orchard work, I researched Bath County records and called genealogists. I tried to track down Dr. Littleton's relatives in hopes they might shed light on his version of the story. I did my best to nail down a tiny measure of certainty about Aunt Cora's apples, with no success.

After several seasons of harvests and ferments, my urge for certainty receded. I became more at ease with the nuances of growing apples and making cider. But I've never become completely comfortable with not *knowing*.

Everyone in the South who grew, noticed, and replicated fruit had a hand in taming southern apples. We know the stories of many of these individuals. The missing stories are empty spaces where unknown people and hidden histories live.

The story of apples grown and selected by enslaved laborers, men and women who chose specific apples and made trees that would outlive them, is a silenced history. But desire drove the making of each that a grower chose to replicate. Cora Gibson's (or Gilmore's) family chose a seedling apple they valued and passed it on through generations through grafting. It might not be a stretch to compare replicating and naming an apple to the pottery created by the artist David Drake in South Carolina before the Civil War.[18] Both offer a window into the desires and forms of resistance exercised by enslaved men and women.

Sometimes desire lives on only in a name . . . such as Aunt Cora's Field Apple with dark red stripes and russeted rays over the shoulder, said to be a fine-grained, slightly sweet apple that ripens in October and is a good keeper.

SHARED

I woke before dawn, full of nerves and energy. In early September 2003, by the time the sun popped over Long Mountain I was outfitted in rubber boots and safety glasses, ready for my first day of pressing apples as a commercial cidermaker. Matt and I had already cleaned and sterilized the tanks, the press, and the grinder. For our inaugural apple pressing, I was in charge of the last-minute checklist.

In a cidery, almost everything begins with a Brute. A Brute is a fifty-gallon food-grade plastic tub on wheels that functions as the measuring cup for most cleaning. I filled a Brute with water and a mixture of citric acid and sulfite, my talisman against spoilage, and began rinsing equipment. By this time I could attach the tricky tri-clover clamps linking hoses to tanks and pumps with one hand, blindfolded. When I connected a juice line to the press pan, the stainless steel basin that collects the freshly squeezed juice, I thought, "This is it. I am really making cider." Half of me wanted to savor the moment, the culmination of years of planning, saving money, and hard work in the orchard. The other half was ready to crank up the tractor.

Apple pressing, even in a highly manual operation like Foggy Ridge Cider, is fast and noisy. The tractor ran constantly, moving bins of apples to the crush pad and tipping them into the conveyor. My secondhand conveyor rattled and groaned as it rolled apples to the grinder, a giant food processor sitting on top of a five-foot-tall platform. The apples plopped into the hopper, fell through the grinder, and exited as what cidermakers call pomace.

The crew pressed Hewe's Crab, Parmar, Smith Cider, Ribston Pippin, and a bin of Grimes Golden apples I purchased from a longtime grower in Cana, Virginia. His orchard was 1,500 feet lower than mine, and his apples always ripened a few weeks earlier. I hoped to fill three 1,000-liter tanks, and I needed plenty of fruit.

When pressing juicy dessert apples like the varieties you find in a grocery store, the pomace is lightly sweet and almost clear. Cider apple pomace, though, is chestnut-colored, full of tannin and intensely sweet apple aroma. I flipped the switch on the grinder and turned on the conveyor. We filled one tub with pomace and replaced it with a second to keep the grinder working. The youngest and strongest person on the press crew shoveled apple pomace into the bags lining the large Squeezebox. We were off and running.

When I planned my cidery, I debated purchasing a rack and cloth press, the old-fashioned vertical contraption that compresses layers of pomace wrapped in fabric. The used Squeezebox I ended up buying is the same design, only horizontal, a sofa-sized collection of food-grade plastic panels lined with bags suspended over a stainless trough. It is a giant juice accordion. The hydraulic press pushed in one direction, squeezing the bags of apple pomace. Juice flowed into the stainless steel pan below. Once the apples yielded juice, the operator flipped the panels to dislodge the now-dry pomace.

By the end of the first hour my hands were the color of tobacco, and I added earplugs to my cidermaking checklist.

The rest of the day was a blur. We filled our tanks and cleaned the equipment. I ran lab tests on my first juice, soon to be cider. As the sun tipped over Tony Goad's pasture, I drove the leftover pressed apple pomace across Pineview Road to Tony's cows.

Ground apples exit the apple press as a "cake," essentially apple bits with almost all the juice pressed out. In the early South, cidermakers mixed this cake with water and fermented the weak juice into a low-alcohol cider called "ciderkin," often made for children. The pressed pomace from my Squeezebox looked like moist granola and smelled delicious. By the end of an early September press day, the back of our farm truck was loaded with cider cake and swarming with bees.

Tony's cows lined the fence, drawn by aromas from the crush pad. Matt opened the gate, and I inched into the crowd of cattle. That's when I found out just how attractive apple pomace is to hungry cows. They pushed against the truck, licked windows and doors, and butted each other for first dibs at the pile of sweet apple bits. Matt jumped on the pile of pomace and began shoveling as fast as he could. We deflected the herd with a small pile of ground apples and then headed straight uphill to lose all but the most energetic calves. By the time we unloaded the pickup, I had a dented truck door and a herd of cows with their noses buried deep in the leftovers from my first press day.

I was sweaty and covered in sticky apple bits. My back ached from shoveling pomace, and I had more than a few itchy bee stings. But I felt drenched in community, the congregation that created this day. My trees, Matt, the harvest and pressing crew . . . even Tony's cows shared in this first day of cidermaking. I had never felt more satisfied by a hard day's work.

I gardened with ghosts in those early days at Foggy Ridge Cider. Though my orchard was new, I keenly felt the spirits of Appalachian farmers who preceded me. Beginning in the mid-1800s, the Spence family grew corn on what was now my cider apple orchard. Cornbread Marshall, in his seventies when I first met him, recalled his childhood when the Spences' sheep clipped the steep pastures on either side of Rock House Creek "as close as a golf course." As a young mother in the 1920s, Carrie Spence gathered chestnuts and sold them for meal. When the chestnut trees died, she and her husband harvested trees and milled them on the site where our house now sits.

My first cider and apple mentors lived in New Hampshire and Vermont, but they were just a phone call away. I often wondered how remote farmers shared information a hundred years ago. How did they learn about a market for their chestnut wood, or how to price a beaver pelt? Southern apples like Albemarle Pippin garnered fame, hitched to aristocratic growers and eaters. But hundreds of southern apples noticed and selected by orchardists all over the South made their names and traveled via a more circuitous network.

In 1785, white aristocratic planters formed the portentously named "South Carolina Society for Promoting and Improving Agriculture and Other Rural Concerns," one of the first agricultural societies in America, a largely Lowcountry rice and cotton group. But before the early nineteenth century there was little organized sharing of general agricultural know-how in the South.

Yet all over the region, southerners were *noticing* which seedling apple trees bore crisp juicy apples in June or set fruit reliably each fall. They observed seedling apples that tasted best, lasted longest, dried well, and made the best cider—and they replicated the apples they most desired through grafting. They named these apples and shared their chosen fruit with friends and neighbors. They bragged about them in letters, diaries, and farm books. Early nineteenth-century planters and farmers eagerly exchanged trees and grafting wood.

Because apples are heterozygous, meaning they don't come true from seed, replicating an apple requires using the tissue of the "mother tree," the tree that's been noticed and named, to create a clone of the desired tree. Every named southern apple shared or sold by a grower was either a sucker pulled up from the mother tree's roots or created as a grafted tree. Grafting joins the living tissue of the "understock," the roots that will support the new tree, with tissue from the variety to be reproduced.

Early southerners usually practiced dormant grafting, which involves joining short sticks of living wood, or scion wood, cut from the growing tips of an apple tree to understock, or rootstock. Apple growers created understock by planting apple seeds or by using native crabapples for rootstock. Orchardists gathered scion wood in winter when trees were dormant and grafted this wood to rootstocks in early spring. Bud grafting used the same principle to join a living bud from the mother tree to a living bud of the rootstock, usually in late summer.

The March 1853 issue of the *Southern Agriculturist* instructed readers to grow rootstock from apple seeds and described "plain and practical" grafting steps for cleft, root, whip, and side grafting techniques. The detailed guide included a recipe for wax used to seal grafts made from "six parts of rosin, two parts of tallow . . . and one of beeswax."[1]

Though they practiced grafting, early nineteenth-century farmers did not understand cross-pollination, insect life cycles, or how to prevent disease in fruit trees. Few practiced crop rotation or soil enrichment. Mendel's experiments in genetics would not be published until 1866. For southerners, the most advanced nursery in the country, Prince Nursery, was far away on Long Island. At the turn of the century, all the tree fruit growers had in the South was each other.

Letters flew among fruit aficionados, offering scion wood, bud wood, and young trees of favorite varieties. Scholarly scientists corresponded with tradesmen. Part-time farmers penned editorials in agricultural journals. Politicians spent hours on "must have" apple lists. These vivid descriptions of southern apples reveal a community of southern growers and their complex desires for apples.

Silas McDowell and Jarvis Van Buren were two of the most prolific letter writers and tree swappers, extolling apples in letters sent between North Carolina and Georgia. In early December 1856, Van Buren petitioned for "grafts next spring . . . of Iola and Nequassey" and foisted an Alabama apple on his friend in North Carolina: "I have [grafts] from almost every Southern state. One in particular you must have, Called the Red Warrior, a native of Montgomery, Ala., verry [*sic*] large weighing 30 ounces & keeps eternally."[2] A few weeks later Van Buren wrote, "I shall send you some grafts of the Queen Apple it is one of the handsomest apples I ever saw; it looks like an ivory ball with a red cheek, hard, fair and glossy as glass."[3]

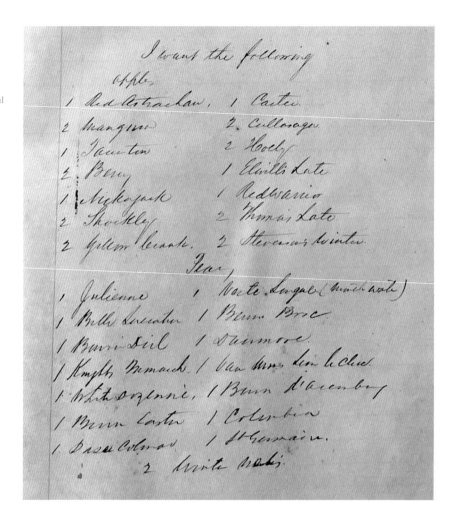

In 1857 North Carolina lawyer and politician Walter L. Steele drafted a list with a phrase I've used many times: "I want the following apples." He noted fourteen apples, including Nickajack, Shockley, Cullasaga, and Red Warrior.[4]

Twenty-three-year-old William Summer began selling fruit trees from his family's South Carolina farm in 1838 even before he founded the influential Pomaria Nurseries. Summer corresponded with orchardists, often responding to more than a dozen letters each day.[5] He collected apple seedlings from South Carolina and other southern states and was instrumental in pushing southern varieties into a larger market. Pomaria's 1856–57 catalog listed 121 apples, and by 1862 Summer offered 319 apples, a remarkable increase in apple varieties, many noticed and selected by the community of small farmers across the Lowcountry.[6]

The owners of southern nurseries, large and small, often learned about local apples from farmers who had grown a special family apple for generations. Early in his apple sleuthing career, author Lee Calhoun learned about the Aunt Rachel or Rachel apple, an excellent early apple grown only in Chatham County, North Carolina. Neighbors and families who valued a big July-ripening cooking apple passed this hyperlocal fruit along for over a century. Cedar Grove Nursery in North Carolina's Yadkin Valley sold Aunt Sally, another family apple, in the late 1800s. Calhoun explains that Sally Caroline Ridings brought this family apple from Virginia to North Carolina when she married a man from Allegheny County. She continued the tradition of gifting root sprouts to her female descendants to carry on Aunt Sally's apple legacy.[7]

Family apples were treasured across the South. Devine is an Alabama family apple grown by Mrs. J. B. Devine and discovered near Gadsden, Alabama, by apple detective and nursery owner Joyce Neighbors. The Devine family brought a root sprout from South Carolina to Alabama in 1895, and this bright-red late-summer apple thrived in its new home. My neighbors in southwest Virginia are fiercely loyal to Virginia Beauty, discovered around 1810 as a seedling tree in the Piper's Gap area of Carroll County. An early enthusiast described this apple as "the very acme of deliciousness among eating apples. . . . It has a distinctive flavor all of its own that clings to the palate and lingers in the memory for a lifetime."[8]

Lee Calhoun writes about the Fairey family in South Carolina and their Schumacher apple. In Virginia the Berriers shared Davidson Sweeting, and the Carters passed along Chimney. The Georgia Farrow family kept the Sam apple going through generations. North Carolina families shared dozens of family apples: the Covingtons shared the Glass apple; the Dixons kept Bud Wolf. The Smiths saved Pinky, and the Nolens passed along their namesake, the Nolen apple.[9]

Family apples and hyperlocal apples demonstrate that southern apples linger in memories for much longer than one lifetime. Passed along as root shoots at weddings, shared as scion wood with neighbors, bragged about every fall—southerners valued uniqueness and were inordinately proud of their local fruit. In *Victuals*, Ronni Lundy describes Appalachian bean varieties that varied from one mountain cove to the next. Lundy notes that site-specific beans raised by multiple genera-

Virginia Beauty from Pulaski, VA, by Amanda A. Newton. US Department of Agriculture Pomological Watercolor Collection, Rare and Special Collections, National Agricultural Library, Beltsville, MD.

tions created a powerful edible culture of connection. The same is true for apples.

The Vernon family in Caswell County, North Carolina, has this connection to the Mary Reid apple. David Vernon operates Century Farm Orchard on hilly land that has been in his family since 1872. David's great-great-grandfather planted the original orchard in the 1880s and 1890s. Each generation grew a wide variety of apples, all with different uses and flavors. "My grandfather kept the orchard going," David said. "It was heaven. They made cider. They made vinegar for the neighborhood and stored it in oak barrels. My aunt loved apples, and her recollections sparked my own interest in finding a way to keep the family orchard going."[10]

David's aunt Martha Rice married and moved six miles away from the family farm to a community where everyone had a Mary Reid apple. He said, "It was the perfect apple for small farmers who weren't selling their fruit. It ripens from July to mid-September; it's good to eat and cook with, and it's a dry apple so it stores well."

David is familiar with the evocative pull of local apples. He said that he can often guess the apple his customers are phoning about by looking at the area code for the call. David explained, "If someone calls and asks for a Bevan's Favorite, they are calling from somewhere on the Kentucky and West Virginia border. When a call comes in for a Tony apple, it's most likely from Cabarrus or Stanley Counties in North Carolina."

David's family doesn't know who Mary Reid was or why a valuable apple carries her name. But he does know his role in preserving this apple. He remembered, "I thought everyone had a Mary Reid apple until I talked to Lee Calhoun and found out there were only two trees left in the entire world." Thanks to Century Farm Orchard, today anyone can add Mary Reid to their "must have" apple list.

Some of the best southern apples were brought to market by small nurseries, nineteenth-century versions of David Vernon's Century Farm Orchard. More than a few southern apples jumped the region's borders and gained fame in Europe and other parts of America. But a rich cultural connection occurred with pass-along trees, apples that began when a southern farmer noticed, then replicated, and then shared a specific tree from a specific community. The hundreds of apple varieties sold in southern nurseries and grown on southern farms were "essentially a rural, populist movement," one that filled the southern apple basket with beloved useful fruit.[11]

GRAFTED

The wise person who said that good wine- or cider-making is "99 percent good janitorial practices" was right. As a new cidermaker, I spent more time cleaning tanks than I did tasting cider. For this inaugural batch of cider, my cleaning protocols paid off. Five days after adding yeast to freshly pressed juice, all the yeasty, fruity aromas of a healthy ferment filled my tidy little cider house.

I had always longed to make cider that expressed the apple varieties I grew in Foggy Ridge's high-elevation orchards. But I also wanted to insert my own aesthetic on the beverage that filled Foggy Ridge bottles. Some cider- and winemakers aim for "natural ferments," juice fermented with ambient yeast, no added nutrients or temperature control. I've enjoyed beautiful beverages made this way and have also tasted many stinky bottles of highly flawed natural wine and cider. I had worked too hard to graft and grow my cider apples to risk my first ferment to a process that felt like rolling dice.

Apple juice pressed from ripe apples grown in the South is usually 14 to 19 percent sugar by mass, expressed in degrees of Brix, a measure of sugar. In fermentation, yeast consume sugar and produce carbon dioxide and alcohol. Cider has less alcohol than wine because apple juice has less sugar than grape juice. In a warm southern fall without temperature control, yeast consume the sugar in a fast ferment that can burn off flavor and aroma. Since I wanted flavorful and aromatic cider, I aimed for a cold, slow ferment.

This meant *lots* of monitoring. I was barely comfortable in my tiny lab with my new skills and ran each test twice to confirm results. These calculations and measurements would eventually become second nature, but for that first batch of cider, angst filled every day. I wove cider duties between client calls from my part-time consulting work. Sitting at my cider house desk in rubber boots, I answered urgent emails about the next project at a New York bank as a timer clicked for a lab test. I had not been this happy in years.

Late one afternoon, a week into that first cider ferment, I stood in the middle of my compact tank room with my arms outstretched. I had worked one fifteen-hour day after another. My income-producing consulting job and the demands of thousands of liters of cider were straining me. But in that moment I could almost touch the tall stainless steel fermenters lining both walls. All the work and worry melded with a full measure of joy. My heart was full to bursting.

At that moment I knew my apple journey had changed me to the core. The orchard, the trees, the cider house . . . all this was more than a new life chapter. My axis had shifted. My feet were profoundly rooted in a *place*, a place that embodied home, a profession, and a community in ways I had never experienced.

Standing in my tank room, surrounded by stainless steel and fermenting juice, I felt elated, as if I was somehow holding all that I had made in my arms. I planted the trees, grew the fruit, picked the apples, and pressed them. I watched over my cider as if it was a newborn. My clothes smelled like sweet ripe apples and baking bread. If this was what cidermaking was all about, I was all in.

———————

One winter in the early 1830s, Jacob Epting, a Newberry County, South Carolina, farmer, taught teenage William Summer how to graft fruit trees. Epting and the Summer family were descendants of the German and Swiss German immigrants who had settled the Dutch Fork area between the Broad and Saluda Rivers eighty years earlier, bringing fruit-growing skills and a tradition of diversified farms to the South Carolina midlands.

William Summer contracted polio as a child and walked with crutches from then on.[1] Jacob Epting's gift of grafting skills changed Summer's life. Summer later wrote, "In our childhood through long years of excruciating agony and bodily suffering, his kindness contained us. He taught us the beautiful lesson of planting a tree."[2]

By age nineteen, Summer had turned his grafting skills into an occupation. Unable to attend college with his brothers, he began grafting fruit trees for sale on the Summer family plantation.[3] By 1840, aided by his brother Adam, William launched Pomaria Nurseries, which would become one of the South's most influential sources of southern-grown fruit trees and ornamentals.

William's connection to trees was deeper than the handy skill of grafting and the potential to add to his family's plantation economy. He seemed more connected to trees than to people. At age thirty-eight he wrote, "Those dozen scions planted in childhood have become old and productive friends; better friends too than mankind has furnished us . . . for they are always faithful and always fruitful."[4] The trees he grafted as a child, and the dozens more he introduced to southern agriculture, occupied an outsize space in William Summer's life.

With Jacob Epting's nudge, apples grabbed young William Summer, captured his imagination, and catapulted him into a lifelong obsession.

The German Lutheran Sommer family immigrated to America and first settled in Philadelphia to work off their indenture. In 1752, William's great-grandfather Johannes Adam Sommer moved to South Carolina's backcountry, a land still populated by Indigenous people who had occupied this land for over 13,000 years.[5] He petitioned King George II's agents for land and began farming 250 acres,[6] land that had been occupied by Native groups including the Catawba, Cherokee, Creek, Shawnee, and Chickasaw.[7] By the early 1800s, "Sommer" had become "Summer" when grandson John Adam Summer III anglicized his name and built the home where William Summer learned to graft.[8]

The Summer plantation was a "small large plantation" with a plantation house, horse and cow barns, a carriage house, and all the outbuildings that a diversified farm demanded. The family used the labor of enslaved people, at one time enslaving as many as forty-four men, women, and children. The enslaved workers grew cotton, corn, wheat, rye, potatoes, and barley; cared for livestock; and provided labor for all aspects of the plantation. William's nursery also employed Irish immigrants, white neighbors, and, as the nursery grew, a Scottish horticulturist.[9]

Today we don't think of South Carolina as a source of apple varieties. But during his life as a nursery owner and apple grower, William Summer brought an astonishing thirty-three southern apples into commercial production, from his own seedlings and from discoveries by growers across South Carolina.[10]

He distributed Carolina Red June, a popular local apple first grafted by a neighbor, Henry Sieber. Author Lee Calhoun describes Carolina Red June as "one of the most important southern apples well into the twentieth century."[11] Pomaria was the first nursery to sell Hoover, an oddly spotted red seedling apple from Edisto, South Carolina, grown in the South from the coast to the mountains. In 1908, a USDA official wrote, "In passing through the mountain sections of North Carolina one sees this variety very commonly. During the fall, it is the one most often brought to the stations for sale to passengers on trains."[12] Pomaria's catalog described Hammond, from Spartanburg, South Carolina, as "equal to the best Newtown Pippin," high praise for any apple.[13]

Some of the most intriguing apples from the Pomaria catalogs no longer exist. Pomaria introduced Aromatic Carolina, a South Carolina seedling apple grown by Johannes Miller, along with Cook's Red Winter, grown by Jacob Cook in Edisto. Andrew Jackson Downing's 1865 edition of *The Fruits and Fruit Trees of America* described the Aromatic Carolina as "highly aromatic" with "exceedingly tender and melting flesh."[14] These apples are now likely extinct, as are Anderson, Augustine, Lever, and Fixlin, all Pomaria introductions. Adam Minnick, a Pomaria neighbor, grew the Ferdinand apple and named it for his father. William Summer described this now extinct apple as "the best winter apple that is for our climate, large and fine flavored."[15] Maverick's Sweet, an intensely sweet apple, was widely grown in the South until the early twentieth century. Two apples named for William's grafting teacher, Epting's Premium and Epting's Red Winter, are also extinct.

A description of the lost apple Susannah tantalizes. This long-storing late-fall apple won a premium in the 1859 South Carolina State Fair apple competition. William Summer was so impressed that he wrote about Susannah in the *Farmer and Planter* as triumphing "over *twenty-one varieties* of choice well-known Southern seedlings."[16] He grafted 400 Susannah trees and charged fifty cents for this apple in his 1860 catalog, double his usual price.

William Summer may have been confined to mid-state South Carolina, but apples expanded his world. In May 1850, he wrote to his friend George Adam Fike about the fruit that arrived at Pomaria Nurseries from around the country: "My occasional articles have I found carried my name beyond the limits of my native state and I have received from this fact, grafts done up in oiled silk by mail from many different states of most superior kinds of pears, apples and other fruits."[17]

When the Newberry to Columbia railroad arrived in 1851, Summer's nursery blossomed. Many of Pomaria's apples originated with South Carolina neighbors and in nearby southern states, but they traveled beyond their home turf. Pomaria shipped apples within South Carolina from Greenville to Bluffton. Pomaria fruit trees and ornamentals headed to customers in North Carolina, Arkansas, Virginia, Florida, Alabama, and Mississippi.[18] Orders ranged from a few trees to enough stock for significant orchards. In 1859, Dr. Gaston of Columbia purchased 100 apples for twenty-five dollars and 106 peaches for twenty dollars plus pears, cherries, plums, quince, and asparagus plants.

By 1860 Summer answered "12 to 28 letters daily," with orders for fruit trees and ornamentals.[19] Pomaria employed agents to represent the nursery in Charlotte, Asheville, Augusta, Mobile, New Orleans, and Fernandina, Florida.[20] Pomaria sold to businesses in New York and Pennsylvania, as well as to the van Houtte horticultural firm in Belgium.[21] A year before the Civil War began, the orchard was valued at $10,000 and Summer expected his profitable nursery "to increase yearly until I can make it what I choose."[22]

The Summers focused on apples, pears, and peaches, but Pomaria Nurseries sold more than fruit trees. Adam handled the ornamental side of the nursery, centered in Columbia. The 1860 Pomaria Nurseries catalog listed over 800 varieties of roses, all adapted to the South.[23] The Summer brothers imported plants from Europe and helped popularize *Magnolia grandiflora* plantings throughout the South.

But William's lasting connection was to apples.

William could have devoted his life to growing wheat or, like his brother Adam, spent his time promoting superior livestock breeds. He could have retreated to his extensive library and penned more articles for the *Farmer and Planter* or *Horticulturist*.

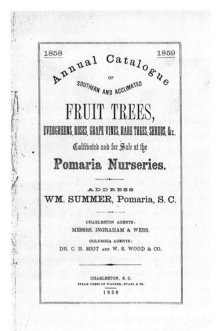

Pomaria Nurseries, Annual Catalogue of Southern and Acclimated Fruit Trees, Evergreens, Roses, Grape Vines, Rare Trees, Shrubs, Etc., 1858–59. South Caroliniana Library, University of South Carolina, Columbia.

But William chose apples. Jacob Epting's "beautiful lesson" connected him to neighbors and the larger horticultural world. Both brothers founded and served as officers in prominent nineteenth-century agricultural groups, including the American Pomological Society and the United States Agricultural Society in Washington, DC. The Massachusetts Agricultural Society made William an honorary member in 1850.

The brothers wrote articles in southern agricultural journals supporting diversified, self-sufficient farms. They believed that the South could "produce within its boundaries the crops and products that would yield economic independence."[24] William's lively apple descriptions in the Pomaria Nurseries catalogs paint an evocative picture of fruit culture. His letters are filled with adjectives portraying fruit flavor, size, and color. His 1860 paper "Essay on Reforesting the Country" detailed ways to revive "South Carolina's glorious forest."[25] Pomaria's vision of southern agriculture mirrored the values of the white landowners who purchased plants from the nursery.

The agricultural self-sufficiency championed by the Summers depended on the labor of enslaved people. Enslaved people grew crops on the Pomaria plantation. They tended pigs and chickens and cared for the horses and carriages. The nursery also employed Irish immigrants who had come to South Carolina to build the Columbia, Greenville and Newberry Railroad, as well as three European landscape gardeners.

Before the Civil War, William Summer employed emancipated freedmen in the nursery and mentioned several freed Black workers in his ledgers. Spencer Valentine, born in Newberry County in 1839, was William's "valued right-hand man in propagation after the war."[26] Yet, pre–Civil War freed Blacks lived circumscribed lives designed to control and subjugate. They could not travel freely or testify against whites. They were required to have white guardians.[27] In the mid-1860s, their limited rights were constantly under threat from increasingly restrictive legislation. The freed Black workers at Pomaria were far from free.

Enslaved people performed much of the labor of this large nursery that offered thousands of trees for sale each year: digging, planting, maintaining beds, and weeding. Older enslaved men, women, and children worked in the nursery all year caring for the orchards and gardens. In winter they dug dormant trees and fertilized with manure. Spring was planting season, time to set out hundreds of sprouted grafts in nursery beds. Enslaved people helped William pack plants for shipment. And all year they watered, weeded, and mulched.[28]

Slavery and the subjugation of Black growers and workers were the context and subtext for the hundreds of southern apples sold at Pomaria Nurseries before the Civil War.

In February 1865, Union soldiers captured Columbia. Pomaria's nursery devoted to ornamental plants burned along with much of the city. The financial loss for the Summers was devastating. William Summer valued the loss of the Columbia property at $115,000.[29] The orchards at Pomaria survived, and later that year he grew wheat on the Pomaria plantation with twelve freedmen and one white worker.

But William never stopped yearning for apples.

In 1867 he wrote, "I have the Nursery here improved and hope to be able to make a good living from it and in time regain something of former prosperity."[30] Pomaria's 1872 catalog offered sixty-one pages of fruit trees and ornamentals, and "only such as are adapted to our climate," including over 150 dessert apples, 9 cider apples, and 10 varieties from Russia.[31] The 73 winter varieties were all southern seedlings.

William's optimism for the nursery after the Civil War played out against the violent assault on the rights of emancipated Blacks in South Carolina. In 1871, as William wrote his nursery listings, white Klansmen in nearby Union County lynched twelve Black men. Racial violence in South Carolina was so prevalent that President Ulysses S. Grant declared martial law in 1871.[32] A wave of racial violence swept the state during the 1876 gubernatorial election.

In 1878 William died of pneumonia contracted on a cold, rainy ride back from a South Carolina Agricultural Society meeting in Charleston. Pomaria's 1878 catalog was its last. It offered 39 apple varieties, a steep decline from the 500 listed in the 1860 catalog.[33] His nephew John Adam Summer inherited the nursery, then valued at $1,050.[34]

Pomaria was the first significant southern nursery, predating the more well-known Fruitland in Georgia by almost twenty years. Pomaria endured for nearly four decades, survived the Civil War, and introduced scores of seedling apples discovered in fields and on roadsides and adapted to the South. Supported by the enslaved and later emancipated Black farmers, Pomaria spread southern fruit across the region and the country—valuable fruit, evocatively described, and inextricably entwined with the legacy of slavery and the violence of the Reconstruction era.

CELEBRATED

Isolation drew me to our farm. There were more wild turkeys than neighbors. The county had a single traffic light and no gated communities. Perched at the base of a graceful green hill, the Foggy Ridge cider house sat surrounded by apple trees on a chip-sealed rural road. But this scenic spot was also a fifty-mile round-trip jaunt to a grocery store. As I approached the first open day of Foggy Ridge's tasting room, my goal of selling cider to visitors at our little cidery seemed ill-considered, and perhaps even reckless.

I had big hopes for our small tasting room. Due to changes in Virginia alcohol laws, distributing cider to restaurants and retailers turned out to be more complex than I envisioned. I wanted to sell cider, but more important, I wanted connection with customers who might care about the complexities of growing an agricultural ingredient and making a craft beverage. After making cider in near isolation for over a year, I wanted to see my hard-won product out in the world.

So I marshaled my marketing skills and networked with local chambers of commerce. I left flyers at nearby inns and even purchased a small ad in a few local weekly newspapers. For our first open day in 2004 I tucked away the bottler and set up display racks and a tasting table. I arranged red folding tables and green chairs on the crush pad. I rolled labels onto my first vintage of Foggy Ridge Cider bottles. And I opened the doors.

The previous week a talented young journalist from the *Roanoke Times* visited the farm. Lindsey Nair and I walked through my first orchard—at that time almost six years old—which was also my test orchard of over thirty varieties of cider apples. We hiked up the steep rows in the new north orchard, dominated by Ashmead's Kernel and the largest planting of Hewe's Crabapples in the country at the time. Lindsey was smart and curious. She asked insightful questions and took lots of notes. She seemed genuinely interested in my vision for making cider that reflected a specific place, the Foggy Ridge Cider farm. And she had a photographer in tow.

Lindsey's article ran in the *Roanoke Times* the day before we opened the Foggy Ridge Cider tasting room. Our farm is far enough off the grid that we don't have daily newspaper delivery, or for that matter any newspaper delivery. A friend called at 8:00 a.m. practically yelling over the phone, "You're on the front page of the features section. A half-page photo. And she called you a 'willowy red head.'"

Well, that felt pretty good. I looked forward to reading the article. What I didn't anticipate is that on that beautiful September day, the first with a hint of fall in the air, scores of people from all over southwest Virginia would decide to take a drive in the mountains. Or that carloads of curious customers would find our little cidery.

By 11:00 a.m. the gravel parking lot overflowed with visitors. Most had never tasted alcoholic cider other than a sweetened six-pack cider version. None had tasted the bitter acidic apples displayed on our tasting table. Many were wine drinkers, familiar with Virginia's growing reputation for high-quality farm wineries. Quite a few asked, "What grapes is this made from?" I tried to explain, "Cider is made like wine, only it's made with apple juice, not grape juice." I talked until my voice grew hoarse, and I poured bottle after bottle of our precious first vintage. At the end of our first open day we had sold close to fifty cases of cider, 10 percent of our entire year's production.

But what surprised me most were the scores of apple stories. Customers wanted to talk about the tree behind Grandma's house that produced tart apples for apple butter. The Maggie Bowman apple from the family home place. Did I know the name of the hard green apple that ripens in midsummer? And this one, told more than once and always with a smile: "Do you know what it felt like to sit in my daddy's lap and watch him slowly peel a deep-red Winesap in one long unbroken peel?"

For months customers entered Foggy Ridge Cider's red front door with Lindsey Nair's article in hand. Most knew nothing about cider. I was ready to tell stories about my southern cider apples, many grown in Virginia for hundreds of years. I was primed to show off my apple press and explain cider fermentation. But my customers wanted to talk, not listen. Lindsey's article struck the emotional chord between people and apples. My new customers came wanting to tell their own apple stories.

I had to learn to listen.

In 1858, Louis Mathieu Edouard Berckmans, a fifty-seven-year-old Belgian physician and botanist, purchased 365 acres in Augusta, Georgia, with outsize dreams for transforming the southern landscape.

A year after landing in the South with his family and collection of pear trees, Berckmans wrote, "I shall not see the time when the South, from Virginia to Alabama, will be considered the fruit garden of America, but I am fully convinced that such a time will come, and that thousands of acres, unfit for cultivation of cotton and corn, [will] all be converted into remunerating orchards."[1]

Augusta seemed an unlikely place for Louis Berckmans's view of a fruit revolution in the South.

Native people had long occupied the shoals below the Savannah River's fall line. Some historians say that Hernando de Soto crossed the river here en route to South Carolina. In 1736 General James Edward Oglethorpe's troops established a settlement to secure the headwaters of the Savannah against the French and Spanish and to serve as a site for trading furs with Indigenous people. By 1739, Noble Jones surveyed Augusta as the second city established by white colonizers in Georgia. When the Berckmans family arrived at this southern edge of Georgia's Piedmont Plateau, Augusta was the second-largest city in the state, with over 16,000 white and Black residents.

The Augusta Canal provided water and power. Paper and textile products traveled west on the Georgia Railroad to Atlanta and Chattanooga. The town was one of the South's most significant manufacturing centers, far from a fruit-growing mecca.

In 1850, almost half—48 percent—of county residents were enslaved people.[2] Augusta was second to Savannah as a Georgia slave trading center. Some 34 percent of families in the county owned slaves.

Cotton was the dominant crop for area planters, and horticulture was not part of the city's or region's economy. But Louis Berckmans had a vision for an altered southern landscape and a son with the skills and drive to carry it out.

On August 22, 1850, some nine months before Louis and the rest of the family landed in America, Louis's son, nineteen-year-old Prosper Jules Alphonse Berckmans, sailed from Antwerp, Belgium, to New York, his French education and weighty name in tow. Traveling on the *Peter Hattrick*, a three-masted ship packed with 243 passengers, Prosper crossed the Atlantic on a largely uneventful voyage filled with calm seas, a few stormy nights, and almost universal seasickness among the passengers. Fourteen privileged travelers occupied private cabins. Prosper filled his room with four trunks, several hunting guns, and a leather-bound travel journal. Here he recorded evocative entries about harpooning porpoises and sunsets that "surpass all descriptions."[3] Thirty-nine days later, he stepped onto lower Manhattan, ready to explore America.

Prosper arrived with extensive horticultural knowledge. He had studied botany in France and attended meetings of the Royal Horticultural Society. He collaborated with Belgian scientist Jean-Baptiste Van Mons on a three-volume work on European fruit and contributed to Van Mons's groundbreaking pear research.[4] Before he was twenty, Prosper built a reputation in European horticultural circles and was positioned to take over the reins of his family's estates.

But the Berckmanses, both father and son, had other plans. Prosper's voyage to America was a scouting trip for this family's expansive horticultural venture.

Prosper visited New Jersey and Philadelphia but quickly found his way to Rome, Georgia, home to a community of Belgian expats. Here he hunted ducks, quail, and possum; marveled at the city's four churches, where "one is free to follow the religion which suits him"; and drank "excellent Bordeaux wine."[5] For the next nine months Prosper toured the South and filled his leather journal with soil descriptions, lists of native plants, and land prices. He examined mines in north Georgia's Habersham County. He traveled on a steamboat down the Mississippi to New Orleans, recording mostly adult, sober impressions at every stop. Only his excitement at killing a milk snake and catching a tortoise revealed the still-young man hiding in an adult botanist's journal.[6] Prosper visited Chicago, St. Louis, and New York, but Georgia captured his imagination.

When Prosper visited Rome the city was sixteen years old, a product of the forced removal of Indigenous people who had occupied this fertile slice of rolling land at the confluence of the Etowah and Oostanaula Rivers. In 1848 a group of Belgian aristocrats led by General Louis Joseph Barthold Le Hardy, Viscount de Beaulieu, had immigrated to Rome, where they planned to farm on what had been a Native settlement. By the time Prosper arrived, Rome had three hotels, 2,100 residents, and a dry goods store "in which one finds everything that is possible to imagine."[7]

The city's energy and opportunities fascinated him.

Prosper would not have known that the decade of the 1850s was bringing a reversal of what had been an exodus from Georgia. By the time Prosper visited Rome, new settlers from other southern states as well as Irish, German, and English immigrants outnumbered those fleeing depleted soil.[8]

In December Prosper traveled by train, stagecoach, and carriage from Rome to Clarkesville, Georgia, where he met nursery owner Jarvis Van Buren. At this stage in his journey, Prosper was more interested in mining than horticulture, but I can imagine these two pomologists discussing fruit trees and enjoying a few late-season apples.

In May 1851, Louis Berckmans and his family left Belgium and land that had been home to their family for generations, their most choice fruit trees in hand. Though Prosper was enthusiastic about his southern sojourns, Louis chose to relocate the family to Plainfield, New Jersey, home to the luminaries of the American horticultural world, including Charles and Andrew Jackson Downing.

In New Jersey, father and son founded a nursery that offered over a thousand pear varieties. Prosper assisted the Downings in revising their work, *The Fruits and Fruit Trees of America*; attended horticultural society meetings; and married Mary Craig, from Plainfield.[9] New Jersey seemed the perfect landing spot for this Belgian pair, but the region's harsh winters were not kind to Louis's pear trees. Just six years after arriving in Plainfield, the Berckmanses moved to Augusta, Georgia, and in 1858 purchased Fruitland Nurseries from Dennis Redmond, editor of the *Southern Cultivator*.[10]

This family's unlikely move from a thousand-year-old aristocratic European estate to a Georgia trading town would shape southern orchards and gardens.

––––––––––

The Berckmanses' northern agricultural colleagues did not share Louis's view of the South's horticultural potential. Downing's 1845 edition of *The Fruit and Fruit Trees of America* included only one apple from the South, Father Abraham. *The Fruit Garden*, published by Patrick Barry in 1851, included 133 apple varieties but referred to only 4 apples as southern: Carolina Red June, Carthouse, "Limber Twig," and "Rawle's Janet," a Virginia apple that he asserted was from Kentucky.[11]

At the time, northern agriculturists were blind to southern fruit culture. When Barry described the Newtown Pippin as grown to "greatest perfection on Long Island and on the Hudson,"[12] he was unaware that southerners had grown this apple for almost 100 years. In the South it had acquired a new name, Albemarle Pippin, an international reputation, and, to many, a superior flavor. Taliaferro, Hewe's Crab, Virginia White . . . these storied southern apples had not yet made the prominent northern fruit books. All over the South, southern apples were hiding in plain sight, appreciated but not trumpeted.

In his influential book on American horticulture, U. P. Hedrick wrote, "Before the Civil War, progress in horticulture in the South was not comparable with that in the North."[13] Hedrick described few nurseries in the South, no large profitable orchards, little landscape gardening, and a paucity of agricultural societies, in contrast to the North.

But the long-held view of the South as "horticulturally challenged" contradicted observations of the South's abundant and diverse native plants as well as early botanic collections filled with European imports. Beginning in 1773, William Bartram's four-year-long exploration of Georgia, Florida, Alabama, and Louisiana yielded a vivid picture of southern flora and fauna. François André Michaux and his father, André, founded a nursery in Charleston, South Carolina, in 1787. In the summer of 1802, François described the rich natural landscape of the southern Alleghenies when he traveled through West Virginia, Kentucky, and Tennessee. Before the nurseries at either Pomaria or Fruitland offered indigenous southern plants, Stephen Elliott praised southern natives in his two-volume work, *A Sketch of the Botany of South Carolina and Georgia*, published in 1821 and 1824. Charleston was home to botanic gardens established in the late eighteenth and early nineteenth centuries, both filled with "indigenous and exotic plants, arranged according to the Linnaean system."[14]

While no nursery at the time exceeded the Prince Nursery, founded in Queens, New York, in 1737, southerners had benefited from local nurseries that stocked imported and "southern acclimated" fruit trees long before the Berckmanses purchased Fruitland. As early as 1750, William Smith in Surry County, Virginia, operated a fruit tree nursery. Vineland Nursery advertised fruit trees from Mobile in 1755. In 1792, Ann Jessup, a Quaker apple enthusiast, offered scions of English apple varieties through Abijah Pinson's nursery in Guilford County, North Carolina. Thomas Affleck founded Southern Nurseries in Mississippi in 1848. Before Fruitland, Jarvis Van Buren promoted southern apples, writing, "I will not hesitate in saying that the choicest apples may be raised from the seaboard to the mountains in Georgia."[15] And William Summer's Pomaria was influential in its southern footprint and, at times, offered more fruit varieties than Fruitland.

In the few years between his family's nursery purchase in Augusta, Georgia, and the start of the Civil War, Prosper Berckmans did what other southern apple growers had not: he put southern apples on the national map.

———————

The financial crisis of 1847, declining cotton prices, and a countrywide depression that lasted through the mid-1840s coincided with a move-

SOUTHERN COUNTRY HOUSES.
"FRUITLAND"—THE RESIDENCE OF D. REDMOND, NEAR AUGUSTA, GA.

ment to address soil depletion and other agricultural issues. Between 1819 and 1860, over 400 agricultural periodicals sprang up in the country, with at least 100 in the South.[16] The *Southern Cultivator*, published in Augusta, Georgia, was among the most significant journals in the country.

By 1853 the *Southern Cultivator* had 10,000 subscribers. Assistant editor Dennis Redmond was an experienced agricultural journalist who brought an editorial bent toward crop diversification and soil regeneration to this southern publication. Redmond had written for the influential *Genesee Farmer* in New York, but he was also a farmer with big dreams for southern fruit.

In 1853 he purchased 315 acres a few miles outside Augusta, between Rae's Creek and the Savannah River in the Bedford community. James L. Coleman, the original property owner, was a planter who in 1850 owned ninety-three enslaved people.[17] He was one of the first Georgia planters to alter the entrenched cotton culture by planting fruit trees.[18] While Coleman experimented with English apples, Redmond advertised trees from this first iteration of Fruitland Nurseries as "especially adapted to this climate."[19]

Redmond used the *Southern Cultivator* to champion southern fruit. Redmond wrote, "We have never failed of a crop," and in a column optimistically titled "Fruits That Never Fail" he boasted that in the South, "it is easy to have an uninterrupted succession of Apples from the first week in June until the following spring."[20] He trumpeted in upper case: "FRUITLAND NURSERY. TEN THOUSAND CHOICE TREES!"[21] Fruitland's outsize marketing had begun.

In the August 1857 issue, Redmond printed an engraving of his home at the nursery and a lengthy description of the design and construction of his 5,500-square-foot concrete house. Redmond wrote that the first concrete house constructed in the South was "admirably adapted to our Southern climate."[22] Situated on a knoll in the Fruitland orchard, the two-story house had twelve- to eighteen-inch-thick walls and an expansive veranda. Ten-foot-wide hallways bisected the living space. The ground floor housed the "working rooms," including a fruit storage room. A cupola on the roof allowed hot air to escape and provided a viewing platform for the orchards and nursery surrounding his home. Redmond owned one enslaved man in 1860, and it was likely that enslaved people provided some of the labor to construct his house at Fruitland.

One of Prosper's first acts after purchasing Dennis Redmond's nursery was to plant a double row of *Magnolia grandiflora* along the drive leading from Washington Road through the Fruitland orchards to the front steps of the Berckmanses' new home.[23] This Belgian family with a thousand-year-old lineage began planting roots in the South.

The Belgian father and son brought deep horticultural knowledge and international connections to their new venture. Prosper immediately took his place at the top of the southern horticultural scene.

Fruitland's first catalog, 1858–59, offered a staggering range of fruit trees and ornamentals, including 6,000 pear trees, "and to be increased to ten thousand."[24] Prosper's name was the only Berckmans on the catalog frontispiece, and his emphasis on the scientific study of fruit trees began in the first paragraph: "Large orchards of bearing Trees of all kinds of Fruit occupy all parts of the farm and offer many facilities to compare and study the influence of soil and aspect upon the same varieties."[25]

Building on Dennis Redmond's nursery offerings, the Berckmanses emphasized plant breeding, introductions of newly imported ornamentals, and fruit trees adapted to the South. Their first catalog offered 120 apple varieties, many that appeared in catalogs with longer lists from Gloaming Nursery and Pomaria Nurseries in the same year. Apples like Equinetelee, Nantahalee, Disharoon, and Nickajack were not new to southern fruit growers. But no southern nursery combined horticultural skill, international connections, and savvy promotion quite like Fruitland. Prosper had a larger megaphone.

Like Pomaria, Fruitland offered a full list of fruit trees, including pears, plums, cherries, nectarines, and peaches, along with grapes, ornamentals, and an extensive list of roses. But Prosper wanted more than a long plant list—he embraced his father's vision of reshaping the southern landscape. Channeling his New Jersey colleague Andrew Jackson Downing, Prosper used horticulture to emphasize his definition of a cultured landscape.

The market for the Berckmanses' horticultural vision went beyond the planter class. In 1860 less than 6 percent of farms in Georgia were over 500 acres. Some 30 percent of Georgia farmers owned between 100 and 500 acres, and these farmers had the education and means to purchase fruit trees and ornamental plants.

And the Fruitland market extended far beyond the Georgia borders. The nursery sold fruit trees and ornamental plants to farmers, lawyers, doctors, and merchants from Georgia to Texas and New York.[26]

On the eve of the Civil War, the 1861 *Fruitland Nurseries, Descriptive Catalogue of Fruit and Ornamental Trees, Shrubs, Vines, Roses, Evergreens, Hedge Plants, Etc.*, published in 1860, included 900 apple varieties, 300 peaches, 1,300 pear varieties—plus over 10,000 pear seedlings from Europe "not tested in the South"—and ornamentals from Belgium, Germany, France, and Japan.[27] In the catalog preface, Prosper Berckmans wrote, "The general impression at the South is that apples cannot succeed. This is a great error; not only can we raise fine apples but we can rivalize and surpass the North in summer as well as late keeping apples."[28] He praised southern seedling apples from "South Carolina, Middle Georgia, Middle and Southern Alabama, [and] Middle and Southern Mississippi," arguing that southern apples perform best in the South.[29]

The two most prominent southern nurseries, Pomaria and Fruitland, fared very differently during the Civil War. After Sherman's troops destroyed Pomaria's Columbia nursery, William Summer declared bankruptcy in 1868. Though he continued to offer an impressive list of ornamental and fruit trees, his nursery depended on South Carolina customers and was unable to flourish in the recession that followed the war.

In Augusta, the massive Confederate Powder Works, consisting of twenty-six buildings along the city's canal, produced gun powder for

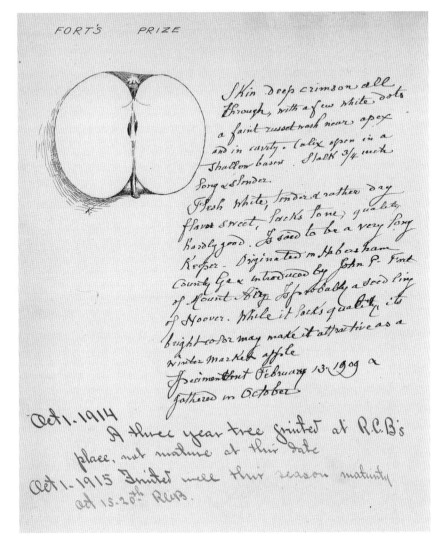

FORT'S PRIZE

Skin deep crimson all through, with a few white dots a faint russet-wash near apex and in cavity. Calix open in a shallow basin. Stalk 3/4 inch long & slender.

Flesh white, tender & rather dry flavor sweet, lacks tone, quality hardly good. Is said to be a very long keeper. Originated in Habersham County Ga & introduced by John P. Fort of Mount Airy. Is probably a seedling of Hoover. While it lacks quality its bright color may make it attractive as a winter market apple. Specimen about February 13. 1909 gathered in October

Oct 1. 1914 A three year tree grafted at R.C.B's place, not mature at this date

Oct 1. 1915 Fruited well this season maturity at 15.20th ReB.

Drawing of Fort's Prize from Prosper Jules Alphonse Berckman's field notebook, 1857. Hargrett Rare Book and Manuscript Library, University of Georgia.

the Confederacy. The city provisioned the Confederate army with cotton and other goods. Likewise, Fruitland Nurseries provided fruits and vegetables to southern soldiers.[30] But the left wing of Sherman's Union troops passed south of Augusta on their way to Milledgeville, the state capital, bypassing Augusta.

Though the nursery survived the Civil War, Prosper did not advertise the Fruitland Nurseries stock from April 1861 until December 1865.

Fruit production expanded in Georgia in the postwar years. Even though the value of his land and nursery holdings decreased, Prosper had the resources to purchase additional acreage and put more land into nursery production. In 1860 he reported owning 360 acres valued at $18,000. By 1870 he owned 500 acres valued at $15,000, including an additional 50 acres of improved land. Cotton was still king in Georgia, but farmers slowly moved toward the diverse horticultural landscape envisioned by Louis Berckmans and other agricultural progressives.

By the 1880s, the nursery mailed out over 25,000 catalogs a year, many overseas.[31] Fruitland's reputation created international interest in its nursery products and in southern fruit and plant varieties. The 1896 catalog boasted that Fruitland shipped plants to foreign markets in Australia, China, Japan, Africa, the East Indies, Brazil, Bermuda, and Europe.[32] By the turn of the century, Fruitland covered 500 acres, including 250 acres of fruit trees and 40 acres of test orchards.[33] Prosper's three sons with his wife, Mary Craig Berckmans, managed a big business that shipped plants all over the globe.

Transforming a landscape requires more than new plants. When Louis Berckmans articulated his vision of the South as the "fruit garden of America" with orchards replacing worn-out cotton fields, southerners had selected acclimated apples for over 200 years.

Prosper Berckmans brought commerce with a capital C to the world of southern apples. He combined superb technical knowledge, deep experience, and international connections with a keen promoter's eye, all backed by the resources of his family's wealth.

Fruitland imprinted fruit on the southern map more powerfully than any other single nursery.

Prosper was a master connector whose correspondence with prominent horticulturists in America and Europe amplified his reputation and influence. He created and led some of the most influential agricultural groups in the South. In 1876 he was a founder of the Georgia State Horticultural Society and served as president for thirty-four years. He was an honorary member of horticultural societies in several states and in France. He served as president of the American Pomological Society for five terms, the highest honor in the agricultural field. In 1889 his horticultural colleagues pushed for his nomination as the first US secretary of agriculture.[34] He reportedly turned down the opportunity because of his opposition to the Republican administration.

Through his voluminous correspondence and networking, Prosper's innovation was his role as an influencer: "He came to know, often intimately, most of the leading horticulturists of his day and was in a position to exchange with them new varieties of trees, plants, and shrubs."[35]

He promoted apple varieties that formed the foundation of commercial apple culture in the South, including Yates and Shockley. Using his French nursery contacts, he imported a Chinese privet shrub used for hedging, *Ligustrum amurense*, which today blankets the South in white blossoms and its distinctive scent. Prosper rode the wave of crop diversification after the Civil War, selling peach and apple trees to planters interested in fruit growing. He introduced several new peach varieties and is recognized as the father of southern peach culture. William Thomas Okie's book *The Georgia Peach: Culture, Agriculture, and Environment in the American South* explores the Berckmanses' central role in the story of this southern tree fruit.

When Barry revised *The Fruit Garden* in 1889, his list of apples from the South grew from four to twenty, including Stevenson's Winter from Mississippi, Carter's Blue from Alabama, and Georgia's Shockley apple.

Just before Prosper Berckmans's death in 1910 at age eighty, the pomologist for the US Department of Agriculture described his name as "a household word to fruit growers. . . . He had done more for American horticulture than almost any other man."[36]

———————

Fruitland faltered at the generational transfer. Prosper was sixty-seven when his wife died. At Prosper's death, ownership of Fruitland fell to his second wife and stepson. Ten years later, the influential nursery closed and the brand name, Fruitland, was sold.[37] While the three Berckmans sons continued horticultural work on national and regional projects, Fruitland Nurseries languished for the first few decades of the twentieth century.

Then Fruitland had an unlikely rebirth.

In 1932 golf champion Bobby Jones and a group of investors purchased Fruitland and created the Augusta National golf course, one of the most exclusive and recognizable golf courses in the world. Though Prosper would never see it, the Berckmanses made one final mark on the southern landscape. Prosper's son Louis Alphonse suggested that each hole of the Augusta National golf course focus on a single southern landscape plant.[38]

Today, members of this exclusive club drive down the avenue of magnolias leading to Prosper's former home, now the much-modified Augusta National clubhouse. Each spring, manicured lawns and immaculate plantings of azaleas, camellias, and dogwoods dominate television coverage of the Master's Tournament, a landscape bare of fruit.

Two influential nurseries bookend the South's golden age of apples— Pomaria in South Carolina and Fruitland in Georgia. Both served as organized experiment stations for discovering fruit acclimated to the South. Both changed the southern landscape with ornamentals and apples. Both existed on land stolen from Native people. Both had links to slavery and were built, in part, with enslaved labor. Eminent men who wrote extensively about farming and influenced the national agricultural dialogue led both nurseries. Both nurseries promoted agricultural reform.

But these two southern nurseries grew from distinct motivations and exhibited vastly different styles.

Today, South Carolina and Georgia seem unlikely spots for an apple renaissance. Commercial apple growing occupies a small corner of Georgia's agricultural map, concentrated in the northern counties. South Carolina's commercial apple footprint is even smaller. But valuable apples once flourished across both states, selected by white and Black southerners and by Indigenous people, apples chosen and imprinted with longing and histories.

I picture William Summer sitting in his Pomaria study, his cane propped against his small upright desk, writing letters to apple-growing colleagues in Edisto or Columbia, exchanging enthusiasms alongside scion wood. I see Prosper Berckmans, his diminutive orchard notebook tucked in a pocket, stalking down orchard rows outside Augusta, scribbling notes and sketching the silhouettes of ripe apples.

As different as these men were, they both celebrated southern apples. Thanks to Pomaria and Fruitland, twenty-first-century apple growers have an opportunity to taste and explore uses for Disharoon, Carolina Red June, Equinetelee, Cullasaga, Junaluskee, and many more.

NAMED

From the top of Lover's Leap, Rock Castle Gorge spread in front of me like a snow globe scene. Brilliant snow and ice coated limbs and trunks of every tree. Evergreens bent low, and ice crystals swirled around my car. This stretch of Highway 58 begins in Stuart, Virginia, climbs the flanks of the Blue Ridge Plateau, and crests just before Meadows of Dan. In my first few years making cider at Foggy Ridge, I made the trip from the Greensboro, North Carolina, airport back to the farm countless times. On each drive I marked my transition from corporate work to farmwork by pulling into one of the several overlooks and inhaling the view.

That February day in 2008, all of Patrick County sparkled in dazzling morning sun. My flight from New York had been late, and I had missed news of the ice storm that damaged power lines and closed schools across the region. As I wound along the ridge, snow swirled and dashed against my windshield. I was so enthralled by the winter scene all around me that I didn't think to worry about a power outage at the cider house or downed trees in the orchard.

I was exhausted, ground down by travel for my wage-earning job, a job where I exercised skills and saw results but one that felt increasingly at odds with growing apples. Rather than being invigorated, as I was by farmwork, I felt leaden and old, worn out by the pull between two very different worlds.

As I inched my way to the cider house past fields coated in sugary frost, I tried to focus on my islands of accomplishment over the last few years: my original orchard produced excellent fruit; the new orchards were healthy and growing. I was making cider and actually selling it, cider that made me proud. And I was learning more each day about how to hone my craft. But every problem seemed like a steep summit. Every stumble set me back hours and even days. A broken chiller and only one repair person within fifty miles. Clogged filters. A stubborn ferment that in spite of coddling didn't move for days. My head knew that obstacles always littered the path to anything new, yet my heart felt defeated by roadblock after roadblock.

When I reached the farm, the cider house had power and my ferments were healthy. In spite of the weather, the chiller repairman was on his way. I sat down at my desk, pulled up a production spreadsheet, and began planning my way out of angst.

I thought about the pruning I did the previous month, my focus on making the best cuts to shape and train my trees to produce cider fruit for decades. One day I was doing battle with a mature Parmar tree in the old orchard, four feet off the ground and pruning saw in hand, when I came face-to-face with a tiny hummingbird nest hidden in a tangle of apple branches. I was so focused on my pruning that without an up-close confrontation I would have missed this little marvel. I thought, "Why am I so overwhelmed? What am I missing in my apple equation?"

As I pored over production plans and orchard yields and looked hard at sales in our new markets, I was certain this work satisfied me. Planting trees, growing fruit, and making cider . . . all these concrete steps added energy to my life. I thought, "I need to spend more time noticing the palpable details of this satisfying work, details that stare me in the face every day, and stop obsessing over the things I can't control."

I also learned that I needed more fruit. With even a modest sales forecast, it was clear we were going to run out of bottled cider in the next year. I expected my two new orchards to yield fruit in the next couple of years. But to make enough cider to create a profitable business, I needed more cider fruit, and I needed help making cider.

I was beginning to understand that creating something new takes a web of connections and support. Like Tommy Stanley coming to fix my chiller on an icy February day. Or the local winemakers who helped me taste cider in blending trials. Most of the apple growers around me grew dessert apples not suited for cider, like Gala, Red Delicious, or Fuji. But maybe I could find a grower with a few Magnum Bonum trees or a block of Old Virginia Winesaps. Perhaps I could find a talented winemaker with time on his or her hands for a part-time cidermaking job.

I needed to expand my web. I had work to do, but by nightfall I had a plan.

Clouds raced across the full moon as I drove the half-mile from the cider house to our house. I put the truck in four-wheel drive and turned up the steep pasture to the new north orchard. The wind howled from the northwest, but after a long week in New York and a day inside the cider house, I couldn't resist feeling the orchard under my feet. Moonlight cast long shadows beside every tree. To the west, swaying trees set off the motion detection lights around the low-slung cider house and formed a gentle brow over the silver rows of Blacktwigs and Hewe's Crabs. Bundled in down and Carhartt, I crunched through the crusty snow. The burden I had carried up Lover's Leap melted away in the cold, clear air.

So far, every step in this venture had both heartened and humbled me. I was ready to walk a little faster.

————————

In October 1895, Deborah Griscom Passmore sat in her Washington, DC, artist studio, watercolor brush in hand, and captured the Pilot apple in an elegant botanical portrait. She painted a hefty apple with dull red skin, subtly striped with orange. The stem sits in a deep cavity. With Passmore's sensitive shading, the dense yellow flesh appears juicy and crisp. This Virginia apple, complete with a dusting of sooty blotch fungal disease, was one of 7,584 watercolor paintings, lithographs, and line drawings of fruit produced between 1894 and 1916 as part of the US Department of Agriculture Pomological Watercolor Collection.

President Abraham Lincoln established the USDA in 1862 as "the People's Department," with the goal of educating farmers and advancing agriculture.[1] Yet from its beginning, this government agency institutionalized discrimination against African Americans, Native Americans, and women, a legacy that continued through the Civil Rights era.[2]

The department added the Division of Pomology in 1886 to document old and newly introduced fruit varieties, act as the authority on fruit nomenclature, and provide guidance to American farmers—in practice, this meant white farmers—on varieties and growing techniques. Over twenty-one artists depicted plants from every state, including many fruits submitted from the South. The USDA used these botanically accurate paintings to create lithographs that illustrated bulletins and agricultural yearbooks. The pomological artists painted 3,807 apples, more than any other fruit.

This government-sponsored fine art educated an American audience about the country's fruit.

It is no surprise that J. W. Porter from Charlottesville, Virginia, provided the Pilot apple that ended up on Deborah Passmore's drawing table. This long-keeping apple originated around 1830 on a farm at the base of Pilot Mountain in Nelson County, Virginia. In *Old Southern Apples*, Lee Calhoun reports that Virginia growers harvested Pilot apples in October and stored them under trees, covered in straw or cornstalks. In spring, they unveiled the still-firm, deeply aromatic apples and packed them in barrels for sale.[3]

Pilot was big, beautiful, delicious, and useful, qualities that made this fruit ubiquitous in the southern Piedmont. But a written description alone did not adequately depict this valuable apple, or any other fruit. Mr. Porter must have been proud of his Virginia-grown Pilot apple to ship a few to the nine-year-old pomology department and have his favorite apple immortalized in a painting.

By the time the Division of Pomology artists began documenting American fruit, Black, white, and Indigenous southerners had been grafting and naming apple varieties suited to their climate and needs for over 150 years. By the nineteenth century, apple nomenclature was a jumble of inconsistent spellings and countless synonyms.

The popular Nickajack apple likely originated near Nickajack Creek in Macon County, North Carolina. Southern nurseries listed this apple by over forty names. Some synonyms described a place, like Dahlonega. Others, like Red Warrior, conferred white nomenclature on an apple grown by Cherokee orchardists.

Pomaria Nurseries promoted the Hoover apple in its 1856 catalog. Over the next few decades, this showy, dark-red apple from Edisto, South Carolina, acquired an impressive list of varied names: Black Coal, Black Hoover, Baltimore Red, Thunderbolt, Watauga, and Welcome.[4]

Even the celebrated cider apple Hewe's Crab carried varied monikers: "Hughes Crab" in a 1741 James City County advertisement, "Red Hughes" in Monticello farm journals, and "Hewe's Virginia Crab" in the 1861 Fruitland Nurseries catalog.

Southern apples documented the human urge to claim and name a special possession. Lee Calhoun often talked about the "pride of ownership" he heard when southerners talked about a family apple or a wild apple with some special quality they had replicated by grafting. A Cook's Red apple that ripened a little later or stored a little longer easily became known as Cook's Red Winter. An apple grown on John Lowry's farm carried the name "Lowry" and passed from family ownership to neighbors and then on to nurseries. Southern apples were the endowment effect in action, with southerners valuing an apple more just because they owned it.

Deborah Passmore's sensitive painting of Virginia's Pilot apple came as southern agriculture was shifting from small diversified farms that served local markets to farms managed as regional businesses. Each apple that Passmore and other artists painted expressed the desire to claim deep ties to a valued variety.

At the same time that Passmore was documenting American apples, improved transportation and the drive for specialized farming prompted apple growers in the South to seek scientific information on how to profitably grow fruit. Nurseries, anxious to offer the "latest and best," protected varieties they viewed as unique. In previous decades, farmers exchanged information—and apples—through horticultural societies, journals, and agricultural fairs. The USDA, land grant colleges, and the Division of Pomology encouraged small-scale farmers and growers to embrace new business models and what were seen as progressive farming practices. Land grant colleges were racially segregated until 1890, when the second Morrill Act required states to demonstrate racial equality in admissions or establish separate institutions for African Americans.

The 1901 USDA yearbook articulated the shift from small orchards with 50 to 100 trees and apples "grown more for family use than commercial purposes" to "orchards of hundreds and even thousands of acres each, and capital in large amounts being invested annually, not only for home markets but for extensive export to foreign countries in fresh and cured forms."[5] This shift to larger, more mechanized forms of fruit growing disadvantaged farmers with less access to capital and excluded those denied access to the financial resources needed for modern orchards.

Over twenty-two years, USDA artists painted scores of apples from southern states. Painters documented Poorhouse, Coffman, Tull, Wallace Howard, and Indian apples from Georgia. They depicted Shipper from Kentucky and Yellow Forest from Louisiana. Ten apples came from North Carolina, including Lewis Green, Trull, Rimmer, Pinnacle, and Florence. Clemson, South Carolina, sent Kinnard, also called Kinnaird's Choice. Half a dozen came from Tennessee, including Waverly, Margaret, and Archibald.

USDA artists painted six apples from James Dickie's orchard in Nelson County, Virginia—Pilot, Royal Limbertwig, Dickie's Favorite, Father Abraham, Peck Pleasant, and Pride of Du Pres. According to Dickie's grandson John Bruguiere, the Pride of Du Pres probably was a hyperlocal apple called Pride of Du Priest, named for Priest Mountain that rises over their eight-generation farm.

Today that banquet is much smaller. The Trull apple that originated in Canton, North Carolina, is extinct. Coffman was once planted from its origin in Lauderdale County, Tennessee, to Mississippi, but

Six apples from the Dickie Orchard in Massie's Mill, Nelson County, VA (*from left to right*):
Pride of Du Pres by Berthan Heiges; Pilot by Deborah G. Passmore; Royal Limbertwig
by Deborah G. Passmore; Dickie's Favorite by Berthan Heiges, 1901; Father Abraham by
Berthan Heiges, 1899; and Peck Pleasant by Amanda A. Newton, 1906.
US Department of Agriculture Pomological Watercolor Collection, Rare and Special Collections,
National Agricultural Library, Beltsville, MD.

this adaptable apple no longer exists. Even the Indian apple, known
more widely as McAfee and documented by W. H. Ragan, author of the
USDA's seminal work *Nomenclature of the Apple*, is lost.

The USDA documented apple bounty in America while promoting
agricultural practices that contributed to the decline in the number of
apple varieties in the South. By 1930, 50 percent of the apples that had
existed in 1880 were extinct.[6] The number of orchards and varieties decreased, but orchard acreage grew as the average farm size increased.
Railroads, improved roads, and new technologies such as canning, refrigeration, and cold storage swiftly changed orcharding in the South.
Policies favored larger orchards populated with fewer varieties.

The USDA Pomological Watercolor Collection captured apple beauty,
but the paintings could not save apples from modernity.

———

When I scroll through the marvelous Pomological Watercolor Collection
on the USDA's website, Deborah Passmore's paintings reveal a sense of

drama and a deep sensitivity to each subject. It's easy to spot her work, and not just because she painted more than any of the other early artists. In her painting of *Amelanchier canadensis*, the serviceberry tree, the pale green leaves and glossy dark fruit seem to wave in a breeze, like the serviceberry tree outside my kitchen window in late May. She painted watermelons, avocados, grapes, and pears. Her lemons make my mouth pucker. Passmore's almost 800 apple paintings inspire me to plant more trees.

The youngest of five in a Pennsylvania Quaker family, Passmore's father was a farmer. Her mother was an educator and a minister in the orthodox Quaker church. After studying art at the School of Design for Women and the Academy of Fine Arts in Philadelphia, Passmore taught art in Philadelphia and Washington, DC. She joined the USDA as an illustrator in 1892 and was soon promoted to chief of the staff artists. Passmore painted for the USDA and in her own studio until her death in 1911.

Her apple portraits show her obsession with capturing plant detail. Passmore used a high-power microscope and spent hours observing specimens. Her close friend and colleague at the USDA Carrie Harrison wrote in an informal biography that Passmore began painting as a small child and attempted to draw and paint flowers with their own juices, which she obtained by chewing the plants.[7] Painting absorbed her. Harrison wrote, "She would sit in a greenhouse on an overturned box, her feet in the wet, and paint and neither see nor hear what transpired around her."[8] Passmore painted apples with a farmer's close and obsessive observation of the natural world.

Her work illustrates the range of apples that crowded the late nineteenth-century southern table. From Arkansas Black with a deep plum-colored skin, to Ardwell, a brown, fully russeted apple sent from Grant County, West Virginia, Passmore's paintings depict a diverse harvest. She painted southern apples with the talent of a trained artist and the eye of a plant lover.

The watercolor project documented thousands of apple varieties while the USDA scientists advised growers to limit their apple palette. Writing in the 1901 USDA yearbook, pomologist G. B. Brackett stated, "The main point in the selection of a variety should be the determination of its valuable qualities as an article of commerce." The author concluded, "One of the most common mistakes made by the commercial apple orchardists is planting too many varieties."[9]

In 1908, a USDA field agent reported that the McAfee apple grew well, fruited in the southern Piedmont and mountains, and was a more reliable producer than other apples for the mountain South. But he added that its "dull red color limited the usefulness of the McAfee as a market fruit."[10]

In 1910, the year before she died, Deborah Passmore painted twenty-two apples. The Abram apple came to her from Tobaccoville in Forsyth County, North Carolina, not far from the Foggy Ridge Cider orchards. Her watercolor shows an oval red-skinned apple with a subtle orange background. By the time she painted Abram, southerners had enjoyed this apple's brilliant white flesh for over 160 years. Her version of Shockley, an apple I grow today, always catches my eye. A yellow blush lights up the margins of this round red apple. Passmore included a brownish bruise on one shoulder and a few dots of flyspeck, a fungal disease common in late-season fruit that affects only appearance. The stem leans left at a jaunty angle. Lee Calhoun writes that Shockley was one of the southern apples "that could be counted on, year after year, to provide southern farm families with apples for eating, cooking, drying and cider."[11]

That same year Passmore also painted Delicious, an apple submitted by the Stark Brothers Nurseries and Orchards Company. She depicted a cone-shaped red apple knobbed at the base with burgundy stripes. This Iowa apple spawned Red Delicious, and we all know that story. Within a few decades after Passmore painted its parent, Red Delicious became the most widely planted apple in America, eclipsing older and, to my

palate, more interesting and valuable apples and reshaping consumers'
tastes.

Passmore and her colleagues documented the big banquet that was
once southern fruit. The USDA artists painted a cornucopia of fruit at
the same time that USDA practices encouraged fruit growers to grow
fewer varieties. Today some of those southern apples exist only in sensitive watercolors, stored in the USDA archives, reflecting uses and memories long gone.

Lost

FORFEITED

Decades-old orchards shelter on the south-facing slope of Bent Mountain, 2,000 feet above Roanoke, Virginia. Drive twenty miles up Bent Mountain in fall and you'll find roadside stands overflowing with what many call the best apples in the state.

Though most Bent Mountain orchards have closed, customers still visit the few remaining farm stands to nab hard-to-find varieties like Jonathan, Winesap, and Grimes Golden. Stayman, a popular dessert apple long grown in the South, loiters in bins alongside modern apples like Gala, Fuji, and Golden Delicious. But to find a Bent Mountain Albemarle Pippin apple, you need connections.

Grown in the South since the 1800s, this esteemed apple was notoriously picky about its specific home. For over 150 years, the south-facing slopes of Bent Mountain have produced the South's finest Pippin apples.

I lusted for Bent Mountain fruit.

Grown well in the right terroir, Albemarle Pippins explode with flavor. While they are delicious off the tree, after a few months in storage the flavors concentrate into a complex stew of tropical fruit, sugary citrus, and tart apple. The juice ferments into cider with a near-perfect balance of tangy and sweet. My own Albemarle Pippins had already created some of Foggy Ridge's best cider. I was determined to get more of this fruit for our cider blends.

On a warm day in early June 2006, I drove forty miles north from Foggy Ridge to call on Ed Witt and his wife, Lorraine. Ed was a spry, compact man with the energy of someone much younger than his eighty-three years. He showed me his ancient apple grader, a long conveyor that divided apples by size. We hiked through his Pippin trees, all with healthy fruit set. Ed was the only Bent Mountain orchardist still growing Pippins commercially, and his views on apple growing showed all the conservatism common to multigenerational tree fruit growers. He farmed his orchard much as he had decades earlier when he first planted southern apples. And he was skeptical about change.

"Lorraine, when was our daughter born?" This was how Ed remembered that he planted his giant Magnum Bonum apple tree over fifty years ago, a tree with a trunk I could barely circle with my arms. Apples are longtime plants, and the Limbertwigs, Grimes Goldens, and Old Fashioned Winesaps in Ed's orchard cradled his life. Each tree held a story, and that day I heard most of them.

Orcharding in the twenty-first century carried challenges new to Ed, and I heard about those too. Ed told me he sold his first quality fruit to customers who drove out to his orchard each fall. He was proud to say, "I've been selling to the same people for over forty years." But he also complained about the low prices that grocery chains paid for his fruit and the rising costs of orchard supplies. He seemed mystified that harvest workers didn't want to work for the same wages they earned a half-dozen years earlier. "People just don't want to work fruit anymore," he said. "I'm barely breaking even."

I explained that making high-quality fermented cider enabled me to pay above-market prices for well-grown, flavorful fruit. Ed was skeptical about my cider venture and hesitant to sell apples to a stranger. I talked to him about expanding his retail business and investigating the H-2A guest worker program. I asked him if he would be willing to graft some of his Red Delicious trees over to cider varieties, apples which would bring a tenfold greater price. But Ed just shook his head.

Since hatching my plan for Foggy Ridge Cider in the mid-1990s I had lobbied Virginia orchardists to grow cider apples, tannic and highly flavored fruit that could command a much higher price than blocks of bland Red Delicious. I was familiar with Ed's resistance to change. After almost ten years of cajoling across the entire state, I had yet to convince a single grower to plant cider apples. And while I had purchased a few bins of Grimes Golden and Winesap from nearby orchards, no grower had yet agreed to contract with me for a large apple purchase.

At the end of my tour of the Witt Orchard, I took a deep breath and asked, "Ed, will you sell Pippin apples to me this fall? I'll pay you when I pick up the fruit, just like your retail customers."

Late that June day I drove back to the farm through slanting light, with gleaming fescue pastures lining the road. I passed abandoned Bent Mountain apple barns stenciled with family names, names of families that hadn't sold apples in decades. Withered apple trees stood in the front yards of a few brick ranch houses, remnants of past Pippin orchards.

I was thrilled to have seen the Witts' old trees. I felt honored to hear the stories behind the fruit, straight from the man who had planted his apples decades ago. But I was also sad. Sad that the way forward for fruit growing was so fraught. Sad that the rootedness of apple growing, the long game of growing trees, seemed to also root many farmers in the past.

Ed Witt's perseverance had kept his Pippin trees in the ground, but his adherence to the past limited his orchard's future.

As I got closer to home I began to think that perhaps I shared some of this orchardist's stubborn streak. Foggy Ridge was growing fast, both the orchard and the cidery, and I was still running the business much as I had in our first few years. I had not changed the way I was working. I was still doing a good portion of every job on the farm. Maybe there was a better way . . . I just wasn't certain what that change looked like.

As I drove down Highway 221 through Copper Hill and the little town of Floyd, I realized I had left Witt Orchard with a couple of certainties in the face of change. That June day Ed Witt put two shining promises in my pocket: a promise from a man I was certain would keep his word, and the promise of well-grown southern fruit for my tanks next fall.

Now, all I needed to do was figure how to navigate big changes for my little cidery.

———————

Apples captured Joyce LaRue Neighbors in midlife, same as me. In 1978, at age fifty-one, she taught herself to graft using a mail-order kit, planted her first orchard in Clay County, Alabama, and changed her life's trajectory.

Memories of her grandfather's Yates, Black Ben Davis, and Stayman trees and her grandmother's fried apple pies inspired Neighbors to chase the flavors and histories of old southern apples. The May apple was her first graft, an old Alabama variety from her father's orchard. When Neighbors retired a few years later from Life Insurance of Alabama, she opened a nursery in her hometown of Gadsden, Alabama, a sanctuary filled with southern fruit.

For Joyce Neighbors, each apple occupied a unique place on the kitchen counter—a flavor, a color, a season. And each had a use. Like Lee Calhoun and scores of southern apple sleuths, Joyce relished the

Summer King apple from Caroline, MD, by Ellen Isham Schutt. US Department of Agriculture Pomological Watercolor Collection, Rare and Special Collections, National Agricultural Library, Beltsville, MD.

hunt for flavorful and useful fruit. She wrote that her first discovery was Summer King, thought at the time to be extinct.[1] This apple likely originated in North Carolina before it migrated to Kentucky, where Summer King was grown commercially in the 1850s.[2] The Neighbors Nursery catalog focused on this apple's Alabama lineage and Joyce's connection to the fruit. Neighbors wrote that a friend from Anniston peddled apple trees for an uncle who owned Collinsville Nursery in Collinsville, Alabama. The friend pointed Joyce to a tree labeled "August Apple." He said tree peddlers often simplified apple names by referring to apples by the month they ripened. The August Apple turned out to be Summer King.

Hiding in a tree peddler's sales book under a faded lithograph of "August Apple No. 4" was a cherished apple that for most southern orchardists was only a memory.

Neighbors described Summer King's smooth greenish-yellow skin, marked with broken crimson stripes. Unlike other nursery lists, her catalog often lingered on flavor and offered details for cooking. She reported that this tender, succulent apple made a good pie and added that in the 1930s and 1940s her grandmother shared fried apple pies with hungry people who stopped by her house for a gift of food.[3] I think it is fitting that her first apple discovery was a pie apple. A fierce desire to preserve varieties full of flavor and usefulness drove Neighbors's apple quest until her death in 2017 at age ninety.

———————

Today we eat over half of our apples as a handheld sweet snack, raw and fresh.[4] But for hundreds of years southerners valued a range of apple flavors and found a multitude of uses for this fruit.

Drying intensifies flavor and sweetness in any fruit. For apples, moisture content drops from 90 percent to around 15 percent, preserving sugar and flavor far beyond a fresh apple's life. Southern nursery catalogs always included notes about the best varieties for drying. The 1871 Albemarle Apple Nursery catalog recommended Annette, Fall Cheese, and Pilot for cooking and drying.[5] North Carolinians preferred Hunge. Keener Seedling was popular in Tennessee as a dried apple.

In the Virginia Blue Ridge Mountain community of Rock Castle, farmers dried apples on racks in apple houses heated by a flue, much like a tobacco drying barn. Sometimes they dried apples on a sheet of iron placed over a low-burning fire in a rock flue or strung them behind the woodstove. Apples like Grimes Golden, with a tart-sweet flavor that didn't turn dark during the drying process, earned a higher price.[6]

Drying apples was an art form celebrated by agricultural fairs. Competitions across the South awarded medals and cups for superior dried apples, like the plate that Miss S. Thompson from Walton County, in central Georgia, received in 1859 for Best Bushel of Dried Apples.[7]

Though drying apples in the warm, humid South was a common way to preserve this fruit, southerners found far more culinary uses for their flavorful apples.

Pomaria's 1862 catalog referred to the southern seedling apples Early Harvest, Green Horse, and Buckingham as superior for baking and pies. Richmond Nursery's 1869 *Descriptive Catalogue of Fruit Trees, Vines & Plants, Cultivated and For Sale by Franklin Davis & Co., Richmond, Virginia* suggested Early Joe, Summer Queen, and Smokehouse for "culinary purposes," all apples that originated outside the South but were widely grown in the region.[8]

Joyce Neighbors's catalog tied apples firmly to the kitchen. Her list included Parks Pippin for jelly, cider, and apple butter. She noted several apples for cooking—Tarbutton, Spice, and Collins June from Georgia and Pauley from Mississippi. She suggested Benham, a Tennessee summer apple, for applesauce and pies. The Limbertwigs received high praise for cider and culinary uses, especially Caney Fork Limbertwig and the aromatic Brushy Mountain Limbertwig. For cider she mentioned Albemarle Pippin, Calvin from Virginia, and Winter Jon, an apple I especially like for fermented cider.

Before refrigeration and commercial canning, seasonal eating was a necessity in the South. Almost as frequently as "prolific bearer," southern nursery catalogs noted when apples could—and should—be consumed. Joyce Neighbors suggested eating Hackworth, a Georgia apple, in midsummer: "After eating the May Apple, we always looked forward

▶ (*Overleaf*)

(*Left*) Photograph of Winesap in bloom by Tony Greatorex.

(*Top right*) Drying apples on a roof in Nicholson Hollow, Shenandoah National Park, VA, 1935. Photograph by Arthur Rothstein, LC-USF33-002189-M2.

(*Bottom right*) Drying apples outside mountain home near Jackson, KY, 1940. Photograph by Marion Post Wolcott, LC-USF34-055582-D, FSA/OWI Collection, Prints and Photographs Division, Library of Congress, Washington, DC.

to eating the Hackworth when it ripened in July."[9] Neighbors's mother asked her to graft a Black Ben Davis because she wanted to recreate the memory of walking home from school past a Black Ben Davis tree and picking an apple in September.[10]

South Carolina's Pomaria Nurseries championed southern apples with stellar keeping qualities: Epting's Red Winter, Buncombe, Bradford's Best, and Pomaria Greening—all "will keep until March."[11]

In the mountain South, apples in many forms remained a significant part of farm family diets well into the twentieth century, as well as a cash crop in both fruit and liquid form. Contrary to common views of the region, Appalachia was far from a subsistence farming economy. Appalachian scholar Wilma Dunaway noted that nine-tenths of farm owners in this region grew agricultural surplus, including apples and cider.[12] In the Rock Castle community, apples were the main cash crop until the 1920s. Farmers sold dried apples and exchanged them for credit at Edwards Store at the northern, higher end of the five-mile-long Rock Castle Road, or at DeHart Store at the southern end. They preserved apples in jams and jellies and stored long-keeping apples with pungent flavor in root cellars dug into the side of steep hills.

But in Rock Castle, it was the "still-house apples" destined for DeHart Distillery's potent apple brandy that garnered the highest praise.

Early southerners fermented and distilled fruit to prevent spoilage and to provide a safe, inexpensive beverage. On an eighteenth-century Tidewater Virginia small farm, a family of six would typically drink 90 gallons of cider and 21 gallons of distilled liquor each year. Large plantations with an enslaved population required 450 gallons of cider and 105 gallons of liquor.[13]

By the late eighteenth century, productive southern cider and brandy apples like Hewe's Crab and Parmar, along with improved fermenting and distilling equipment, brought cider and brandy making into most Virginia small farms and plantations.

Southern wills and estates often included brandy, both apple and peach. Robert Tate's Newcastle, Virginia, estate in 1777 offered "All his Household and Kitchen furniture, Stock of Cattle, Hogs and Sheep, fine Peach and Apple Brandy" for sale.[14] In eastern Virginia, William Rives offered "the well accustomed ordinary where I now live, in Suffex county, . . . containing about two hundred acres of land . . . also a quantity of very good APPLE BRANDY."[15]

In a region with few roads, transporting apples in the form of brandy was practical and profitable. Joseph Earl Dabney writes in *Mountain*

Spirits, "By the mid-1700s, columns of steel blue smoke poured from hundreds of stills over the six-hundred-mile backcountry along the Appalachian Mountain chain."[16] Corn whiskey was most common, but early apple crops that would not store well over winter headed to the still.

Nurseryman Jim Lawson remembers north Georgia brandy makers using whatever apple variety they could get their hands on, though they favored Limbertwig. His brandy-making neighbor asserted, "Limbertwig is the best apple to put in a barrel."[17] Nursery catalogs praised several southern apples for brandy—Georgia's Yates apple often carried the description "good for cider and brandy." Gilpin, called Carthouse in the South, was also popular for cider and brandy, as was Gregory, a Virginia apple now extinct. In 1872, *The Southern Apple and Peach Culturist* recommended Horse and Gregory as cider and brandy apples for Virginia's Isle of Wight County, a coastal region with an average elevation of sixty-two feet.[18]

Well into the twentieth century, orchards full of brandy apples lingered throughout the South, especially in the Appalachians.

Today most people know Rock Castle Gorge as a hiking trail on the Blue Ridge Parkway in southwest Virginia's Patrick County. I hike this strenuous eleven-mile route in late fall when I can enjoy views over the Woolwine community's apple orchards and again in early spring to count trillium species that flourish along the many creeks. The trail begins at 3,572 feet on a high ridgeline and winds 1,700 feet through rocky switchbacks into a steep, shaded valley. Rock Castle Creek and a few smaller tributaries spill into the bottom of the gorge. For a decade I hiked this trail unaware that a few falling-down stone chimneys and one white-frame farmhouse represented a thriving mountain community that once made a living largely on trees.

In the late nineteenth and early twentieth centuries, apples blanketed Patrick County, from fertile mountain coves to the slopes of the Blue Ridge Plateau, many grown in thermal belts that protected fruit from late frosts. By 1901 the county had 375,000 apple trees and several large orchards. Orchards like E. C. Tudor's on Bull Mountain, the largest orchard in southern Virginia, grew apples familiar to southern orchardists, including Buckingham, Horse, Parmar, Ben Davis, and Vine, a late-season apple that originated in Patrick County.[19] Patrick Orchard contained 400 acres of apples with "one cove of especially favorable land set in Pippins."[20]

Rock Castle growers hauled apples down Rock Castle Road, today a portion of a hiking trail. Appalachian families like those in the Rock Castle community lived on chestnut trees and apples.

In 1889, Fleming DeHart founded DeHart Distillery in Patrick County to produce corn and rye whiskey and apple brandy. The Danville and Western Railroad arrived in the county seat of Stuart in 1884, the year the town was incorporated. The rail line transported crossties, tanbark, lumber, chickens, eggs, and apples, both fresh and dried.[21] The county's Black and white residents had access to a more robust town than today's twenty-first century Stuart, with multiple stores, taverns, tobacco factories, shops, and a newspaper office.[22] DeHart Distillery shipped Patrick County rye whiskey, corn whiskey, and brandy across the country.

DeHart produced 100-proof brandy from Rock Castle and other Patrick County apples that sold for $2.10 per gallon in gallon-sized jugs and $2.00 per gallon in four-and-a-half gallon kegs.[23]

Rock Castle residents were proud of their "still-house" apples. These varieties typically ripened in summer and, like most summer apples, did not store well. Six legal distilleries operated in Rock Castle, but most apples headed to DeHart's.[24] Mack Conner's twenty-five- or thirty-acre orchard, located at the halfway point on Rock Castle Creek on a southeast-facing slope, was one of the largest orchards in the Rock Castle community.[25] His prosperous orchard helped build a two-story frame house that still stands today alongside a hiking trail, surrounded by poplars and oaks, with not one cultivated apple tree in sight.

In 1914 Virginia held a vote on state Prohibition. Patrick County residents voted 471 for Prohibition and 1,055 against, but the statewide vote passed with 60 percent in favor.[26] When Prohibition went into effect in Virginia in 1916, DeHart Distillery closed. DeHart had paid well for old "still-house" fruit, and Prohibition dealt a blow to Rock Castle's economy and to decades-old orchards. While the production of alcoholic beverages in Patrick County likely increased after Prohibition, illegal stills produced cheaper corn whiskey rather than apple brandy.

In March 1932, a strong winter storm pounded southwestern Virginia. Ice and sleet fell for two days in near-zero temperatures, followed by a heavy snow that brought down telephone and electric lines, closed roads, and destroyed orchards. The storm severely damaged Mack Conner's Rock Castle orchard. His descendants believe the storm and the loss of his trees led to his death—Mack contracted pneumonia during the storm and died two days later.[27] The same year, Mack's son, Wyatt Conner, left his family home in Rock Castle to work in a textile mill near Burlington, North Carolina.

Prohibition closed DeHart Distillery and hastened the loss of southern apples grown in communities like Rock Castle.

Nursery catalogs from the early twentieth century document the forfeiture of southern apples. The 1861 Fruitland catalog praised the Horse apple for drying, Chestatee for cooking, and Shockley as "the best keeping apple we possess."[28] This issue listed 11 summer apples, 10 fall apples, 20 winter apples, 3 apples specifically for cider, and an additional 160 apple varieties. By 1937, Fruitland listed only 7 summer, 3 fall, and 8 winter apples, a 90 percent decline. Cider apples had disappeared from the list, along with descriptions about cooking or drying. The newly popular Delicious apple received the most press: "A popular Western apple, but equally good in any other section. . . . A splendid market Apple, as keeping and shipping qualities are of first rank." The catalog remembered Shockley—"ripens in August and will keep until the following summer"—but southern apples and their many uses began to disappear.[29]

In her ninety-year life, Joyce Neighbors witnessed the decline of southern apples with varied flavors and scores of uses. She wrote about the chicken houses and small industrial plants that replaced the family farms that grew cotton, fruit, and vegetables in her Alabama county. She praised the modernized county hospital but lamented the loss of apples.

In her lifetime, southerners lost most cider varieties. The best of the brandy apples disappeared. When farm families moved to cities, they stopped drying apples and making apple butter. In the lifetime of a long-lived apple tree, the southern apple basket shrank to a few varieties, almost all chosen for fresh eating.

I believe this loss diminishes our world. Eating only fresh apples, consuming the same varieties all year—this, I believe, narrows our experience. We are not just eating from a shallow bowl; we are missing the opportunity to connect with our past through this fruit.

The cornucopia of southern apples inspired Joyce Neighbors to devote half her life to old southern apples. She hoped that "others will consider doing the same thing."[30]

I wish more southerners today would act on her desire.

DISPLACED

Foggy Ridge Cider sits on a rare stretch of flat road near the intersection of three southwest Virginia counties rich with family names endemic to the region. Nearby mailboxes announce "Quesenberry" and "Goad." Further on are "Mabry" and "Sutphin." My 1,200-square-foot cider house perches on the edge of the farm that will forever be known as the "old Spence place." The low-slung metal and concrete building holds a decade of apple dreams wrapped in double-jacketed stainless steel fermenters.

The promise of Ed Witt's Bent Mountain Albemarle Pippins gave me hope that I could shape my dreams into reality. But by 2007, I knew I needed talents I didn't yet possess. I wanted a cidermaking partner who knew more than I did about fermentation and was expert at production planning. Someone who could not only help me solve problems but anticipate them.

The perfect package of skills and experience arrived with Jocelyn Kuzelka. Jocelyn studied biochemistry as an undergraduate at Virginia Tech and then earned master's degrees in viticulture and enology. She worked for large wineries in New Zealand and, recently, for a small winery nearby in Floyd County. We had met at tasting events where her discerning palate and articulate flavor descriptions impressed me. She knew how to grow fruit and was an expert winemaker. Our casual connections convinced me that learning motivated Jocelyn every bit as much as it did me. Friends introduced us, and our informal consulting arrangement grew into a creative partnership.

Jocelyn took charge, in a good way. She tightened our fermentation protocols and organized production planning. She suggested I purchase a few new pieces of equipment, but she also understood the modest scale of what we were attempting at Foggy Ridge.

And Jocelyn was strong. This five-foot-two-inch powerhouse could hoist bales of rice hulls and shovel pomace for hours. She immediately gained the respect of the entire Marshall family by her ability to repair equipment and navigate our steep roads with a tractor load of heavy cider. No drama queen, Jocelyn, when greeted with the scores of problems that arose each day, would reliably comment, "No worries."

The best part of working with Jocelyn was her palate. Blending trials involve tasting scores of combinations of ferments. Jocelyn could identify and describe flavors that were only a vague hint to me. She zeroed in on the best our fruit could offer, and our cider improved dramatically. With fruit from the Foggy Ridge orchards and Ed Witt and with Jocelyn's strong guidance, I hoped to grow my cidery in size and quality.

"Finally," I thought. "Everything is under control."

Jocelyn lived almost forty miles away, a precipitous drive down Lover's Leap into Patrick County. She visited the cider several times a week, but the day-to-day monitoring and cellar work meant I often worked alone in the cidery.

One cold April night, two-inch juice lines lay coiled on the tank room floor, curled in lazy loops like fat bucatini. Early on it had taken weeks for my overwhelmingly verbal brain to grasp the mechanics of inlet valves, pressure, and outlets, used to properly sterilize the filter and successfully filter a tank of cider. Now, after a few years of practice, I could assemble that filter blindfolded. My tiny tank room, as efficient and compact as a ship's cabin, was crowded with twenty-five feet of hoses filled with cider. What looked like chaos, or a plateful of giant spaghetti, was a carefully designed effort to create a bright, flavorful sparkling drink.

But that night the filter was not cooperating, and I was on my own. At 8:00 p.m. I still didn't have cider in the tank.

A southern Appalachian spring can break your heart. At an elevation of 3,000 feet, Foggy Ridge is in the southernmost Zone 5 horticultural region. That's a plant geek's way of saying my orchards are in Virginia, but the weather can act like Chicago. Late April is a fraught time. Ramps push up through skunk cabbage in wet corners of every mountain holler. Sulfur-yellow mountain cress lines roadsides and carpets the orchards. Nights dip below thirty degrees, but sunny days rush spring into life.

Mountain cress is a tough, lusty plant. The bitter leaves, shaped like tiny iced-tea spoons, live under snow. Frost shrivels the plant, but on a sunny day, tender new growth leaps out of the cold ground. An alphabet of vitamins pack the peppery cress, and like the Indigenous people and colonists before me, in early spring I couldn't get enough of this taste.

Nor can the pollinators. I sow mountain cress under my apples to tempt bees from hives and holes. The blooms create bright yellow stripes in the orchards, as if I am growing rows of rapeseed, not tree fruit. Usually the stout cress bounces in April breezes, but tonight a cold wind that smelled like snow bent the tender plants sideways. The weather report said a nor'easter was coming. Not good news for an apple grower.

Sometimes experience and planning aren't enough to control outcomes. After following two hours' worth of protocols to prepare the tanks and filter for a run of cider, a plug of sediment clogged the pads. Another hour of far-too-slow filtering convinced me to start over. I broke down the filter, cleaned and sterilized it, and refilled the line with cider. I lost gallons of my favorite blend, a bone-dry cider crafted from Hewe's Crabapples that spoke of the orchard. Jocelyn always said that making good wine or cider is "99 percent good janitorial practices." I smiled and thought it's a good thing that I enjoy process because even on a dark, cold spring night, you can't skip a step.

Just then I did miss a step: in slow motion, as if I was watching myself on film, I hooked my boot on a coiled hose and fell to the concrete floor. I landed hard on my hip and then on my elbow before my head crashed to the floor. I lay in a heap, my heart racing, my mouth full of blood, half on the wet floor and the rest of my body wrapped in juice lines. My eyes filled with tears, and I thought, "I am so lucky." I had worked years to learn this craft, to grow cider fruit, to earn the money to build this cider house. I had cajoled fruit from neighbors and recruited skilled colleagues. I had done all I could to make my apple dreams come true.

At that moment, all I could think was, "I'm so lucky to be lying on the cold wet floor by myself at ten o'clock at night during a late April snowstorm that may ruin my apple crop for the season."

I recovered from my tumble in the cider house, but my orchards didn't fare so well in the three-day nor'easter. Apples are most vulnerable to frost damage during the pink bud stages of bloom. Biting wind and several nights below twenty-eight degrees destroyed the crop on my early blooming apples, along with most of the apple crop in three southern states—which made my precious Hewe's Crab cider from the previous harvest, now resting in temperature-controlled tanks, all the more important to my nascent cider business.

After almost a decade of education and apprenticeship, I was still decoding the apple cipher. In my search for certainty, I was learning how easy it is to misstep, how forces beyond my control could derail even the most sturdy plans. I was beginning to see how little agency fruit growers possess.

Will Messer's apple house nestled into a hillside near Coggins Branch in the northwest corner of Haywood County, North Carolina. Thick stone walls over six feet tall and two feet thick supported the imposing two-story building. From early September through spring it housed apples destined for markets outside the twin valleys of Little Cataloochee and Big Cataloochee, on either side of Noland Mountain. In 1915, Messer built his apple house to last, with hand-hewn chestnut sills and siding and a split-oak shingle roof.

In the southern Appalachians, apple houses provided insulation and ventilation. Messer dug the first floor deep into a hillside to moderate temperature. Early in the harvest season, windows and floor vents opened to trap cool air at night. The second-story walls formed a sandwich of two layers of chestnut siding, six inches apart, filled with sawdust. Apples from Messer's three orchards rested in rows of storage bins made from sawmill strips on one-inch spacing, with sawdust in the bottom of each container.

Throughout fall and into early spring, a wave of rich, sugary apple aromas greeted everyone entering the ground-level door. During harvest the apple house functioned as a gathering spot for the Cataloochee farm communities. Family members and local workers hauled in fruit, unloaded ripe apples, and carted empty bins back to the orchards. As the season progressed, a yeasty aroma of fermenting fruit filled the air.

During September, I imagine more than a few harvest workers took a bite of a sharp-tasting Jonathan, an apple that originated in New York but was widely grown at higher elevations in the South. In October, Stayman dominated the storage bins. The mountain South was "Stayman country," and this all-purpose fruit made its way into pies and apple butter in Cataloochee kitchens. Winesap, one of the most popular apples in the region, was the last apple to land with a satisfying thud in Messer's chestnut wood bins. For more than half the year, this busy apple house rang with the aromas and sounds of apple harvest.

Will Messer and his Little Cataloochee neighbors were not the first to pull sustenance from this remote mountain area.

Apple House from the Upper Will Messer Place relocated to the Oconaluftee Farmstead.
GRSM05077, Great Smokey Mountains National Park, Swain County, NC.

For centuries the Cherokee people hunted the woods and balds around the Cataloochee valleys and fished Cove Creek. The Cataloochee Trail connected Cherokee communities in what is now Waynesville, North Carolina, and Overhill towns near present-day Crosby, Tennessee.[1] In the mid-eighteenth century, the European fur trade reached even isolated areas of the southern mountains. By 1740, as many as 150 traders based on the South Carolina coast bought pelts from white trappers as well as from Indigenous people in this part of the Appalachians. The Cherokee people who hunted in Cataloochee could have been part of this exchange, which brought apples to Indigenous groups.[2]

From 1721 to 1775, under pressure from white settlers encroaching on their lands, the Cherokee people were forced to relinquish over 60,000 square miles in the southern foothills and mountains. In 1791, the Treaty of Holston ceded Cherokee land in the Great Smoky Mountains of North Carolina and Tennessee to white ownership. White farmers, mostly from North Carolina and Tennessee, began moving into the Cataloochee area in the 1820s. Cattle drovers came first, followed by log homes, cornfields, and apple orchards of small farmers. By the 1850s, there were enough white settlers to establish a voting percentage and the township of Cataloochee.

Apples grew in the narrow valleys of Little Cataloochee and Big Cataloochee. Orchards hugged the thermal belts, the bands of warm air on sunny slopes, and at least a handful of apple trees surrounded every dwelling. Most of the early homesteads included small apple houses for storing "keepers" for winter use.

Messer's apple house occupied prime territory in Little Cataloochee. His father-in-law, Dan Cook, was one of the first settlers in the area. Between 1856 and 1860, Cook built a sturdy log home in a fertile flat meadow next to Coggins Creek and half a mile from the Little Cataloochee Baptist Church. He was a skilled carpenter who liked to carve, and his grandchildren remember the one-story house filled with handmade furniture, including a spindle bed and a corner cabinet with a moon and star design carved from his favorite cherrywood.[3] Apple trees surrounded his home.

Harriet Cook was as skilled and enterprising as her husband. She raised eight children, wove cloth and sewed clothes, preserved food, and was an expert forager.[4] She passed along skills to her children and helped harvest apples each fall.

In 1891, the Cooks divided their property among three of their children. Their daughter Rachel took over the homeplace and "promised to care for her father and mother as long as they lived."[5] Three years later, Rachel married William "Will" G. B. Messer.

By 1900, the Cataloochee settlement had a population of 800 and 150 homes.[6] Most residents had moved from Tennessee and North Carolina; all were white and almost all described themselves as farmers. Half the residents rented farms. Farmers grew corn, hay, and a little burley tobacco and raised cattle. They sold their crops in markets like Waynesville, North Carolina, and Knoxville, Tennessee. Everyone referred to the two communities as "Catalooch," and, though hard to reach, this world was not isolated. Families subscribed to newspapers and purchased goods from the Sears, Roebuck, and Co. catalog and in towns outside the valley.

At the turn of the twentieth century, apples changed the economy of this mountain community.

Settlers from North Carolina could have brought varieties like Cullasaga, a popular southern apple named for the Cullasaga River seventy miles south of Cataloochee, or Fall Pippin, often called Carolina Pippin, a popular early winter apple suited to mountain orchards in the South. South Carolina's Pomaria Nurseries sold apple trees to customers in western North Carolina and employed a sales representative to cover Greenville, South Carolina, and areas west.[7] Farmers in nearby Waynesville, North Carolina, planted orchards in the early 1800s for cider and apple brandy and grew Winter Jon, a popular cider apple.[8] In the 1890s, Pomona Hill Nurseries in Guilford County, North Carolina, sold sought-after southern apples including Kinnaird's Choice and Carolina Beauty that likely traveled west to Cataloochee.[9]

By the early 1900s, improved roads and the growth of lumber camps in the Smoky Mountains created a viable commercial market for the apples from these two small valleys. Will Messer, John Burgess, and Mack Hannah planted the most prosperous commercial apple orchards in Cataloochee. Family members recall scores of apples, including Stayman, Jonathan, Black Hoover, and Stark Red Delicious.[10] Traveling tree salesmen from Stark Brothers Nurseries were a common sight in mountain communities, peddling varieties such as Stark Golden Delicious, Black Ben Davis, and Winesap. The 1901 Stark Brothers Nurseries and Orchards catalog described the ideal site for Winesap apples, one that mirrored the place and people of Cataloochee: "Needs rich, moist soils. . . . A good table and cider apple, and its fruitfulness makes it a favorite."[11]

In 1915, Messer's 600 apple trees were producing over 2,500 barrels a year, and he needed storage and a place to sort fruit. He sited his apple house in a central spot in Little Cataloochee, about fifty yards southeast of his wife Rachel's homeplace, Dan Cook's original log home.

Sorting and grading apples on long tables was a community event. Wives, children, and tenant workers packed apples in barrels for shipping and stacked them high in the ground-floor storage bins. The long-storing varieties, like Winesap, headed to sawdust-lined bins on the second floor. The large logging camps at Crestmont, Sunburst, and Mt. Sterling purchased apples for $0.50 to $1.50 a bushel.[12] Apples traveled from Messer's apple house to Charlotte and Gastonia, North Carolina; Greenville, South Carolina; and Knoxville, Tennessee.[13]

I can easily imagine Messer's apple house—the sound of apples tipped into wooden barrels, the smell of rotten apples sorted from solid fruit. Even with a forklift and tractor, my own apple storage shed was a scene of barely controlled chaos each fall. Messer's apple house faced northwest, and I can picture workers bundled against a cold north wind in late October. But Messer was an industrious and entrepreneurial man with a busy mind. He operated a successful sawmill and gristmill, made and sold caskets, installed a cattle scale, and ran a stockyard. He created a market for Cataloochee apples and "could make anything out of iron or wood."[14] I believe his apple house full of southern fruit ran as smoothly as nearby Coggins Branch.

———

While apple trees connected the Cataloochee community with a world of commerce beyond Noland Mountain, trees, or the people who sponsored their wholesale harvest, functioned as a destructive agent of change. From the 1880s to 1920, prompted by declining timber stands in the Great Lakes and Northeast and by increased rail access to rich southern Appalachian forests, the "era of industrial railroad logging" altered the trajectory of this and many other mountain farming communities.[15] Environmental historian Donald Davis states that in 400 years, "the single greatest human activity to affect environmental and cultural change in the southern Appalachians [was] industrial logging."[16] Once railroads made timber extraction profitable, corporations backed by foreign and northern investors purchased huge tracts of the southern mountains for clear-cutting timber, often from virgin stands.

Timber operations provided a local market for Cataloochee apples, but they brought environmental destruction to the Appalachians and contributed to the decline of southern orchards.

Narrow-gauge rail lines snaked up steep hillsides. Giant steam-powered cableway skidders hauled huge logs across slopes, removing vegetation and creating a path for erosion. Fires increased, fueled by piles of slash, the downed limbs and treetops left by loggers. In 1891, between 800,000 and 1.2 million acres of woodland burned in North Carolina alone. Bare hillsides, scoured by rail lines and skid-paths, created soil runoff, erosion, and flooding. By the early 1900s, a joint investigation by four federal agencies determined that industrial logging in the southern mountains had caused topsoil loss, erosion, and the destruction of streams and rivers.

The solution was to preserve southern forests. In March 1911, Congress passed the Weeks Act, which allowed the federal government to purchase land to preserve the headwaters of streams and rivers.[17] Federal land acquisition in the southern mountains began.

Though the Weeks Act eventually allowed federal acquisition of more than 20 million acres of land, timber extraction in the southern Appalachians did not end in 1911. The US Forest Service purchased most land from timber companies, including land already clear-cut. The Forest Service mandate was to "manage land," which included the right to harvest timber, a practice the agency continues today.[18]

At the same time, the desire to conserve forests and protect waterways coincided with the juggernaut of southern tourism to accelerate demand for eastern national parks. Automobile registrations increased from 458,000 in 1910 to 23 million in 1930.[19] Improved roads and increased car travel stoked the tourism industry, especially in Virginia's Shenandoah Valley and in Asheville, North Carolina, and generated support among business interests for national parks in southern states.

In contrast to national forests, national parks sought to "preserve unimpaired the natural and cultural resources . . . for the future enjoyment, education and inspiration of this and future generations."[20] National parks, like the Shenandoah National Park, the Blue Ridge Parkway, and the Great Smoky Mountains National Park, would consist not just of land full of timbered and virgin forests but of land long occupied by people, farms, and apples.

In 1899, Dan Cook was living in his well-built log cabin and Will Messer had planted apple orchards when business owners in Asheville, North Carolina, along with politicians and business interests from five other southern states, formed the Appalachian National Park Association. This group first sought federal funding for a national park in the southern mountains, but after six years of unsuccessful lobbying, it changed tactics and names. The "Appalachian Natural Forest Reserve Association" pushed all the right buttons—the concept of a national park that preserved forest land in the South located close to growing tourism centers captured the imaginations of politicians in North Carolina, Tennessee, and Virginia.

When the National Park Service was formed in 1916, a year after Will Messer built his apple house, the stage was set for the marketing, fundraising, and mythologizing that led to the Great Smoky Mountains National Park and other southern parks.

Timber and pulp companies owned much of the land for the proposed sites for southern national parks. The sites also encompassed many mountain farming communities with thriving economies and deep-seated histories. The battleground was staged: city-based business concerns, powerful timber and pulp companies, and small southern farmers fighting over landownership and land destiny.

The battle was far from an equitable match.

North Carolina and Tennessee political and business interests lobbied Congress for a national park in the Great Smoky Mountains, at one point employing a professional public relations firm.[21] In 1925, Congress passed the Temple Bill directing the secretary of the Interior to define boundaries for a national park in the Great Smoky Mountains and the Shenandoah. Funding for land purchases was left up to the states. Political lobbying and consumer marketing—plus two large donations from John D. Rockefeller—resulted in funds to purchase land for the Great Smoky Mountains National Park. Beginning in April 1928, North Carolina directed the state Park Commission to begin acquiring land for the North Carolina portion of the park.

Pulp and timber corporations owned 85 percent of the land in the proposed park, and they vehemently opposed land acquisition. Suncrest Lumber Company owned 32,853 acres; Ravensford Company owned 32,709 acres and was the last large tract purchased in 1934.[22] Litigation by timber companies was so extensive that the North Carolina attorney general hired extra staff.[23] The machinations of acquiring land, especially during an economic depression, included a decade of dramatic twists and turns, charges of financial mismanagement against the Park Commission, independent audits, a bank failure, bribery, and a Supreme Court decision.

The farmers and orchardists who resisted a park in the Great Smoky Mountains had few supporters and a tiny voice. The small landowners who occupied 15 percent of proposed park land faced a public relations campaign that painted mountain residents as happy to receive a good offer for their subsistence farms. Land acquisition displaced over 5,665 people in what became the Great Smoky Mountains National Park.[24]

In her collection of family memories about Cataloochee, Hattie Caldwell Davis described the shock and anger her relatives felt when they learned they would have to leave their farms and orchards. Cataloochee residents missed the "sweetest, coldest water in the world."[25] They regretted leaving family homes and land with good fishing and hunting and productive orchards. As a young woman, Davis was shocked to see men and women with twisted faces and puffy eyes, openly weeping as they watched neighbors pack their furniture in trucks and leave the valley. Stories full of emotion about being cheated out of farms and long-standing orchards have spread through generations.

In Little Cataloochee, James and Melissa Hannah resisted selling their land and in 1931 took their case to superior court in Asheville, North Carolina. For 100 acres of land that James's father had purchased in 1857 for $400, including one of the most productive orchards in the area, the Hannahs received $1,650.[26]

———————

Some 350 miles northeast of Cataloochee, in another mountain apple-growing region home to small farms, a similar struggle played out in Virginia's Shenandoah Valley. Powerful tourism interests, led by George Freeman Pollock, owner of Skyline Resort, joined with the *Harrisonburg News-Record*, a regional newspaper owned by politician Harry Byrd, to support a national park in the Virginia Blue Ridge Mountains. Byrd supported the park as governor and senator. The 1925 Temple Bill that paved the way for the Great Smoky Mountains National Park did the same for a park in Virginia's Blue Ridge Mountains.

Frustrated by the prospect of negotiating over 3,000 tracts with individual landowners, the Virginia state legislature passed the Public Parks Condemnation Act, controversial legislation that allowed the government to file a single condemnation suit in each of the eight counties included in park land, and to appraise the land with a court-appointed board.[27] In 1927, William E. Carson, head of the State Commission on Conservation and Development, began surveying 4,000 private tracts in proposed park land.[28]

Unlike the broad acreage acquired for the Great Smoky Mountains National Park, the Shenandoah property stretched 100 miles along a narrow strip on top of the Blue Ridge Mountains. White farmers had occupied this land for over 250 years. Though absentee owners and timber companies owned most of the park land, almost 2,000 people lived inside the park boundaries on farms, big and small. The tracts acquired by the Shenandoah National Park painted a portrait of productive orchards in what was promoted as an area "free from commercial activities."[29] Sue Eisenfeld, author of *Shenandoah: A Story of Conservation and Betrayal*, states that 40 percent of land acquired by the park consisted of farms, productive pastures, and orchards.[30]

Contrary to the stereotyped image of isolated mountain folk living primitive lives, Shenandoah's communities included profitable orchards, gristmills and sawmills, schools, post offices, and stores. Mail-order consumer goods filled homes, along with pharmaceutical glass, varied kitchenware, store-bought shoes, and even records.

The prosperous apple economy included a stave mill for making apple barrels, legal distilleries that produced corn liquor and apple brandy, bunkhouses for orchard workers, and packing sheds, plus many orchards, large and small. In Page County, Zada Kemp Shenk had 135 acres of apples and peaches. Edgar Merchant in Warren County owned 92 acres with 18 acres in apples.

Surveys of small farms illustrate how ubiquitous apples were in Shenandoah park land: Marvin Sours owned 30 acres with fifty trees; Mattie Cave had 37 acres including fifty-five apple trees and ten cherry.[31] Land tract descriptions paint a picture of orchards populating almost every cleared slope, cove, and hollow.

In the Shenandoah, surveyors valued orchard acreage higher than pastureland or farmland. Shirley Carter's 707 acres in Rappahannock County on the headwaters of the Jordan River were deemed worth $9,580, with 45 percent of that amount coming from her 35 acres of orchards.

Many of the pre-1935 homesteads in the Shenandoah had seedling orchards, but Eddie Wood in Page County had four acres of York apples, an apple widely grown in the Shenandoah for processing into applesauce, canned apple slices, and cider vinegar. York apples create a yellow, jewellike applesauce, with enough acidity to offset this apple's natural sweetness.

As was true in Cataloochee, some residents protested land acquisition for a national park and others welcomed offers for their land. But the farming demographics were different in the Shenandoah: less than 40 percent of residents owned the land they occupied, and only 7 percent of park land was owned by full-time residents.[32] The area had a long tradition of landowners in the more fertile Shenandoah Valley leasing mountain property to farmers who carved a living from mountain slopes at the crest of the Blue Ridge.

Cider and apple stand on the Lee Highway, Shenandoah National Park, VA, 1935. Photograph by Arthur Rothstein, LC-USF33-002196-M4, FSA/OWI Collection, Prints and Photographs Division, Library of Congress, Washington, DC.

The Shenandoah park scheme included government support to relocate families to one of seven resettlement areas in Page, Madison, and Greene Counties with new homes, acreage—and a mortgage. Twenty years later, no relocated families remained on the government-sponsored relocation farms.[33]

A total of 197 landowners qualified for compensation, but only 34 people received more than $2,000.[34] About a third of families on soon-to-be park land accepted payment and left immediately. But 350 families remained on their farms and orchards from 1934 to 1938, living on what had become federal land, under strict guidelines about how they could use the land their families had occupied, some for centuries. Those who stayed had to petition the federal government to prune their apple trees.[35]

Robert Via, who owned 154 acres including apple orchards, protested the land acquisition in a lengthy court case. In November 1935, the US Supreme Court dismissed the case.[36]

In 1935 Virginia presented the Department of the Interior with deeds to 199,173 acres. The 105-mile-long national park opened in 1936, welcoming visitors to what was called a "wilderness area." Today, the only physical reminders of over 250 years of white settlement and prosperous orchard communities in the Shenandoah National Park are crumbling chimneys, one restored cabin, and over a hundred small cemeteries. Abandoned orchards still yield windfall fruit.

In 1930 Will Messer accepted $35,405 in a condemnation settlement from the North Carolina Park Commission for his land and buildings. His 340-acre farm included three productive orchards full of southern apples, a twelve-room house with hot and cold running water and acetylene lights, several barns, two mills, and an apple house built to last several lifetimes. He believed his property was worth twice the price paid by the Park Commission, but, like most farmers, Messer chose not to litigate. He didn't want to "take a chance with a picked jury [since] you never can tell who anybody is going to marry or what a jury will do."[37] Between 1930 and 1934, Messer and his family moved to Caldwell County, North Carolina, 150 miles east and 3,000 feet lower.

On September 2, 1940, at Newfound Gap on the Tennessee–North Carolina border about fifty miles west of Cataloochee, President Franklin D. Roosevelt dedicated the Great Smoky Mountains National Park. In the next year, over 1 million people visited the park.

The white settlers in Cataloochee had created a community with only a hundred-year life span. Will Messer's apple house, built to last over a century, housed apples for less than twenty years.

The Park Service burned most of the buildings. Dan Cook's house collapsed in 1975. The park collected some of the timbers and relocated and restored Rachel Messer's homeplace in 1999. The top floor of the apple house was removed and sold in the 1950s, likely for the chestnut wood. Once exposed to the weather, mortar between the thick stone walls crumbled. Ruins of Will Messer's apple house still stand across the road from the original location of Dan Cook's log home. Today, visitors to the Mountain Farm Museum at the Oconaluftee Visitor Center can see relocated homes and buildings that portray a reconstructed version of an Appalachian mountain community, including a handsome stone and hardwood apple house, empty of the sounds and smells of apple harvest.

TRANSPORTED

My grandmother Dovey Annis liked pretty things. Her dresser overflowed with dime-store lipstick and face powder. She never missed her weekly beauty shop appointment for a "set," a surprisingly soft mound of blue-gray waves that framed her face and lasted, unchanged, for seven days.

She grew daffodils on a high bluff between my grandparents' farmhouse and Highway 29 in Troup County, Georgia. Each spring Grandmother filled milk jugs, canning jars, and every vase she could find with dozens of daffodil varieties. When she passed, all the cousins spent a Sunday afternoon digging bulbs in her daffodil field. For almost forty years, I've planted Grandmother's bulbs around every house I've owned.

Today her old-fashioned "daffs," as she called them, grow under the big oak tree by the Old Orchard. They cover a steep bank at the cider house and line the spring by the driveway. She liked the showy, big trumpet daffs, especially the vibrant yellow blooms. My favorites are the dainty, small-cupped daffodils with creamy petals and deep orange trumpets. She grew dozens of varieties, and I like to think a tiny bit of Georgia soil clings to my Virginia daffodils.

Daffodils were blooming all over the farm when Jocelyn and I faced a long table laden with two dozen French squares in April 2009. These small, thick-walled, square-sided bottles held permutations of cider blends. Jocelyn had spent hours manipulating spreadsheets filled with fermentation and production records. We both pored over months of tasting notes. The decisions we would make in the next few hours would determine the quality of the cider we had to sell in the next year.

Beverage makers need good palates to create complex drinks, whether wine, cider, beer, or spirits. Jocelyn excelled at blending trials—she detected delicate flavors and minute flaws. Maintaining aroma is one of the most difficult aspects of making cider, and Jocelyn could detect the most subtle aromas, ones that we could amplify in our blending. Best of all, she described flavor with a vocabulary I vividly remember. When Jocelyn talked about a cider blend, she told a story that created an evocative image of fruit and beverage.

In those early blending sessions Jocelyn and I spent hours tasting cider blends and scribbling notes. We kept a laptop open to calculate production volumes. Jocelyn would suggest, "What if we added another 10 percent of Albemarle Pippin to this blend?" I lobbied for putting 2,000 liters of Ashmead's Kernel in our most popular First Fruit cider. Each diversion required returning to Jocelyn's spreadsheets to calculate production and revisiting my sales projections to see if we might actually sell the cider we created.

My little cider business was turning into a big cider business—I had expanded our orchards and was purchasing Winesap and Gold Rush apples from local growers. My glass order, the annual shipment of empty bottles, used to arrive in a small tractor trailer. Foggy Ridge Cider's glass now showed up in an enormous eighteen-wheeler that we struggled to back into the loading dock. As we bottled more cider each year, every decision carried more risk.

While Jocelyn mixed the next set of blends, I walked off nervous energy and struggled to keep my worries in check. Jocelyn and I were determining what our entire cider production would taste like for the next year, cider I was responsible for selling.

With each round of tasting, my worries bloomed into anxieties. I was keenly aware that the decisions I was now making mattered more. Fear often accompanies growth and change; I thought of Ed Witt and other apple growers who calculate orchard risks and felt a renewed empathy for the judgments they confront each year.

One of the biggest tasks of my life has been to understand my apprehensions and tame them. The task of turning the samples contained in dozens of French squares into delicious cider blends pushed all my anxiety buttons.

But Jocelyn was not one to agonize. She provided a steady rudder for my tendency to over-examine. Whenever I threatened to careen into space, Jocelyn's phrase "No worries" brought me back to earth.

That night, Jocelyn and I wrapped up the blending trials around 8:00 p.m. Snow was predicted, the last snow that always arrived in late April alongside apple blossoms. I locked the cidery and drove the half-mile curving route back to our house. Deer crowded the gravel driveway and barely shifted as I passed. A raccoon waddled into a ditch and then turned two shining eyes toward me. At the top of the drive, a flash of red fur streaked across my high beams—a fox, suspended in mid-flight.

At home, I filled a few pails with water. I shrugged off the tension in my shoulders and pulled on a down jacket and warm gloves. For two hours I picked Grandmother's daffodils under a full moon. Snow-flakes swirled in the dark sky and settled on the pale yellow petals and creamy trumpets. In my cozy kitchen with the last fire of the year blazing, I filled every vase I could find with Georgia daffodils. The next morning the house smelled like spring, full of the season's change. Full of possibility.

Tall, spindly apple trees covered in pale green leaves swayed in the back of the wagon as it bumped over ruts on the Oregon Trail. Six oxen pulled the oversize flatbed loaded with two twelve-inch-deep wooden boxes filled with 700 fruit trees. In April 1847, Sweet June or Summer Bell-flower would have bloomed inside the fence of hickory slats that pro-tected the seedlings from livestock. Henderson Luelling's remaining six wagons held enough food, clothing, tools, and cooking utensils to supply his party's seven-month journey from Iowa to Oregon. His eight chil-dren and pregnant wife, Elizabeth, rode on top of the piles of posses-sions or walked alongside the wagons. Luelling's convoy of twenty-two people headed west just as daffodils bloomed and pink buds swelled on his young apple trees.

Inside the traveling nursery, Luelling's dreams of apple orchards nes-tled in Iowa soil.[1]

Henderson Luelling grew up in Randolph County, North Carolina, steeped in horticulture. Born in 1809 into a prosperous Quaker com-munity, Luelling learned to graft "as soon as he was old enough to whit-tle."[2] His father, Mescheck, grew apples and sold fruit trees. Even as a boy, Henderson would have been familiar with seedling apples and an array of named southern varieties like Ralls Janet and Smith Cider.

His Piedmont community was also home to English apples. In 1792, Ann Jessup, a Quaker minister from Guilford County, North Carolina, visited her daughter in Scotland and returned with grafting wood for about twenty English varieties, including Golden Russet, White Pear-main, and Red Cheek Pippin.[3] Jessup and Abijah Pinson, a skilled orchardist, established the first nursery in the area using her grafting wood from English fruit and from some southern varieties.

The Luellings were committed abolitionists. Motivated to escape a

Henderson Luelling.
Oregon Historical
Society, Portland.

slaveholding state, his family moved to Indiana when Henderson was thirteen. His father continued diversified farming, but apples increasingly captured young Henderson's attention. By his early twenties, he and his brother, John, operated a fruit tree nursery that supplied Indiana homesteaders for whom an apple orchard was an essential investment.

In 1837, twenty-seven-year-old Henderson Luelling moved farther west to Iowa with his wife and family, toting a collection of southern fruit. John followed a few years later, and the brothers founded the Cedar Grove Botanic Garden and Nursery in Salem. By 1840 the Luelling brothers offered 36,000 fruit trees for sale, including 45 apple varieties.[4] They delivered trees to customers within a twenty-five-mile radius and hauled large orders of 1,000 or more trees to Burlington and Fort Madison on the Mississippi River. In a few years, the enterprising brothers "changed the countryside in southeastern Iowa into a center of apple growing."[5]

Grown on rootstocks available in the nineteenth century, an apple tree took seven to ten years to bear a significant fruit crop. Homesteaders were eager for apples that produced fruit from June through fall and preferred nursery-grown trees at least two years old. A one- to two-year-old apple seedling was called a whip or a "maiden tree." A well-grown whip was three to four feet tall with "feathers" or small limbs already forming a scaffold for fruit.

Nurseries sold apple seedlings when they were dormant, after leaves had fallen and before the trees leafed out in spring. In late fall the Luelling brothers dug dormant whips, washed soil from the tree roots, tagged them, wrapped bundles of trees in heavy cloth, and stored them in a cold cellar until sold. Farmers planted the bare-root apple trees in early spring before buds began swelling.

Iowa held Henderson for just a decade. He read about Colonel John C. Frémont's travel to Oregon's Columbia River and was familiar with published accounts of the Lewis and Clark expedition from the early 1800s. He certainly envisioned the potential for apples in the Pacific Northwest because in 1845 he began planting fruit trees in a special nursery plot in preparation for another move. He sold land to raise funds and gathered a group of like-minded neighbors and fellow abolitionists who saw possibilities at the end of a long journey west.

In April 1847, Henderson Luelling transplanted 700 maiden trees into his two nursery boxes, including North Carolina apples and Ann

Jessup's English varieties, for a total of twenty-one different kinds of apples, six pears, five cherries, three peaches, and three grape vines.[6] Henderson believed his custom mixture of Iowa soil and charcoal would hold water better than soil alone.[7] He tucked black walnut and shagbark hickory nuts into the soil, loaded the boxes on his biggest wagon, and pointed the oxen team toward Oregon.

Some southern apples never left a valley or a county and were so welded to a specific spot that deep connections persist today. But many have traveled far from their roots in the South for centuries. Apples followed colonization in the South—North Carolina and Virginia apples moved to Tennessee and Kentucky. Georgia apples traveled to Mississippi and Texas. Quakers in Guilford and Surry County in North Carolina took Jessup's apples with them when they migrated to Ohio, Indiana, Illinois, and Missouri.[8]

Henderson Luelling was not the first to grow *Malus domestica* in the Pacific Northwest. A venerable apple tree planted from seed at Fort Vancouver in 1827 lived for almost 200 years. Before 1846, the British Hudson's Bay Company planted orchards in the Oregon Territory and traded fruit and seeds with Indigenous people.[9] A decade before Luelling arrived with his traveling nursery, a member of the Nez Percé tribe planted a seedling orchard in present-day Asotin County, Washington.[10] But Luelling was the first to ferry grafted trees, including southern apples, across America with the intent to start a commercial nursery.

As it turned out, apples grew very well in the Pacific Northwest.

Apples have the widest geographic range of any tree fruit. They grow from southern Alabama to Canada; they prosper in damp, misty climates like southern England and in hot, humid southern states. In order to produce fruit, apples require a dormant period that is set in motion by low temperatures. The term "chill hours" or "chill units" refers to the number of hours in a year between thirty-two and forty-five degrees Fahrenheit. Most apple varieties need 500 to 1,000 chill hours. Some apples from the Gulf South, like Shell of Alabama, have chill requirements as low as 300 hours. This cold sleep triggers hormonal growth inhibitors that prevent fresh growth in winter. A dormant period enables development of fruit buds, which begin swelling when apples break dormancy, or wake up, in spring. Apples need this annual cycle of sleeping and waking to bear fruit.

Apples grow best in climates with sunny, warm days, cool nights, adequate rainfall or irrigation, and enough days with temperatures under forty-five degrees to meet the chill requirements of the varieties grown. The Pacific Northwest turned out to be near-perfect fruit territory, a fact that would not bode well for southern orchards.

———————

Railroads changed the movement of apples around the South.

Before rail travel was common, transporting apples required time and labor. Today a bushel of medium-sized apples packed in a cardboard box weighs about forty-eight pounds. In the nineteenth century, orchardists packed apples in wooden barrels that held about three bushels. Harvest crews filled barrels in the orchard and then rolled them onto wagons. On steep mountain slopes, horse- or mule-drawn sleds called "ground slides" transported apples to flat roads, where barrels were transferred to wagons. Heavily laden wagons made slow progress on poor roads. As late as the early twentieth century, transporting apples from Will Messer's Little Cataloochee orchard to Knoxville took more than a day.

Southern rail construction lagged the North, but in the 1850s every state in the South doubled its rail mileage.[11] The Virginia Central Railroad ferried apples and other agricultural products from the Shenandoah Valley over the Blue Ridge Mountains to Clifton Forge and the James River.[12] The Virginia and Tennessee line cut a gap through the Blue Ridge Mountains from Lynchburg to Bristol, Tennessee, and carried dried apples in fourth class along with ginseng and sacks of flour, lard, and beeswax.[13] Rail lines that extended from central Virginia into the southwestern counties established the foundation for a southern winter apple industry that lasted over eighty years.[14] In West Virginia and areas of the South with rough terrain and poor roads, railroads existed well into the twentieth century as a means for transporting goods like coal and heavy agriculture products like apples.[15]

Railroads moved apple trees as well as apples. When the Newberry to Columbia, South Carolina, line opened in 1851, Pomaria Nurseries began shipping fruit trees to customers in Mississippi and Arkansas.

Before the Civil War, enslaved people, either owned by the railroads or leased through contractors, built and repaired the South's railroads, loaded goods, and worked on rail lines. Historians estimate that at the start of the Civil War, 76 percent of the South's 118 railroads used enslaved labor.[16]

When railroads were rebuilt after the Civil War, some plantation owners who had relied on enslaved labor turned to growing apples, which required less hand labor than cotton or tobacco. Beginning in 1869, Moscow Carter planted 389 apple, pear, and peach trees on his

family's Franklin County, Tennessee, farm. He shipped Kinnaird's Choice, Summer Queen, and Early Harvest to Georgia markets on the Nashville to Decatur railroad.

Apples took a slow route west on Luelling's ox-drawn wagon, but soon after the transcontinental railroad was completed in 1869, apples boomeranged back, packed on railroad cars destined for Chicago, New York, and other eastern markets.

Rail transport, favorable growing conditions, the availability of nursery stock, and horticultural know-how contributed to rapid orchard expansion in the Northwest. In the 1880s and 1890s, apple growing declined in the East, but western orchardists planted industrial-scale orchards to supply markets thousands of miles away. Regions like Washington's Wenatchee and Yakima Valleys shipped railcar loads of apples east, in direct competition with southern fruit. When refrigerated railcars were introduced in 1887, the economies of scale for western apples only improved.

Refrigerated cold storage was developed in the 1890s and changed the way apple growers thought about the type of fruit they grew and how they sold it, a move that further disadvantaged southern apples. Since apples are climacteric, continuing to convert starch to sugar after harvest, growers have always sought ways to slow the natural decay that begins when apples leave the tree. In most of the South, warm temperatures remain into fall, and southern orchardists prized long-keeping varieties like Abram, Arkansas Black, and Ralls Janet that hung on the tree until late fall and stored well into spring.

Farmers grew these "keepers" and stored apples in their own versions of cold storage. Apples sheltered in root cellars dug into the side of hills. They spent the winter in handsome apple houses with stone foundations. They rested in trenches, covered with straw, dirt, and wooden boards, and lay tucked away in stone hearth pits.

By the 1910s, refrigerated cold storage replaced these nineteenth-century options and introduced a complex set of conditions that increased the power of the western fruit industry that Henderson Luelling helped spawn. Storing apples at thirty to forty degrees Fahrenheit slowed ripening and allowed growers to sell fruit all year. Refrigerated storage facilities sprang up near railroad depots in every apple-growing region, including the South. But the larger West Coast apple growers had the size and organization to create the first cooperative storage buildings and packhouses. The stage was set for national brand-making of western apples.

Some apples store better than others. Increased use of cold storage meant that the West Coast orchards began to grow apples that maintained flavor and texture after months in a cooler. Henderson Luelling came from a North Carolina farm family that valued four seasons of apples, but technology and transportation pushed rapidly growing apple regions like the Northwest toward growing a few varieties that survived cold storage and long-distance travel.

In just a few decades, the rich mix of apples that Luelling and other nurserymen carried west transformed into a handful of varieties that stood up to months in a refrigerator and survived a long train trip.

A final factor influenced the ascendency of western fruit and the decline of apples in the South. Southerners had always packed apples in wooden barrels. Cooperage businesses supported the apple industry in the South, a region with no shortage of timber. Harvest crews loaded barrels in the orchard and then transported the full barrels to apple houses, where they were rolled into place. Barrels were efficient and easily moved, but apples on the bottom of the barrel were often bruised from the weight of the fruit. A damaged apple spreads rot in a closed container. For decades, southern nursery catalogs cautioned growers to loosely pack apples to avoid spoilage.

Western growers had fewer hardwood trees for constructing barrels, but they did have softwood trees they could use to manufacture smaller, lighter crates. After World War II, apple packing shifted from barrels to crates, and the West quickly capitalized on this change.[17] Since the softwood crates were not as sturdy as hardwood barrels, growers harvested into large bins and then transported the bins to a packing shed, where workers loaded apples into the smaller crates. Western growers were among the first to create large packing cooperatives.

Smaller apple containers resulted in fewer damaged apples. Perhaps even more important, they created marketing real estate for western apple brands.

Retailers found they could display apple crates more effectively than wooden barrels. Shop owners arranged the containers in windows and along storefronts, providing ideal billboards for western fruit cooperatives. The early co-op apple brands like Apple Kids, Good Pickins, and Dainty Maids portrayed a uniformly white version of apples, with rosy-cheeked children cheerfully biting into brick-red apples. The Chief Joseph brand showed a stereotyped Indigenous man bookended by two red apples.

Western apple branding established an aesthetic standard for what became the country's most popular apple, Red Delicious. Images of a steeply oblong apple with a pointed "sheep's nose" on the blossom end and a deep red color came to define the epitome of a desirable apple, an image that worked against southern growers. Dark-red color and oblong shape are difficult to achieve in warmer growing regions with a less dramatic diurnal swing, the temperature difference between daytime highs and nighttime lows.

The South lost orchards and apples not in a steep plummet but in a series of declines, like a roller coaster trending downhill. While transportation and technology sped western orchards' domination, they also helped southern orchards, and many southern apple-growing regions expanded orchards in response to new markets reached by railroads. The number of Virginia orchards, for example, increased 100 percent between 1895 and 1900.[18] But change is complicated—the promise of growth in apple commerce carried obstacles that many southern orchards could not overcome.

Framed against the giant western apple industry built on industrial-sized orchards, cooperative production, and marketing and competing with technological advances like cold storage and rail shipping, the South's severely disadvantaged orchards declined.

Seventy-two years after Luelling settled in Oregon's Willamette Valley, the region had 100,000 acres of apples.[19] In 1902, the first refrigerated railroad cars in the Northwest transported Grimes Golden, Ben Davis, and Arkansas Black, three apples widely grown in the South, from the Willamette Valley to Seattle. By 1920, neighboring Washington State surpassed New York as the top apple-producing state in the country. Today Washington produces 65 percent of the apples grown in the United States.

Henderson Luelling's apples demanded attention every day of his cross-country trip. The rough trails and precipitous river crossings jostled the roots in the shallow soil and increased evaporation. Sixteen-year-old Alfred Luelling recalled watering the trees sometimes twice daily.[20] Walnut and hickory seedlings sprouted among the apple trees. Clover bloomed in the wagon bed. By July 1848, when the trees were in full leaf, the Luelling party encountered freezing temperatures in the Rocky Mountains and then, in August, snow on the Bear River.[21] To ford powerful Oregon rivers, they transferred the two nursery boxes to a smaller wagon. In November the group spent a month building flatboats to ferry 100 miles from The Dales down the Columbia River. Once the trees dropped their leaves, Luelling dug them from their boxes, washed soil from the roots, and bundled the naked trees in heavy cloth.

On November 17, 1847, seven months after leaving Iowa, the Luelling party reached the end of the Oregon Trail.

On December 10, a week after Elizabeth gave birth to the couple's ninth child, Oregon Columbia Luelling, the family moved into a log cabin on the Willamette River, a few miles south of today's Portland. Luelling likely dug a pit and covered the tree roots with soil for the winter. Family accounts say that of the 700 trees, 400 or 500 survived.[22] These peripatetic trees, many with origins in the South, kick-started the Northwest apple industry.[23]

Word spread quickly among fruit-hungry farmers. Some accounts say that settlers traveled over a hundred miles to procure Luelling fruit trees for fifty cents to one dollar per tree.[24]

Luelling was a restless man. Six years after traversing the Oregon Trail with his traveling nursery, he moved to California, again with fruit in tow. But his apples, some with a whiff of southern soil, took root in the Northwest and inspired an industry that crushed southern orchards and dominates apple commerce today.

ALTERED

I was finally finding a seasonal rhythm at Foggy Ridge. After I pruned the orchards in late winter, Jocelyn and I created the cider blends. Spring was all about protecting blooming trees from fire blight, a bacterial disease that can severely damage apples. We bottled cider in summer during the week and then did a quick changeover to operate a tasting room in the same space on weekends. A handful of local teachers traded rotations in the tasting room, sharing their knowledge and enthusiasm about apples and cider. Fall was the rush of harvest and starting ferments that lasted through winter.

Friends often asked me what my favorite season was at our farm. I'd sometimes say the obvious: late summer and fall, when one apple variety after another matured and I sampled a different flavor every day.

But the truth is, I liked the surprises of early spring.

A southern Appalachian spring might offer a foot of snow followed by a balmy sixty-degree day. Fifteen-mile-an-hour winds out of the northwest made for unpleasant tractor driving. Then the next day could dawn still and sunny, warm enough for fishing. I relished the changing days and the charming "spring ephemerals," plants that bloom and procreate in sunny woods before deciduous trees create shade.

But no matter the season, the cold concrete cider house floor always chilled my feet. Even my uniform of Icebreaker long johns under a Carhartt jacket and topped by a down vest was never toasty enough. From October through May I kept a space heater running under my desk in an attempt to keep my toes warm enough to climb ladders and check cider blends.

In early spring 2010, with Virginia bluebells blooming by the creek and cider maturing in stainless steel tanks,

I focused on the task of selling cider. Virginia had by now created a work-around for the state's complicated distribution laws so that wine- and cidermakers could sell directly to restaurants and shops. I had cultivated customers in local markets and Charlottesville. My husband, Chuck, formed a distribution company in North Carolina that sold our cider in Durham, Chapel Hill, and Raleigh. With expanded production, I could consider distributing outside the South.

I had a plan but still faced obstacles to selling our carefully crafted cider blends. Foggy Ridge Cider was almost always the first "fine cider" in the market. I spent more time educating than selling, and after landing an account the education continued. I honed my spiel to restaurant staff, timed to fit a few minutes during setup on a Wednesday or Thursday night. I was a pro at sharing Cider Wheel tasting guides with wine retailers. But every day I felt the difficulties of being a pioneer beverage maker in the South.

Early one chilly spring morning the cider house phone rang. Caller ID showed Chilhowie, Virginia, a town I'd never heard of. I picked up the phone and heard, "This is Charlie Berg. I'm calling from Town House restaurant and I'd like to serve your cider." That was a first. A restaurant actually calling to ask to buy my beverage.

While I listened to Charlie talk about Chefs John and Karen Shields and their small-town fine-dining restaurant, I frantically googled "Chilhowie" and "Town House." Gradually I realized this was the tasting menu restaurant I had read about in *Food & Wine* magazine. The chefs hailed from Chicago and had come with high-flying food pedigrees to this former textile town just off Interstate 81. John Shields had cooked at Alinea restaurant, and Karen had been head pastry chef at Charlie Trotter's. They were clearly setting a high bar in little Chilhowie.

Selling cider to talented chefs with connections outside Virginia fit my expansion plans. When I asked when I might drive over to let the Town House team sample our ciders, Charlie said, "We're closed today. I thought I might just drive to your place right now." OK. Another first.

A few hours later a car pulled into our soggy gravel parking lot. A handsome, elegantly dressed young figure got out. I don't think Foggy Ridge Cider had ever hosted a man in a dark sport coat, gray slacks, and black turtleneck, much less a woman as striking as the one on his arm, his wife, Anastasia, who walked into the cider house outfitted in three-inch heels, a miniskirt, and a white fur jacket. I was instantly a fan.

Charlie and Nastia turned out to be warm, smart people. We stood on the cold cider house floor and talked for over an hour. We shared childhoods spent in rural areas and a passion for food and beverages.

Nastia was from a small Russian town and knew how to cook every part of a pig. Charlie grew up in a small community close to Chilhowie. I was excited to hear about the elegant tasting menus that John, Karen, and Charlie were creating at Town House.

In those days I was often frustrated by conversations with beverage professionals and even with customers who visited the cider house. Cider was new in the South, and cider made by an orchardist with all the care that a winemaker puts into wine had never been attempted here. People asked, "Why isn't this sweet?" Or, "Why don't you sell this in cans?" Often, I felt as if I was shouting over a vast gulf.

Charlie *got* what I was doing at Foggy Ridge. He understood why I was standing on a cold concrete floor in early spring, tasting each tank of cider. He knew why I had spent the last two months climbing trees with pruners and loppers. He knew that work in the orchard was as important as the cider aging in stainless tanks.

By this time Foggy Ridge Cider was in the news—the *Washington Post* had written a glowing article, as had regional newspapers. *Southern Living* and *Local Palate* also covered our cider. But on that spring morning with flowers blooming all over Virginia, when Charlie and Nastia showed up at the cider house, I felt discovered. And even better, *heard*.

Over the next year I expanded our Virginia footprint to Richmond and Northern Virginia. I talked to distributors who could sell our cider in New York and Washington, DC. But my best sales call was always to Chilhowie. Charlie, Karen, and John invariably greeted me with something special: A handful of wild asparagus John had foraged on a roadside. A scoop of Karen's basil ice cream. Charlie always sent me home with a bottle of a wine I'd never heard of that I knew I'd enjoy.

I had found something rare, colleagues who really *heard* me. Who *recognized* and valued cider made with care from fruit grown in the South. This version of selling cider was not a transaction but a beautiful meeting of the minds, even a friendship.

It was easy to recognize the revelatory flavor packed into a Golden Harvey, a squat apple barely two inches around. Every time I bit into this diminutive flavor package I tasted a surprise: sweet ripe pineapple in one bite, spicy cooked quince in the next. Called Brandy Apple in its Herefordshire, England, home, southerners grew Golden Harvey for cider and for the kitchen but mainly for extraordinary flavor.

For over 300 years, the South's great seedling orchards offered a smorgasbord of flavor. Golden Harvey makes delicious cider and brandy.

Grimes Golden is sweet but mild enough that a hungry person can eat two apples in a sitting. Albemarle Pippin's complex flavor satisfies after just a few bites. Terse nineteenth-century southern nursery catalogs devoted valuable copy to describing flavor, such as Sweet Bough's "sweet, sprightly taste" and Augustine's "exceedingly rich and pleasant flesh."[1] Flavor, along with keeping qualities, drove southern apple selections for centuries.

Then, in less than fifty years, dramatic changes in agriculture and society altered the value that southerners placed on flavor. In the late nineteenth century, orchards that had met the needs of families and local communities became commercial enterprises, driven by the need for efficiency and profit. The South's rich orchards full of hundreds of apple varieties, from coastal Virginia to upstate Mississippi, stumbled on the road to the twentieth century, tripped in large part by a southern apple called Ben Davis.

———————

In 1850, farmers made up over 60 percent of America's labor force.[2] Today we envision this agricultural era populated with small diversified farms that met the needs of a farm family, with a few crops or livestock grown for nearby markets. But this view of the self-sufficient farm belies the commercialization of agriculture and orchards that accelerated in the mid- to late nineteenth century.

By 1860, farmers produced over 80 percent of all products exported from America.[3] Farmers increasingly viewed themselves as business owners in search of profitable commerce, not simply as crop cultivators or orchardists with a few dozen acres of trees. The nineteenth-century "golden age of pomology"[4] thus resulted in large orchards across the South, concentrated in regions where apples could be most profitably grown at commercial-scale production.

By 1870, apples were an important part of Tennessee's economy. Commercial orchards in Middle Tennessee around Nashville and Spring Hill grew early varieties like Early Harvest, Duchess, and Red June. Mountain orchards produced late-harvest apples.[5]

Virginia orchards stretched from the Tidewater and Chesapeake through the Shenandoah Valley and into the Blue Ridge Mountains. From 1895 to 1900, the state's tree numbers increased 100 percent, driven in part by agricultural speculators who advertised a 50 percent return on investment.[6]

Commercial orchards in North Carolina, South Carolina, and Georgia planted Yates, Shockley, and Gano, mostly in higher elevation areas.[7]

By the early twentieth century, Berkeley, West Virginia, and neighboring counties in the Appalachian Apple Belt produced one-fourth of the apples grown in the United States.[8]

Commercial orcharding in the South led to larger orchards managed with the scientific knowledge of the time. Whereas farm orchards had existed in virtually every corner of the South other than the southern portion of the Gulf states, southerners increasingly planted commercial orchards in regions where apples could most profitably be grown in large quantities for export outside the region. As southern orchards grew in size, the number of varieties grown in those orchards shrank. And eventually, the flavor of southern apples altered.

The Ben Davis apple epitomized this shift from small diversified farms with many apple varieties to large commercial orchards concentrated on a few.

In 1799 two Virginia farmers, William Davis and John D. Hill, moved to what is now Butler County, Kentucky, and settled in Berry's Lick near Davis's brother, Captain Ben Davis. Hill later traveled to either Virginia or North Carolina and returned with apple seedlings. Captain Davis planted one of Hill's trees, and the tree bore large, attractive apples that stored extremely well. Davis then planted an orchard with grafts from this tree. His apples quickly gained acclaim throughout Kentucky and Tennessee and took on his name. Hill's relatives took the Ben Davis apple to Illinois; other settlers carried it to Indiana, Missouri, and Arkansas. By the Civil War, millions of this southern seedling apple had taken hold in orchards throughout the country.

Ben Davis spread quickly and begat many versions of this mythical beginning, with several states claiming bragging rights for what some called "the joy of the nurseryman."[9] North Carolinians referred to Captain Davis's apple as Carolina Red Streak. Growers in southern Alabama called it Thornton. Kentucky fans conferred three names: Kentucky Red Streak, Kentucky Pippin, and Kentucky Streak. Illinois Red, Baltimore Red Streak, New York Pippin . . . every state that grew Ben Davis wanted to claim it.

The first widely published description of Ben Davis was Andrew Jack-

Ben Davis apple from Fauquier, VA, by Mary D. Arnold. US Department of Agriculture Pomological Watercolor Collection, Rare and Special Collections, National Agricultural Library, Beltsville, MD.

son Downing's 1865 edition of *The Fruits and Fruit Trees of America*. A few years later, the *United States Department of Agriculture Pomology Bulletin of 1898* said that Ben Davis was "more extensively planted in commercial orchards in the United States than any other variety."[10] By 1905, S. A. Beach, author of *The Apples of New York*, asserted that Ben Davis "is the most important variety known in the apple districts of the vast territory which stretches from the Atlantic to the Pacific between parallels 32 and 42."[11]

Why was this thick-skinned, colorful apple so popular? Ben Davis flourished in a variety of soils over a wide territory, from Georgia to Maine and Michigan. Pomologists refer to apples that bear fruit early in life as "precocious." Ben Davis was extremely precocious. Some apples are biennial, meaning they crop only every other year. Ben Davis was an annual bearer. It bloomed in late spring and avoided frosts that could destroy young fruit buds. Fruit remained on a Ben Davis tree until fully ripe. Ben Davis stored well without refrigeration, and the apple's thick skin and firm flesh did not bruise easily.

Within a decade or two after Captain Ben Davis planted John Hill's trees, his namesake apple appeared in nursery lists from Winchester, Tennessee, to Jackson, Mississippi. By 1877, this seedling fruit from North Carolina traveled all the way to Colorado.[12]

In Iowa, where it sold for a higher price than Jonathan, Winesap, and White Winter Pearmain, growers called Ben Davis "Old Reliable."[13] In Georgia, Prosper Berckmans described Ben Davis in his 1897 Fruitland catalog as having "fair quality" but "keeps extremely well." Wm. C. Geraty's nursery on Young's Island, South Carolina, praised Ben Davis as "one of the surest and heaviest bearers and best keeper of all."[14] The term "mortgage lifter" appeared in many advertisements for the Ben Davis apple.

Ben Davis was a handsome apple with highly colored yellow skin washed a bright red. Dark-red stripes gave rise to the term "striped" or "streak" in some of this apple's many appellations. It showed well in market displays and printed advertisements.

This variety was ideally suited for farming on an industrial scale. It was not, though, an apple that burst with flavor.

Ben Davis required a long growing season and when grown in northern states did not ripen fully, which likely contributed to its reputation for poor flavor. But Ben Davis had plenty of detractors all over the country. A fifth-generation Virginia grower described Ben Davis to me as "you're better off eating the cardboard box it's packed in." Nursery catalogs described it as "not particularly flavorful," "bland," and, at best, "mellow." In *Old Southern Apples*, Lee Calhoun repeats this quote:

"Very popular with hotel keepers. Few patrons have the hardihood to bite into one."[15]

By the early twentieth century, Ben Davis's reputation for poor flavor began to dominate discussions of this widely planted apple. In his welcome address at the twenty-ninth session of the American Pomological Society in 1905, J. H. Neff wondered "whether the proper penalties will ever be inflicted on [Ben Davis's] inventor . . . even though it sells better in London than Jonathan, Bellflower, and Grimes Golden."[16]

Ben Davis was the starting gun for apples chosen for qualities other than flavor and use. Though it did not cause the slippery slope that led to bland apples like Red Delicious, it signaled the forces that altered values about flavor and prompted the loss of southern apple varieties.

Ben Davis, the southern seedling apple that spread so quickly across the country, epitomized the commercial mindset that came to dominate apple selection and production. An apple had to be eye-catching and survive shipping without damage. It must store well so the fruit could be grown in large quantities and sold over many months. The variety must produce early and reliably, resist disease and late frosts, and be easy to maintain in the orchard. With industrial-scale production, growers' view of apples shrank to a narrow lens.

The early nineteenth-century diversified farm, the farm of "old agriculture," aimed to wrest as many crops and food sources from the land as possible, with a portion sold or bartered and the rest consumed by the farm. The commercial farm, the "new agriculture," was an industrial venture specializing in the most profitable product that could be produced on that site.[17]

In the world of new agriculture, the South had no comparative advantage in producing apples.[18] The Northwest's advantages in climate, terrain, and infrastructure led to this region dominating apple production. When cold storage was introduced in the 1890s, western fruit headed east by the train carload. The South's apples had to alter to fit the new economy.

Southern apple growing increasingly concentrated in regions where apples were the most profitable crop that could be grown. Orchardists discarded old varieties grown for centuries and specialized in apples that met the criteria for a commodity product, criteria touted by the USDA bulletins and, after the 1914 Smith-Lever Act that established the Cooperative Extension Service, promoted by local extension agents.

Southern orchardists also altered the way they grew apples. If southern orchards could not compete in the market for beautiful, cheaply

grown fruit, they could produce large amounts of fruit suitable for processing.

West Virginia, Virginia, and North Carolina growers were especially aggressive in transforming orchards to produce fruit for applesauce, canned apples, fresh apple juice, and vinegar. A processing orchard does not need to grow perfect fruit. Prices are lower for processing fruit, but production costs are lower as well, due to fewer orchard sprays and other factors.

Some southern orchardists pivoted to apple processing in ways that transformed apple-growing communities. In 1911 the National Fruit Product Company began processing fruit from the famed Apple Pie Ridge in Berkeley County, West Virginia. By 1915, the Cumberland Valley Fruit Products Company used up to 150,000 bushels of West Virginia apples to produce 10,000 barrels of apple cider vinegar.[19] Three large processing plants in this state—National Fruit Product Company, C. H. Musselman Company, and Knouse Food Cooperative—were among the largest fruit processing plants in the world. These, along with five smaller companies, processed half of the West Virginia apple production, 12 million bushels of apples each year.[20]

White House Foods opened a vinegar plant in Winchester, Virginia, in 1909. By the mid-twentieth century, Shenandoah Valley orchards sent nearly half of their apple crop to processing plants like White House.[21] Around the same time, Gerber and Seneca established processing factories in Henderson County, North Carolina.

Processing orchards increasingly grew a few apple varieties suited for canning, applesauce, juice, and vinegar. In less than fifty years, old diversified orchards populated with flavorful, useful apples that ripened all year evolved into a standardized orchard industry.

———————

The South's loss of rich apple diversity was mirrored across the country. In the early 1800s there were over 6,700 apple varieties widely grown in America. In 1892, the Cornell botanist Liberty Hyde Bailey surveyed fruit tree nurseries and found 735 varieties available for purchase. In 1910, a second survey found only 338 apple varieties available, a 54 percent reduction. By 1970, less than eighty years after Bailey's first survey, only 10 percent of the apple varieties he had recorded remained in nurseries.[22]

Even the seemingly indestructible Ben Davis was replaced by a more flavorless apple in southern orchards.

In the 1870s, a Quaker orchardist in Madison County, Iowa, Jesse Hiatt, recognized a valuable seedling apple growing from the roots of a bellflower tree and named it Hawkeye.[23] The 1907 USDA yearbook reported that Hiatt sold the rights to market this apple to the Stark Brothers Nurseries and Orchard Company. Stark Brothers introduced Hiatt's seedling apple as "Delicious" in 1895.[24] Delicious, which evolved into more than fifty cultivars sold as Red Delicious, met the criteria for commercial apple production—it grew quickly in many climates and produced a medium to large apple. It was hardy and survived late freezes. Delicious grew upright and bore a full crop of fruit annually. The apple, even before apple breeders modified its color and shape, had attractive, glossy red-striped skin that shined when polished.

But the Delicious apple, even the early version available in 1907, lacked a quality Americans had already begun dismissing—flavor. The USDA yearbook stated, "Though lacking such marked and distinctive quality as characterizes our best apples, such as Esopus, Jonathan, Northern Spy, Grimes and Yellow Newtown, this variety is acceptable to most palates."[25]

By 1925, a Delicious orchard was worth twice the value of an orchard full of Ben Davis.[26] By peak production in the 1980s, almost half the apples grown in the United States were Red Delicious.[27] Ben Davis and Red Delicious did not on their own alter the shape and flavor of southern orchards, but they did signal the push of modernity that meant the end of diversified orchards and thousands of varieties full of flavor and uses.

In the fifty or so years around the turn of the twentieth century, the South lost mixed orchards filled with an array of pink and white blossoms from April through May. Southern growers forgot about Early Harvest, a delicately flavored apple that bruised easily but tasted like spring smells. The southern orchard was diminished for having fewer Magnum Bonum apples, a tender, finely grained apple with a perfect balance of acid and sugar. Even Ralls Janet, an apple that bloomed late, stored well, and offered a juicy mouthful of ripe apple flavor deep into winter, fell out of favor. It was too small and not red enough to suit the demands of the industrial orchard. Southerners increasingly grew apples to meet the demands of commerce, not the palate. Hundreds of southern apples were no longer recognized or heard.

ABANDONED

Foggy Ridge Cider was starting to hum. Customers flocked to our weekend tasting room, especially when the Dogtown Pizza oven arrived on a flatbed trailer. After I made countless market visits to Richmond, Durham, and other food-centric cities, Foggy Ridge was now the dominant fine cider in North Carolina and Virginia. I landed distributors for Washington, DC, and South Carolina. With increased production, I could head to New York, the mecca for beverage producers seeking a national reputation.

The two new Foggy Ridge orchards were yielding fruit. Each fall I counted on bins of highly flavored Foggy Ridge apples as the basis for all our blends. Jocelyn and I had big plans for Ed Witt's pristine Bent Mountain Albemarle Pippins. Two part-time farmworkers helped keep the farm and orchards in shape. Wayne could fix any piece of equipment and drove our four-wheel-drive tractor on slopes so steep they gave me vertigo. Antonio, a lifelong farmer, showed up like clockwork for weekly orchard and garden chores.

The urge to notice the natural world around me, to grow an agricultural ingredient and turn it into something special, like a delicious bottle of sparkling cider . . . this was my driving force. I adored my new chef and beverage friends, people who were doing in their own restaurants what I was trying to achieve at Foggy Ridge. But while I was good at marketing and selling and even somewhat enjoyed the national sales director hat I frequently wore, the expanding business side of Foggy Ridge challenged me.

Production spreadsheets and distributor conference calls took so many hours each week that I felt I was back in the banking world. By now Jocelyn carried most of the cidermaking load, with my contribution limited to monitoring ferments on weekends and blending trials. I had completely abandoned my rare quiet time on the patio overlooking the orchard.

When an email popped up from *Mother Earth News*, I was ready for a reboot. I had written a few articles on cider for this iconic magazine and was a regular contributor to its blogs on food and beverage. "Would you be interested in pouring Foggy Ridge Cider at Blair House and the State Department in Washington for a Magazine Publishers of America December holiday event?" Hell, yeah.

I should have expected that an event involving *Martha Stewart Living* and *Dwell* would be over-the-top. We started at Blair House, the president's official guesthouse. I was stationed in the Jackson Place Sitting Room, decorated by *Mother Earth News* and *Natural Home* with an environmental theme. Cornucopias of heirloom corn, wheat, and apples covered every surface. I poured Foggy Ridge Cider while servers passed dove-shaped cookies ("Handmade!" shouted the press release) and apple-themed appetizers. Organic tea in recycled cups, chocolates on recycled glass trays, natural quartz crystals on the tree decorated with fair trade ornaments . . . and this was just the hippie magazine room.

Designers transformed six rooms in the stately Blair House, each reflecting the personality of the sponsoring magazine. While a server spelled me at the tasting table, I walked through each room, my mouth agape at the planning and work that went into every corner.

After appetizers, the event organizers bused us to the State Department, in the Harry S. Truman Building, where excess was again on display in the Diplomatic Reception Rooms. Foggy Ridge Cider was at each staffed bar, so I was free to wander. The Air Force String Quartet performed for magazine and State Department staff. Elegant gingerbread houses topped tables loaded with holiday food. I stood four feet away from Secretary Hillary Clinton, Oprah, and Martha Stewart, a career highlight, I have to say. But best of all, there was a full moon over the Potomac.

In my many visits to Washington I had never noticed the dowdy Harry S. Truman Building on the corner of C and 21st Streets. Though filled with priceless American antiques, the state rooms we visited that night felt a bit frumpy, decorated like a prosperous bank executive suite from the 1980s. After the sensory overload of Blair House, I was underwhelmed. Until I found the terrace.

The State Department's top-floor terrace overlooks the Lincoln Memorial, Washington Monument, and, best of all, the Potomac. That early December night an enormous moon rose over the river and painted Washington in a cold, clear light. I had endured nightmare

logistics to make this event—rushing from a meeting in New York to
fly to DC in time for the reception. I planned to take the last shuttle to
LaGuardia that night so I could work another day in the city before flying back to Virginia. Standing on that terrace, glass of cider in hand, I
felt full. But it was not quite the full I expected.

Two nights later, I walked through the old orchard under that same
moon. An owl flew through the trees so close I could hear its wingbeat.
Creatures scurried in the tall grass in front of me, and a few red eyes
shone along the fence. My boots pushed through leftover snow, and I
smelled the cold winter air with a hint of lichen. This experience filled
me.

The owl. My trees. Rock House Creek running fast below me. I knew
this was my tribe.

The trip to DC was a business win. Over the next year many of the
magazine contacts I made that night covered Foggy Ridge Cider and
did so in an authentic way due to our personal connection. I sold cider
to the State Department for a few events. And I have savored the memory of Hillary, Oprah, and Martha singing Christmas songs with a gos-
pel choir a few feet from me.

That long crazy night with the moon over the Potomac was a win,
but I was beginning to think I might not want to compete in that
contest.

———————

Southerners lost apples when distilleries closed and when national
parks arrived. Southern apples traveled west and helped found an
apple-growing industry that hastened the decline of orchards in the
South. Railroads, refrigerated storage, and the growth of highways altered commerce in ways that disadvantaged southern apple growers. At
the turn of the twentieth century, the rich array of flavors in the southern apple basket fell out of favor. Southern orchards became segregated
in the mountain South, where apples could most profitably be grown. In
the end, southerners abandoned their own apples.

The South's farm orchards in the early to mid-1800s teemed with life.
Trees flowered from April through early June with an artist's palette of
blooms: pale pink petals striped with deep rose on Early Harvest, Hewe's
Crabapple's brilliant white blooms. Each spring I can't resist dipping
my face in apple blossoms to inhale sweet and spicy fragrance. It might
be my imagination, but each variety seems to emit a slightly different
scent, lush aromas that filled the rows of nineteenth-century southern
orchards. Bees fed on flowers and swarmed the blooming trees. In many
southern orchards, chickens, pigs, or sheep grazed under the trees.

The South's first apples came as early as May. Pomaria Nurseries advertised Early May, an "excellent cooking apple," as ripening in South Carolina by the twentieth of that month.[1] Southern orchards boasted a big roster of June apples: Red June, Striped June, Yellow June. Southerners ate fresh apples all summer—delicious ones like the Georgia apple Julien, which ripened in July. In midsummer, growers in south Alabama harvested Shell, a juicy apple with a faint pear flavor. By September, south Georgia orchards were harvesting Taunton, a showy apple with cherry-colored skin. In the narrow window between late summer and fall apples, North Carolinians picked Magnum Bonum. West Virginians harvested Grimes Golden. In Tennessee, the deep-red Kinnaird's Choice came off the trees in October.

Southerners made apple butter with a blend of fall apples like Buckingham, Kittageskee, and Nickajack. They dried the Horse apple and other densely fleshed fruit in drying houses and on metal roofs. In November, southerners picked hard, tart apples like Ferdinand, Shockley, and Mattamuskeet and stored them through winter until the flesh turned yellow and the flavors matured. In late fall Mississippi, farmers harvested Stevenson's Winter. In Tennessee, they picked Limbertwig.

Opening the door to a southern root cellar or an apple house released a wave of luscious apple aromas—sugary, yeasty smells that brightened a cold season. In Georgia, Yates kept until April, just before the May apples ripened and the southern apple harvest began again.

Anyone who grows apple trees knows their unmistakable shape against the winter sky, the way their branches twist and bend. Growing a tree confers years of intimate knowledge, like the precise color of blooms and bark, the sound of leaves in summer wind, and the exact moment fruit ripens and falls to the ground. Apples imprinted their story onto every southerner who worked in an orchard, whether it contained a few trees or a few hundred.

In less than the span of a lifetime, southerners abandoned this rich orchard heritage.

America's pomological greats Patrick Barry, Charles and Andrew Jackson Downing, and Liberty Hyde Bailey connected fruit to home life.[2] They emphasized the bond between people and trees and associated long-lived apple trees with values like permanence and industry. The South's horticultural and agricultural associations, such as the Virginia Horticultural and Pomological Society and the Pomological Society of Georgia, published research and scientific observations conducted by fruit-growing bankers and physicians, as well as by full-time farmers. These journals documented a world of close observation by individuals engaged in hands-on cultivation of fruit: growers who wanted to share their knowledge.

The majority of southern orchards were home orchards, with apples grown for use on the farm and for sale in markets that could be reached by wagon, barge, and later by regional railroads. In the 1800s, fruit tree growing in the South was overwhelmingly practiced by white landowners as part of a diverse farm economy and in the mountain South by Indigenous farmers.

When I was planning the first orchard at Foggy Ridge, I found it easy to be seduced by Bailey's musings about apples as "characteristically a home-tree."[3] Prosper Jules Alphonse Berckmans drew evocative line drawings of apples and recorded sensitive descriptions of flavor in his handwritten Fruitland Nurseries journals. It was hard for me to resist the portrait he painted of apples like Equinetelee, which he called "a magnificent fruit,"[4] juicy and rich with a red cheek and crimson stripes. But as Gilbert Fite states in *American Farmers: The New Minority*, "The good old days on the farm were not good for millions of American farmers."[5]

Increased opportunities and greater income in urban areas, coupled with economic pressures on farming, enticed farmers to move to cities. In 1860, farmworkers made up 60 percent of the American labor force. The value of farmland and buildings was six times the value of the country's manufacturing.[6] But by 1890, off-farm migration had reduced farm labor to about 43 percent of the labor force, then 30 percent in 1910. In 1900, farm income was 40 percent of income for non-farmworkers.[7]

The opportunities for city-based manufacturing jobs grew at the same time that the complexities of farming multiplied. In the late 1800s, pests and disease began to threaten the economic viability of many orchards. Virginia orchardists first wrote about apple rust in 1889, a fungus infection that damages leaves. A destructive bacteria called fire blight (*Erwinia amylovorus*) spread like wildfire through southern orchards. The disease turns the growing tips of branches brown as if they have been scorched. Fire blight disperses on damp, warm days during bloom, a common environment in southern orchards.

New insects arrived, bringing a host of orchard threats. San Jose scale entered California from Asia in the 1880s, and by 1895 this tiny sucking insect had reached the South. A single female produces thousands of offspring that suck life from leaves, fruit, and twigs. The plum curculio dined on fruit, especially apples and peaches. The female pierces the apple, creating a round wound, and lays eggs just under the skin, causing the fruit to drop before it ripens. This powerful pest still damages twenty-first-century orchards.

Several monumental government initiatives accelerated the shift from small farming populated with diverse crops to farming as a large-scale commercial enterprise.

President Abraham Lincoln signed the Morrill Act in 1862, creating the US Department of Agriculture, calling it the "People's Department." The USDA's mission was to "acquire and diffuse among the people of the United States useful information on subjects connected with agriculture in the most general and comprehensive sense of that word, and to procure, propagate, and distribute among the people new and valuable seeds and plants."[8]

The Hatch Act in 1887 established federally funded experiment stations, with pest control as a top priority. These acts shifted the science of apple growing from amateur horticultural societies to the federal government. USDA experiment stations advocated the latest science in orchard sprays and recommended an increasingly narrow list of apples.

The USDA envisioned a productive orchard as an efficient business. To operate efficiently, orchardists had to gain a scientific understanding of pests and diseases. The modern orchard required mechanical sprayers and equipment for transporting large quantities of fruit. Orchards were no longer simply places where apples grew—they became industries with associated infrastructure, including packhouses for sorting and boxing apples, refrigerated storage, and housing for orchard workers. Growers needed capital, which required bigger orchards to spread out the capital investment required to grow fruit profitably. Farmers formed cooperatives to share packing, transportation, and marketing costs. Orchards became more complex, while apple varieties declined.

The North Louisiana Agricultural Experiment Station in 1890 recommended what today seems like an extraordinary number of apple varieties for this Deep South state: thirty-five varieties, including local apples like Yapp's Favorite and Hackett's Sweet. By 1908, the Louisiana orchard report stated that apples "cannot be grown for commercial purposes."[9]

Between 1900 and 1910, America lost 25 percent of its fruit-bearing trees.[10] Nursery catalogs documented the decrease in apple varieties. In 1918, Stark Brothers offered 95 apple varieties in its catalog and through tree salesmen who traveled the South; its 1935 catalog included only 19 apples. On the eve of the Civil War in 1861, Fruitland Nurseries offered over 300 apple varieties; the 1934 catalog for this Georgia nursery offered just 18.

The twentieth-century orchard was big and standardized. Growers planted single apple varieties in large blocks of trees, all shaped the same, all blooming the same color and ripening at the same time. Other than the pollinators spaced among the main crop, these rows of highly productive apples painted a uniform picture, a tidy sea of a single color, fragrance, and flavor.

Southerners abandoned farms for cities. Orchards lost habitat to urban sprawl and manufacturing. Disease and insect pressure complicated apple growing, raising the costs and knowledge required to profitably grow fruit. Improved transportation increased competition from other apple-growing regions. USDA policies pushed standardized apple varieties and advantaged larger orchards located outside the South.

The North Carolina Agricultural Extension Circular for 1936 recommended a short list of apples for that state's commercial and home orchards—Yellow Transparent, Red June, and Horse for summer apples; Magnum Bonum, Golden Delicious, and Stayman for fall.[11] The publication reduced the abundant crop of winter apples long grown in North Carolina to just four—Winesap, Shockley, Yates, and Mattamuskeet. The 1939 circular was even more succinct—only six apples made the list.[12]

In this abandonment, southerners lost their passion for growing fruit for flavor or for a special use. The region lost the unique shape, size, fragrance, and taste of its hundreds of apple varieties acclimated to the South. As southern orchards shrank, southerners lost their literacy for fruit growing.[13] They forgot the sound of an apple hitting the orchard floor or the first taste of a June apple. In one generation, they abandoned varieties that had been grown and loved for many generations. They stopped *seeing* apples.

They lost their apple history.

Revived

PRESERVED

In early September 2013, I was standing on the cold concrete floor in the cavernous Atlanta Gift Mart, a world away from ripening fruit. Foggy Ridge Cider was the lone cider in a sea of wine and spirits at my Georgia distributor's annual trade show. Over the next six hours, I knew the 1,200 sommeliers and shop owners would be more interested in the latest French rosé than in a beverage most had never tasted. But I was determined to tell the story of cider with a point of view—cider made from special apples that expressed the terroir of my southern orchard. At least the distributor provided cushioned anti-fatigue mats at each tasting table.

Over the last few years, Foggy Ridge Cider's growing reputation fueled expansion to New York and Washington, DC. Thanks to beverage professionals who appreciated our focus on fruit and carefully crafted cider, Foggy Ridge found homes in fine dining restaurants, casual cafés, and small wine shops. Some sommeliers and shop owners I counted as friends. Some even visited the farm to help with harvest.

Our expanded sales in Charleston, South Carolina, were equally satisfying thanks in part to an excellent distributor and a hearty endorsement from Chef Sean Brock. Sean was making big waves at Husk, his collection of restaurants devoted to all things southern. Like our friends at Town House, Sean *got* what we were doing on our mountain farm. In turn, his knowledge of Appalachian food culture inspired me to explore southern apples more deeply.

But other than Charleston, I was having trouble breaking into the Deep South beverage market. That's why I was spending a perfect September day standing on concrete in a massive trade center talking myself hoarse.

The Georgia trip had already included a few highlights . . . and disappointments. I spent two days with young, curious sales reps visiting accounts in Atlanta and Athens. At that time the Georgia market offered only commercial beer–style low-alcohol ciders made from apple juice concentrate. We found a handful of restaurants and a few shops that embraced our orchard-centric cider, and I felt hopeful that we might get traction in my home state.

The week before I flew to Atlanta, the small boutique Georgia wine distributor I had joined a few months earlier announced it had been purchased by a huge wine conglomerate. Not good news for a niche beverage like fine cider. The sales reps who took me out on "ride withs," account visits that included cider sampling, were confident that "things will only change in the back room." After years in the corporate world, though, I knew it was only a matter of time before this distributor's focus shifted.

But persistence is one of my strong suits, so here I was pouring cider in an Atlanta convention center for what quickly became clear was a virgin cider market. For my final career, my life on the farm, I had always wanted a big, long project. Growing apples gave me a sense of being part of a broad sweep of time. Making cider with the slow careful process we used at Foggy Ridge had a similar rhythm—I was creating something that could give pleasure from fruit grown in the South for hundreds of years.

Pouring cider for over a thousand increasingly inebriated people did not carry the same satisfaction.

For the first hour, sales reps brought the most promising buyers to my table. I talked to decision makers and made a few sales. For the next five hours I poured cider to restaurant servers and taproom staff who asked, "Is this made from red apples or green apples?" When they tasted our crisp dry cider, Serious Cider, the blend that the *New York Times* had chosen as "best dry cider" in a recent review, their faces puckered. "Give me your sweetest cider," they demanded. Even our fruity Stayman Winesap blend was not sweet enough for palates raised on Coca-Cola.

By 5:00, the mescal and vodka producers had the longest lines. I resorted to chatting up the winemakers on either side of my table and checking my watch. A condition of participating in this event was a hefty entrance fee and the promise not to exit early.

At closing time, I packed my sample case and rode to the Atlanta airport with an aching back and throbbing feet. The bitter weariness that trailed me home was even more weighty than my sore body. For years I felt that my work away from the farm was in service of the orchard and cider. On the farm, small experiences and close attention to growing and making filled my days. Now Foggy Ridge's growth was pushing me into larger arenas, spaces that fueled commerce but held fewer satisfactions. I was doing the big things for Foggy Ridge—creating markets and building a brand. But I was less focused on the small observations that, for me, made up a rich life.

On the drive up the mountain from the Roanoke airport I tried to forget the soul-crushing trade show. I thought about the difference between my relationships in Charleston and New York and my experience at the Georgia convention center. My day of talking and pouring cider had been a performance that lacked authenticity, one that left a sour taste in my mouth.

By the time I got back to the farm, the sun was setting over Tony Goad's pasture. His Black Angus cows looked like dark rectangles on the brilliant green field above the cider house. I walked to the Old Orchard, the first trees I had planted so long ago on a handful of cold November days. The trees towered over me now, full of ripening fruit. I bit into a Grimes Golden, knowing it would be too starchy. I hoped a whiff of this apple's delicate flavor might wash away my bitterness and revive me. I watched goldfinches feeding on seed heads. I noticed fox scat full of the season's last berries beside the tractor gate. A hawk glided through the orchard on a final hunting run before dark, his rusty tail glowing in the warm light. After a week in a world of big commerce, I found I desperately missed my wide place in the world.

The South's apples began with farmers who closely observed their fruit and replicated apples that reflected their desires for flavor and need for sustenance. Southern apples evolved into a vehicle for commerce, commerce that faltered as agriculture modernized. Today, twenty-first-century southern orchards are preserving and reviving old apples in ways as haunting and unexpected as that red hawk's last swoop through my apple trees.

No one has contributed more to preserving southern apples than Lee Calhoun.

Lee was a nursery owner, author, and mentor to countless apple growers. He knew that apples reveal themselves over decades through lived experience—the physical labor of pruning and harvesting, the taste memories of fresh and cooked apples. "When I started searching for old southern apples, I found they were hiding in plain sight," Lee said. "And people missed the apples. . . . The elderly southerners wanted others to know about their trees, how they used the fruit and how the trees kept them alive."[1] The southern farmers Lee met knew apples in their hands and mouths, not through a book.

Lee counted himself lucky to be among the last generation of southern nursery owners to know the elders who remembered apples from the turn of the twentieth century.

Lee was born in 1934 in Raleigh, North Carolina, and moved to Mt. Airy as a child with his widowed mother. She taught school in this small North Carolina community on the border of apple territory. Today, generations-old orchards climb the steep slopes of the Blue Ridge Plateau a few miles north of town. Lee's first apple memory came from the schoolyard at Mt. Airy's Flat Rock Elementary School: "We were poor," he said, "but we had plenty to eat and clothes to wear. I saw children who came to school with no shoes or warm clothes. One fall a local orchardist dumped a load of Stark Delicious apples in the schoolyard, and we ate those apples for months."[2]

Small-town rural life suited Lee. In high school he joined an Explorer Scout troop where he hiked and camped with friends in all weather. Lee's tenth grade biology teacher, Miss Claire Freeman, ignited his interest in science. "I've never lost the wonder," Lee remembers. "I've always had a question mark in my brain. I've always wanted to know, 'Why is it that way?'"[3]

Lee attended North Carolina State University, where he met his wife, Edith, whom he unfailingly referred to as "the love of my life." When Lee joined the army, the couple lived in Germany, Japan, and Madison, Wisconsin, where Lee earned a master's degree in bacteriology. When he retired from the army as a lieutenant colonel in the mid-1970s, the Calhouns moved to Pittsboro, North Carolina, and built a house on fifteen acres. His apple journey began with planting three trees from the Stark Brothers catalog—Red Delicious, Golden Delicious, and McIntosh.

Soon after, he met a neighbor who said the magic words: "When I was growing up we had apples you never hear of now." Lee recalled, "The fact that there were apples grown here fifty to sixty years ago that had disappeared intrigued me." He heard the longing for this lost fruit, and, as he said, "I saw the chance to rescue a history that was slipping away."[4]

Lee taught himself to graft from a *Sunset* magazine article. When he started searching for old southern apples, Lee thought there were perhaps a dozen or so trees to rediscover and revive.

"When I spotted an old tree I'd knock on the nearest door and ask if they knew what it was. Fortunately, southerners, older rural southerners in particular, have long memories. They'd often know the variety and what it was good for." Lee listened to members of a disappearing generation familiar with their grandparents' fruit. He found ten varieties, then thirty, then fifty. He recollected, "In addition to looking for the physical trees, Edith and I started looking for information on the history of the apples."[5]

Lee and Edith knew that for southerners, apples resonate with what the Welsh call *hiraeth*, a wistful longing that infuses memories as valuable as the apples' sweet flesh.

By 1986 Lee and Edith had founded Calhoun Nursery with over 400 southern apple varieties, many discovered on winter drives on rural roads in North Carolina, Georgia, Alabama, and other southern states. The Calhouns also began researching apple history at the National Agricultural Library in Maryland. In 1995, Lee published the couple's meticulous research in his classic work, *Old Southern Apples*. Soon after, I showed up at his nursery bearing a copy of his book and a long list of questions about southern apples.

———————

Some 370 miles southwest of Pittsboro, nurseryman Jim Lawson began his apple journey, like Lee, with just a few trees. In June 2021, I visited the ninety-six-year-old apple grower in his nursery storefront in Ball Ground, Georgia. Surrounded by dusty grafting tools and decades-old nursery catalogs, I heard echoes of Lee's curiosity and engagement with the world of southern fruit.

Jim recounted that he was ten or eleven years old when he planted his first apple tree. As is true for every event in Jim's life, a story was attached. He recalled, "Mr. Webb from Ellijay, Georgia, had a nursery at the time. He'd load up his A Model Ford pickup with bundles of apple trees and drive down the road selling them. He stopped at my granddad's country store. I started looking at those trees, and my grandmother slipped me a little money to buy some."[6]

He continued, "I set those four trees out at the edge of a cotton field, and there wasn't a one of them that was true to the label." One turned out to be Rambo, an apple that originated in Pennsylvania and was widely grown in the mountain South and Shenandoah Valley. Like Lee, Jim wanted to know the history behind the names and uses of the apples he grew. Jim said that in Gilmer County, Georgia, people called Rambo the Ellis apple or the Forward Streaked apple. Some called it the Weaver apple after the man who first planted this variety in the area.

Jim said,

That Rambo tree stood here for years. Everybody around here got apples off it to make apple butter and can apples. Rambo was a real hot apple in Gilmer County for making brandy. I sold a tree to a man who was a moonshiner and he said, "I might never make another drop of brandy, but I'd like twenty-five of that old Forward Streaked tree. That's an apple if you beat it up and put it in a barrel, you'd better start building your furnace right then because they'd be worked out [meaning fully fermented] in a few days."[7]

As a rural southerner surrounded by farms full of apple trees, Jim grew up in a web of agricultural connections with apples woven into the lives of people around him.

As in Lee's case, a few trees led to a nursery. Jim worked in the local marble mine and in sawmills. He farmed on the side and in the early 1970s opened Lawson's Nursery "as a hobby," he said—a hobby that got out of hand. Jim and his wife, Bernice, eventually mailed over 10,000 nursery catalogs a year. They drove to the Atlanta airport to pick up truckloads of rootstocks and shipped trees to every state in the country and Canada.

Jim counts his successes not in the number of trees he sold but in the varieties he revived. He rediscovered the Disharoon apple, which was likely a Cherokee apple that Jarvis Van Buren collected in Cherokee orchards and sold in nearby Habersham County. Van Buren's 1859 Gloaming Nursery catalog described Disharoon as an autumn apple, "yellow, large and first rate."[8] Jim grafted and sold Tarbutton and Tanyard's Seedling, both Georgia apples that had been shared by families through root cuttings for generations.

A Gilmer County neighbor asked Jim to graft his Tenderrind apple. Jim remembered, "He said he was afraid something was going to happen to that Tenderrind tree and it was the only one he knew about. The tree was huge and split up the middle. It liked to kill me because I had to climb way up into the top to get good grafting wood." Years later Jim sent fruit from this grafted tree to a pomology convention at Cornell University's Geneva, New York, experiment station. "Those people were real excited about that Tenderrind," he said. "They called it Tenderskin and said they thought it had been lost forever."[9]

Jim connected apples with people and with how people used their fruit. He found Calvin, an old Virginia brandy apple, in Kentucky, along with August Start and Summer Queen. Yellow Striped June came from a customer whose wife liked to fry slices for breakfast. Bernice liked

◀
Nurseryman
Jim Lawson and
scenes from
Lawson Nursery,
Ball Ground, GA.

Scarlet Stayman for cooking in late fall. Jim made cider with Yates. He said, "Limbertwig is the best to put in a barrel."[10]

Even in his ninety-seventh year, the excitement of discovery inhabits Jim Lawson. When I asked him about the largest apple tree he had ever seen, his bright blue eyes sparkled and he launched into a story about an enormous old tree still standing on a nearby farm that measures eight feet ten inches around with "apples so rough you could sandpaper a piece of furniture" with them.[11]

Both Lee and Jim shared apples and knowledge with Alabama nursery owner Joyce Neighbors and Tom Burford from Virginia. For decades, letters and grafting wood made the circuit among these apple preservationists, often filled with detailed history. Lee thanked Tom for Nickajack and Hoover grafting wood, apple varieties that Tom originally obtained from Jim. Joyce shared the Granny Neighbors apple with Lee, named for her mother, accompanied by its origin story—her father found this delicious summer apple with "a distinctive flavor" growing in a trash dump fifty feet from a Hackworth tree.[12] Joyce shared the Devine apple with both Lee and Jim along with the story of the Devine family who passed this apple along for over 100 years by sharing root suckers with family members. A strong thread of curiosity runs through their years of correspondence, undergirded with the generosity of apple growers who wanted nothing more than to preserve southern varieties.

———————

Preserving apple varieties in danger of disappearing requires curiosity and generosity but also scientific organization of facts. In 1886, the US Department of Agriculture knew that the carefully rendered botanical paintings in the Pomological Watercolor Collection could help identify and preserve American fruit. A botanical illustration is a scientifically accurate portrait that shows distinguishing features to aid plant identification. For apples, systematic pomology meticulously identifies those features.

Andrew Jackson Downing's *Fruits and Fruit Trees of America*, first published in 1845, bemoaned the "chaos in nomenclature" and praised the Horticultural Society of London for providing order to apple names. Rather than colored illustrations, Downing showed apples in outline because he believed an outline was more characteristic—more "typical," as botanists say—than a portrait. He carefully described each apple characteristic in this order: the size and shape of the fruit, skin color, stem shape and the size of the cavity that holds the stem, the shape of the calyx or blossom end of the apple, and then a description of the apple flesh, aroma, and flavor.

In *Systematic Pomology*, published in 1925, U. P. Hedrick defined an exhaustive list of options for each characteristic, identifiers that pomologists still use to describe fruit. Apples are not merely round. If you cut an apple in half longitudinally, it is easy to see that in addition to being round, apples can have an oblate (squat) or ovate (egg-shaped) form. The shape can be elliptical, oblique, or, like the Accordion apple, ribbed. An orchardist in Winchester, Virginia, who sells fruit to Walmart told me his company is penalized for sending asymmetrical apples. He informed me of this while holding a big Rome Beauty apple rejected because it was slightly lopsided.

Stems can be long and slender, short and thick, clubbed when thick at the end, or lipped when tucked under a sliver of apple skin. I easily recognize Harrison in a box of mixed fruit by its tall, sturdy, upright stem that seems too imposing for this small cider apple. The stem end of an apple is called the cavity, a part of an apple rich with identifying clues. The cavity is deep, medium, or shallow in depth, and broad, medium, or narrow in width. The sides of the cavity can be furrowed or ribbed; the cavity skin can be a different color than the apple skin, as is true for the russeted cavity and shoulders of an Albemarle Pippin.

The blossom end, or calyx, intrigues me most. The withered blossom can be obvious in some varieties. In others the calyx segments are so open you can almost see inside the fruit. The tips of the shriveled blossom can turn inward, connivent, or outward, reflexed.

The core and seeds contribute valuable information for apple identification. If you slice an apple around the equator you see the carpels, the tough sacks that hold seeds, plus a thin pale-green line circling the core. This core line can form a perfect circle around the seed cavity, or it can travel in a graceful elliptical stroke from cavity to calyx. Seeds are plump and skinny. A white fluffy material covers some. Apples with deep-red skin color often have burgundy-colored seeds. Burford Red Flesh, named for Virginia nurseryman Tom Burford, sports beautiful carmine-colored seeds.

For apple preservationists like Calhoun, Lawson, Neighbors, and Burford, properly identifying an apple was a complex task.

Some apples have a rough outer skin called scarfskin, which can be rubbed off. When I polish a Hewe's Crabapple on my shirt sleeve, this tiny cider apple gleams like a gem. Arkansas Black's thick skin has a characteristic bloom, a grayish coating that can be easily buffed off. Many factors affect apple color—where the apple grows on a tree, nighttime temperatures, soil nitrogen, and how long the apple was allowed to hang on the tree. Lee Calhoun taught me to think first of an apple's ground-color, the background color, which is usually a shade of green or yellow. With this image firmly in mind, it is easy to define the over-color, which can be striped, splashed, washed, or streaked in a wide range of colors: brick red, fire-engine red, burgundy, pink, lemon yellow, gold, all shades of green, and even a warm orange. In early fall, from a distance Black Amish apples look like black globes hanging among glossy green leaves.

Many famous southern apples—especially late fall and winter apples—are russeted, a brownish-red color, often slightly rough, that overlays what is usually a green ground-color. Many southerners call any russeted apple a Rusty Coat, though a Tennessee nursery listed a specific Rusty Coat apple in 1916.[13]

Apples have dots, or lenticels, often referred to as the pores of apples, since apples continue to respire after harvest through their lenticels. Some apples have as many lenticels as I have freckles.

Apple flesh can be stark white, creamy yellow, tinged with yellow, or even red-fleshed throughout or just close to the skin. Americans like crisp apples, and when the cells break cleanly with a loud crunch, pomologists call this "breaking flesh." The British prefer their apple flesh melting and believe flavor is best when apples begin to soften. I love tasting a Parmar when it falls from the tree and the pillowy flesh tastes like apple custard.

Once an apple sleuth analyzes an apple from shape to color, from cavity to calyx, it's time to describe the most difficult attributions— aroma and flavor.

Most pomology books describe apple flavor on a spectrum from sweet to sour. Cidermakers think of the triad of sweet, acidic, and astringent, and want all three in cider fruit.

Descriptions of apple aroma always disappoint me. "Aromatic" fails to evoke the piquant fragrance of a ripe Limbertwig or the musky scent of Winesap after a month in the cellar.

Southern apple preservationists like Lee Calhoun and Joyce Neighbors used scientific terminology but also embellished their texts with a personal imprint. This description of the Devine apple from Joyce Neighbors's 1998 catalog, a catalog that came to me from Lee Calhoun, combines science with the deep attention of experience:

> DEVINE Origin and true variety is unknown, but a sprout of it was brought from South Carolina to Gadsden, Alabama, in 1895 by Mrs. J. B. Devine's father. It had been in her father's family for many years prior to 1895. . . . Fruit is medium to large; shape is roundish conical; skin color at about four weeks after bloom is same red color as Carolina Red June at maturity; it then changes

to a greenish-yellow and as it matures the color appears red, with light red stripes and splashes, with most of the red being toward the cavity end. A little scarfskin radiates from the basin with small patches near the basin. . . . Flesh is greenish-white, fine grained and very slight tart subacid when ripe. It is a good early ripening apple and has been kept in Mrs. Devine's family now for 100 years by each family grafting a new tree when the old one appears to be declining. I had the privilege of doing the grafting the last time in 1992. Ripe mid to late July.[14]

When I was planning Foggy Ridge Cider's first orchard in the mid-1990s, only Calhoun Nursery offered an exhaustive collection of southern varieties, each carefully vetted and scientifically described. Most orchardists viewed old apples through a nostalgic lens. Older varieties were simply about preserving history or maintaining a family tradition. I'm thankful that today more than a few preservation orchards are providing more than a sanctuary for old varieties.

When Lee and Edith closed their nursery in the late 1990s, they donated their collection of over 400 southern apple varieties to the state of North Carolina. Orchard manager Jason Bowen stewards the Southern Heritage Apple Orchard at the Horne Creek Living Historical Farm outside Pinnacle, North Carolina. His pristine orchard filled with over 850 dwarf trees protects the genetic material of southern apples that flourished for hundreds of years. But this collection is also a vibrant center for apple education.

"People understand that we've lost a lot by not raising some of these old southern varieties," said Lisa Turney, site director for Horne Creek Farm. "Young people, especially, are interested in learning how to grow apples for flavor but also for their history."[15]

University of Georgia history professor Dr. Stephen Mihm grew up in Connecticut, where local markets offered a wide variety of northern apples. When he moved to Athens, Georgia, as a professor of history and director of undergraduate studies, apple trees were among the first plants he grew on his eight-acre historic farm. A neighbor gave him a copy of Lee Calhoun's *Old Southern Apples*, which sparked his interest in not just preserving old varieties but finding commercial uses for them today. In 2018, he received a USDA grant to create the Heritage Apple Orchard at the Georgia Mountain Research and Education Center in Blairsville, an orchard populated with apples that originated in Georgia or were widely grown in the state.

According to Mihm, "As much as preservation is interesting and fun and romantic, we are at the tail end of the efficacy of that effort.

There is a real danger that some of the most valuable southern apples could die out. I wanted to preserve apples but also get people to plant them."[16]

And he means more than backyard orcharding. Mihm is asking generative questions about the twenty-first-century iteration of southern orchards. "In many cases these old varieties were grown commercially on a significant scale and are very well suited to different climates," he said. "The genetic resources are valuable as well. These benefits can take us out of the 'isn't that quaint' realm into an orchard project that can benefit growers today."[17]

Mihm teamed with Joshua Fuder, University of Georgia Cooperative Extension agent for Cherokee County, to install the orchard and create a template for educating orchardists, home gardeners, and extension specialists. Josh's enthusiasm for rediscovering valuable varieties reminded me of Lee Calhoun and Jim Lawson, whose Lawson's Nursery operated about sixty miles east of Blairsville. Josh said, "The *Georgia Market Bulletin* wrote an article about the orchard and since then, the calls have flooded in. People still know where the old trees are."[18]

In 2021, Josh and his team planted over 100 apple varieties widely grown in the South, many originating in Georgia. Tanyard's Seedling, Tarbutton, and Rabun Bald are local to north Georgia. Cullasaga and Nickajack were ubiquitous in nineteenth-century Georgia and North Carolina orchards. He planted Mattamuskeet, an apple I first read about in Gloaming Nursery's 1859 catalog. When I peruse Josh's apple list, I want to plant Terry Winter and at least one or two of the four Limbertwig varieties for their cider potential.

In late fall of 2021, the Georgia Heritage Apple Orchard invited Dan Bussey, author of the seven-volume *Illustrated History of Apples in the United States*, to teach extension specialists how to properly identify apple varieties. The group learned about descriptors for the apple cavity and calyx. Bussey explained stem size and placement and provided tips on how to navigate the confusing issue of skin color. When the USDA began the Pomological Watercolor Collection project in 1886, apple growers across the county sent a flood of apples to Washington, DC, for identification. Today, Fuder addresses the stream of old southern apples

▶

Georgia apples (*clockwise from left*): Disharoon from Habersham, GA, by Deborah G. Passmore; Yates apple from Lamar, AL, by M. Strange; Rabun Bald apple from Oconee, SC, by Amanda A. Newton; Shockley apple from North Carolina by Amanda A. Newton.

US Department of Agriculture Pomological Watercolor Collection, Rare and Special Collections, National Agricultural Library, Beltsville, MD.

32546
Disharoon
D Haskell
Demorest, Habersham Co. Ga.

J. G. Passmore
10-12-04

79701
Yates
J. H. Young
Vernon
Ala.

m. Strange.
1 — 4 — 15
2 — 5 — 15.

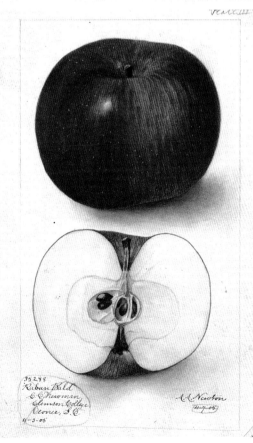

59523
Shockley
Deacon Taggart,
grower Squires & Goulds,
Oak Ridge, N.C.

A. A. Newton.
10-8-'12
10-11-'12

35288
Ribun Bald
C C Newman
Clemson College
Oconee, S.C.
11-3-05

A. A. Newton
4-7-05

flowing into this preservation orchard with an interactive spreadsheet to help his twenty-first-century team put names to fruit.

Both Horne Creek Living Historical Farm and the Georgia Heritage Apple Orchard aim to be much more than "apple zoos." Through education, by providing trees to commercial and home growers, and by continuing to search for old apples thought to be extinct, these are living orchards.

David Anderson, tribal horticulturist with the Eastern Band of Cherokee Indians, has planted orchards of apples connected to Cherokee traditions in Kituwah (Mother Town) in the North Carolina mountains and at the Nikwasi mound site in Macon County, Georgia. His young trees include apples long grown in the southern Appalachians like Junaluska (named for Cherokee leader Junaluska), Nickajack, Cullawhee, Indian Winter, and Green Pippin. David seeks knowledge from tribal elders who have grown apples for decades. His orchards aim to save varieties and educate tribal members, but his vision includes community building: "I want the whole community involved and not just at the tribal center. The older farmers are aging out, and I hope this project will give the younger generation knowledge to grow their own fruit."[19]

Orchard preservation and the revival of southern apples take place in surprising places.

National parks and historic properties preserve southern apples. The Orchard at Alta Pass near Spruce Pine, North Carolina, grows Aunt Rachel, Grimes Golden, Early June, and Limbertwig, as well as modern apples. This preservation orchard includes apples used for drying, like Wolf River, a large bright-red apple that originated in Wisconsin and was popular in western North Carolina and Virginia.

Lee Calhoun got a tip from an Oregon apple enthusiast that Carter's Blue, an Alabama apple long considered extinct, was growing in the National Fruit Collection in Kent, England. The British received this apple from France in 1947. The French trees came from Fruitland Nurseries in Georgia around 1860.[20] The circle completed when grafting wood returned from England to Calhoun Nursery in North Carolina, having traveled far from the original tree.

Preserving apples can at times seem banal, an exercise in nostalgia. But preservationists like Stephen Mihm, Josh Fuder, Jason Bowen, and David Anderson know apples resonate with meaning. They know that a deep-seated connection to people and place lurks behind quaint names. And that southerners' *hiraeth* is longing not just for apples but for what apples once gave us and we no longer hold.

SPECIALIZED

I entered farming with clear eyes. Granddaddy's rag-
gedy farm with its ailing tractor and a fence that constantly needed mending showed me early on that agriculture was a messy, complex endeavor.

But some yearning part of me had romanticized apple
growing and cidermaking.

And it was romantic. Each fall I luxuriated in the
sounds of apples tumbling into a harvest bin. I anticipated my first bite of ripe fruit, each variety offering
unique flavor. When Jocelyn and I filled scores of French
squares with cider blends, I felt the magic. Adding just a
few parts more of Hewe's Crab transformed a forgettable
cider into a beverage that tasted like a fall orchard smells.
I felt deep satisfaction working shoulder to shoulder with
our rotating crew of interns to fill a clean stainless steel
tank with a blend of cider made with fruit from my trees.

But Foggy Ridge's success in the market and our expanded production meant far more hours running the
business than growing trees or making cider. At the farm
I pored over bottling records and supplier invoices. I
headed to my desk each morning dressed for orchard
work, thinking I could exit after handling a few emails,
only to realize that by quitting time I hadn't left the office.
My consolation was a view of Limbertwig trees.

Some nights I sat on the couch, a cat draped over my
lap and a book propped open, waiting for the satisfaction
of a hard day's work to creep into me. Often I felt only the
tedium of one phone call after another. My days seemed
bereft of creativity, lacking a sense of possibility.

As a child I loved swinging high on our backyard swing
set. If I pumped my legs and swung my body hard enough,
at the top of the arc I could see across our roof all the way
to the curve in our street and then our neighbor's white

brick wall. I felt joy at the top of that swing when I saw my familiar neighborhood from an unfamiliar place. Somehow that pause at the top held possibility, the chance for something new.

Foggy Ridge Cider's orchards were over sixteen years old by this time. The realities of a growing business were eclipsing the promise embedded in growing fruit. I knew myself well enough to recognize that I had hauled my*self* from a corporate city life to this dream of a farm—in every role I've ever occupied, I am far more fulfilled as a creator than a maintainer. I entered orcharding and cidermaking as someone who has always loved nothing more than the top of a swing, the chance to see the familiar with new eyes, the possibility of creating.

Somehow, in the midst of growing and maintaining a business, I needed to recapture joy and the feeling of possibility. Perhaps Sue Carter could help me accomplish this.

I first met Sue a few years earlier through a joint tasting room in the nearby small town of Floyd. Several local wineries and a mead maker teamed with Foggy Ridge to staff a weekends-only tasting bar right across from the alcohol-free Floyd Country Store. We hoped this high-traffic location would inspire tourists to visit our businesses. Sue managed this operation with a warm smile and unflappable attitude.

Sue had retired early from a banking career in the Midwest to move back to her husband's hometown near Floyd. She was a logistics and operations pro. In seconds Sue created spreadsheets that I would struggle with for an hour. She offered a skill set we needed at Foggy Ridge, and after a few visits to the farm I was able to convince her to join Foggy Ridge as a part-time general manager.

That next week we wrote all the orchard and cider tasks on Post-it notes. We included orchard and cidery jobs but also the trade shows and market visits that had plagued me. By the end of our planning session, color-coded Post-its covered the stainless steel tasting table, each one representing a task in the orchard or cidery.

Our experienced farm team could easily handle the orchard plus take care of our 250-acre farm. The combination of a part-time cellar helper, our latest intern, and Jocelyn could cover most cidermaking duties. I would take care of weekend ferments and join major workdays in the tank room. In our new plan, Sue managed the weekend tasting room and cidery operations. That left the very big category of "sales."

In real estate, "highest and best use" is a concept that refers to a property's most profitable use. Like it or not, Sue and I decided that the highest and best use of my time was selling Foggy Ridge Cider.

In our early years I picked apples on every harvest day and sold every bottle of cider. When we grew production enough to distribute beyond our corner of Virginia, I made sales calls in North Carolina and northern Virginia. For me, this work was more educational than promotional. I wanted beverage professionals to not just purchase Foggy Ridge but buy into cider as a category. I wanted them to understand that cider, like wine, begins with agriculture. I always took samples from other cidermakers so I could talk about cider styles, apples suited for cider, and fermentation practices. My market visits lasted far longer than the typical ten or fifteen minutes of tasting and purchasing. By now, I counted many buyers as friends.

I was selling not just our cider but the *idea* of cider made by a southern farmer from unique apples that reflected a specific place in the South.

Sue's guidance made perfect sense—customers wanted to learn about cider, and they wanted to learn from the person who was most intimately connected with the orchard that produced the fruit.

We labeled my new role "chief proselytizer." I was not thrilled. My latest soul-crushing sales trip had discouraged me, and I envisioned more of the same in new markets unfamiliar with cider. I already missed the expansive sense of possibility that came with creating an orchard and building a young cidery—I was afraid that taking on a greater sales role would only push this further aside. I knew that at my core I was a creator, not a maintainer. But Sue was right, and I wanted Foggy Ridge to grow and succeed.

A few days later I pointed my car to the airport, again full of regret at leaving the farm. Chimney smoke snaked across the highway in a thick white rope, just twenty feet off the ground. Crusty poplar leaves drifted into the road. Burgundy Virginia creeper leaves wound around barbed-wire fences, sure signs of a change in the season.

This trip offered a promising visit to Nashville. Chef Sean Brock's beverage director, Kenny Lyons, wanted to add our entire line of ciders to their soon-to-open restaurant, Husk Nashville. As I wound down the mountain I pictured flying to Nashville and meeting the young, eager staff at Husk. I had known Kenny for years through Husk Charleston and was happy to congratulate him on this new role with the company and the chic new restaurant. I envisioned a creative conversation with the Husk staff. I was sure Kenny would have a few beverages to share with me, and I looked forward to tasting the Husk menu. I had as much knowledge to gain as I had to impart—perhaps I could find creative conversations in Nashville.

Slowly, on that two-hour drive to the airport, a realization seeped into me. I had been fighting change, a change I needed to embrace if Foggy Ridge Cider was to persist. I began to envision my sales role not as a recitation of facts and tasting notes in the service of converting buyers to cider. Rather, I could use my time in the market to receive knowledge as well as impart it. The beverage professionals I was visiting understand fermentation, the value of fruit, and how to match food and drink. They were all master storytellers who nudged their customers into trying new drinks by painting a picture of flavor and history. I could use my time to learn, to build relationships, even friendships. I could embrace change in a way that just might fill me rather than deplete me.

I drove down the mountain determined to embrace change. I hoped to recapture the sense of possibility and find a way to make it last.

———————

Last week at the Laurel Fork Clinic I heard a woman say, "Daddy's been gone twenty-eight years and I still miss him every day." My father died over thirty years ago, and I still think of him weekly. Memories, buildings, and trees last longer than we think. Wild apple trees line the holler along Rock House Creek below my first orchard, some over seventy years old. For decades Carrie Spence made delicate, pink-tinged apple jelly from these knobby, misshapen apples, some with red-streaked flesh. They are far too acidic to eat, but I occasionally tossed a few bushels into a cider blend. Just because I hate to neglect a persistent tree.

Some things last. But to survive into the twentieth century, southern orchards had to address new orchard diseases and market competition, both domestic and international. They had to adapt to consumer preferences and integrate new technology. They had to find business models that worked with increased costs to grow apples and lower prices for fruit. To endure into future generations, southern orchards had to change.

In less than a lifetime, southerners forfeited and abandoned their apples. The forces of modernity displaced, moved, and changed southern fruit. Southern apples became part of a centralized supply chain that demanded consistency. Farm orchards transformed into commercial enterprises. The only question was: What form would those commercial orchards assume?

———————

For many growers around Winchester, Virginia, the answer was summed up in the phrase "minimal input, maximum output." In the early twentieth century, W. S. Miller in nearby West Virginia led the southern shift to processing fruit by planting massive orchards in the Apple Pie Ridge region. The Miller orchards sold fruit to food processors like National Fruit

Product Company and the Cumberland Valley Fruit Products Company.[1]

Orchards in the apple-growing region that included Winchester, West Virginia, the Virginia Piedmont, and the Appalachians grew one-fifth of the country's apples. More than half headed to processing companies.[2]

For over fifty years, growing processing apples offered a profitable model for southern orchards. In Winchester, located on the eastern cusp of Apple Pie Ridge, this direction created an industry and shaped a town.

Consumers purchasing apples in a grocery store or at a farm stand value appearance. They expect big, pristine apples with bright color. Fruit destined for vinegar or applesauce get a pass on perfection. Smaller apples with a few smudges of sooty blotch or a small bruise still create delicious apple products like juice or canned apples. Growers can grow processing fruit with fewer sprays, called "inputs," to control surface fungus. Processing orchards often consist of large blocks of the same apple variety that can be managed with a standardized plan. A processing orchard is all about reducing growing costs and gaining the greatest production.

Processing fruit growers choose varieties that result in tasty applesauce and produce big crops annually. The mantra "minimal input, maximum output" meant that some southern orchards had a spot in an increasingly competitive apple market.

Robert Solenberger's Fruit Hill Orchard illustrates a family's commitment to land and their nimbleness in forging a modern apple empire.

In the late 1800s, John Thwaite, an English immigrant, purchased land in Frederick County, Virginia, and planted an orchard. Thwaite could have chosen the area for its large Quaker community, or perhaps for its flourishing apple orchards. Albemarle Pippin orchards were planted near Winchester as early as 1860.[3] His son, J. Fred Thwaite, planted more apples, and when his daughter Louise married Hugh Solenberger, their wedding present was a hundred-acre orchard. Like many multigenerational growers, Louise and Hugh's son Robert thought he wanted nothing to do with the apple business. But in 1959, at age twenty-three and after he gained an engineering degree, Winchester's orchards tugged hard on him, and Robert returned to plant more apple trees.

By the early 1990s, Solenberger's Fruit Hill Orchard covered over 3,000 acres. Frederick County produced more apples than any other county in the South. Orchards founded by Governor Harry F. Byrd Sr. in neighboring Clarke County had over 5,000 acres planted in apples with some rows more than two miles long.[4] Glaize, Bowman, Miller . . . dozens of multigenerational orchards, big and small, supplied some of the largest food producers in the world and supported a plethora of apple-related businesses in and around Winchester.

Orchards and apple-related businesses grew in tandem.

In 1915, National Fruit Product opened a vinegar plant in Winchester, and the company expanded its apple offerings with applesauce, jelly, and apple butter. In 1939, Bowman Apple Products took over a New York–based fresh apple and applesauce business near Winchester and expanded into canned apples, applesauce, and other apple products. Bowman eventually packaged private label apple products for Walmart and Safeway before selling its multi-generational apple business to the French company Andros Foods in 2011.

National Fruit Product Company, Capitol Brand Apple Cider Vinegar label. Stuart Bell Jr. Archives, Handley Regional Library, Winchester, VA.

As early as 1915, the C. L. Robinson Ice and Cold Storage Corporation stored 80,000 apple barrels. Winchester Cold Storage boasted in big block letters on the side of its brick building that it offered the "Largest Apple Storage in the World."[5] Green Chemical Company formed in the 1930s to supply spray material and other supplies to orchards in Frederick and surrounding counties. The Frederick County Growers Association built a labor camp on Fairmont Avenue near downtown Winchester. Barrel companies, apple dehydrators, bushel and box companies . . . apple-related businesses dominated Winchester and surrounding towns.

Robert Solenberger liked nothing more than to be outside, working in his orchard. His daughter Diane Kearns described her father's connection to the land, a connection she shares: "Dad expanded and followed the big-business processing path, but he also loved and cared for what happened to the land. He wanted lots of land to be productive, and growing processing fruit was the way to do this."[6] With National Fruit Products two miles down the road from Fruit Hill, a processing orchard offered a profitable route for this southern orchard.

York Imperial was one of Robert Solenberger's favorite apples. Commercial orchards in Virginia and Pennsylvania grew York Imperials for export to England until import restrictions destroyed the export market in the early 1930s.

Even if you have never bitten into a York apple, you have almost certainly consumed one in the guise of applesauce or canned apples tucked inside a pie. York Imperial's yellow flesh makes a fine-grained golden apple sauce, and the slices maintain their integrity when processed into pie filing or canned fruit. Lee Calhoun pointed out that the core is small, so there is plenty of processing flesh in every York apple.

York Imperial's fable-ridden history attests to its adaptability and hardiness—some reports say the original tree grew in a rubbish heap outside York, Pennsylvania, and yielded apples that, hidden among the fallen leaves, remained edible into spring. When Charles Downing christened it the "Imperial of Keepers" around 1850, "York" became "York Imperial."[7] Southern nursery catalogs often sold this apple as Johnson's Fine Winter. Lawson's Nursery catalog described York Imperial as "outstanding for baking pies, also good in cider. Keeps extra well."[8]

Growing processing fruit for large fruit-processing companies was good, until it wasn't.

The profitability of processing orchards began to decline in the 1990s. The big processors faced competition from foreign juice and concentrate.[9] Apple prices declined while production costs increased. Processing orchards began reducing their investment in new plantings and were slow to modernize orchard operations, such as installing high-density orchards.

Fruit Hill remained profitable because Robert Solenberger was nimble—he had always grown mostly York but also had "swing varieties" that could go to a packinghouse for "fresh pack" or, if the price was right, to processing. But by 2012, he stopped planting new blocks of apples.

Solenberger's daughter, Diane, envisioned a new direction for Fruit Hill. Like her father, she never thought she would remain on a Winchester orchard. "If you had asked me in high school, I would have said, 'I'm running as far away as possible and I'm never coming back,'" she recalled. Diane graduated from Wake Forest University in North Carolina and then earned a master's degree in physics from Boston University. She took a break and returned to the orchard to earn money for further graduate work. "I came back to computerize Dad's accounting and started working in the orchard doing whatever was needed. It turned out I liked it."[10]

Like her father, Diane feels a deep connection to the land.

Whenever I listen to Diane talk about her trees, I hear the strong vein of curiosity about the natural world that flowed from nursery owners Lee Calhoun and Jim Lawson. "When I look back on my life," she recalled, "I realize that everything for me has always revolved around being in nature. The natural world fascinates me. I want to know how it works." Diane, too, has a big question mark in her brain.

Her connection to the natural world prompted Diane to begin investigating organic apple growing, a challenging prospect for the humid Shenandoah Valley. "When you go out into the woods and come upon these old trees, there's not a codling moth to be seen," she said, referring to one of the most destructive apple pests. "I started thinking about this."

At the same time that Diane began exploring alternative ways of cultivating fruit, the market for processing fruit was beginning to decline. She remembered, "The transition started in about 2012 to 2013. Everybody knew there was a death knell in the processing business, but nobody talked about it." In 2016, she planted an experimental organic orchard on five acres of the Fruit Hill land.

"When you plant an organic orchard, you need to have a market before you plant. The processors here in Winchester are extremely hungry for organic fruit," Diane said. She gained organic certification for her new orchard in 2021 and sold her first harvest to Andros Foods for organic baby food.

While her father focused on quantity and a standardized approach to growing big blocks of single apple varieties, Diane said that growing organic fruit is "a different mentality—you will have reduced productivity. The apples won't look perfect. But by paying attention to what's going on in the orchard, you can reduce spray costs and grow trees with strong immune systems."

Organic orchard consultant Mike Biltonen describes growing fruit organically as working with the environment and not against it.[11] Organic orchardists need to know the life cycles of every insect that might damage fruit. Viral, bacterial, and fungal pathogens attack apples, so organic growers must be aware of how and when each emerges and how to prevent or remedy diseases. To work with the environment, organic growers develop an extensive knowledge of apples, from their root systems and the health of the soil to how insects and diseases affect the trees every month of the year. Conventional growers use this knowledge too, but organic production eschews chemical sprays, or "inputs," that are highly effective against insects and disease but are not rated organic.

To put this complex set of knowledge in perspective, Cornell University scientists list twenty-nine insects, fifteen diseases, and six classes of weeds representing dozens of weed species that exist in orchards east of the Mississippi.[12]

All this attention pays off in increased fruit prices and the "psychic income" of seeing a diverse orchard thrive. "When I walk in the organic block, I see lichens and other fungi. I see insects I've never seen before. The floor of the orchard looks different—we've planted clover as a ground cover to fix nitrogen and take the place of herbicides," Diane stated.

In Diane's words I hear an echo of other courageous growers who want to not only revive southern fruit but expand what we know about southern apples. When she said, "I'm trusting the ethos. I'm not sure where this is all going to go . . . it's a continual story. I'll never know all I need to know," I hear a curious mind embracing change.

———————

Less than three miles from the Fruit Hill orchards, David Glaize walked me through the brick and concrete building that houses Glaize and Bro. Juice Company, the latest iteration of the Glaize Apples family business. I was immediately transported to our noisy press days at Foggy Ridge Cider, with a grinder running full-blast all day filling the air with bits of apple flesh, a press squeezing juice from pulp, and the unmistakable aroma of fresh-pressed apples.

David's juice operation employs a Goodnature SX-280, a beefier version of the hydraulic press I operated at Foggy Ridge beginning in 2004. As the southern cider industry expanded, David and his brother, Phillip, began selling apples to cidermakers from the family's 600-acre fresh-pack orchard. In 2010 they topworked, a technique of grafting a new apple variety to an existing mature tree, a block of Fujis and Yorks with cider-specific varieties including southern apples like Hewe's Crab as well as English cider apples like Bramley's Seedling, Yarlington Mill, and Porter's Perfection. With an urgency that is common to this orchard family, they quickly seized the opportunity to provide juice to southern cidermakers while adding a profitable new venture for Glaize Apples.

"I started selling apples to cidermakers," David recalled. But within a few years, new entrants into the cider industry no longer wanted to process apples. "By 2017, most cidermakers didn't want apples; they wanted juice."[13]

David's father, Phil Glaize Jr., had to be convinced that the cider market was worth investing in a juice-pressing operation. But his own experience in taking over a family orchard business from an earlier generation weighed on him. "Open-mindedness is very important. I've come across many people in family businesses who think, 'This should be done the way Daddy did it.' Each generation needs to be brave enough to make the best decision they can make at the time," Phil said.[14]

Courage has paid off for the Glaize family. Today Glaize and Bro. presses juice from the Glaize orchard for cidermakers, both cider apples and conventional dessert fruit that would otherwise be culled from the company's fresh-pack operation. The brothers juice apples for nearby orchards that want to sell their apples as fresh juice. And, since founding Old Town Cidery in 2021, David and Phillip make cider for their tasting room in downtown Winchester and supply nearby shops and restaurants.

Old Town Cidery lists the apple varieties inside each can or bottle, a distinction David wanted to make with his cider venture. "I wanted a cider brand that represents the apple business," he said.

Like the families behind nearby Fruit Hill, the Glaizes have a deep southern orchard history. In 1798, George Glaize moved to Virginia from Reading, Pennsylvania, and purchased 473 acres a few miles west of Winchester, the first of many purchases for this land-hungry family.[15] According to family accounts, this early generation's profession as charcoal burners led to the lumber business, which eventually led to planting orchards on cleared land. When George's great-grandson Frederick L. Glaize Jr. planted the family's first commercial orchards around 1927, rather than grow processing fruit, he took the path of growing fresh-pack apples for the wholesale market.

Today, Frederick's grandson Phil Glaize and two great-grandsons David and Phillip operate the multifaceted businesses behind the long, low red-brick facade labeled "Fred L Glaize" on East Piccadilly Street in Winchester.

Since the late 1800s, southern orchardists have utilized apple packinghouses, often cooperatives serving several orchards. Apples arrived at the packhouse in bulk bins, usually large wooden bins with orchard names stenciled on the side. Inside, workers hand-sorted apples into grades like "Fancy" or "Extra Fancy." When mechanical conveyors and sorters became available along with improved transportation, the apple-packing business took off. Boxes of washed, shiny fruit headed to domestic and foreign markets. Five-pound plastic bags of apples appeared on roadside stands and in grocery stores.

Phil recalled, "My grandfather always said, 'The one thing that separates you from other orchards is the packinghouse. Don't let it go.' Packing has helped us keep the business going." The family developed an early export market to England and the Caribbean. In the 1980s, Phil sent apples to Brazil and built strong markets there and in Cuba with the company's Old Home brand. In 1962, Glaize built one of the first controlled atmosphere (or "CA") storage facilities in the South to store apples in a low-oxygen environment to retard ripening.

"For fresh packers, outlets are everything, and you need a lot of them. Markets come and go, and you have to keep your eye on all the markets," Phil said. "You always need a place to take your apples other than the cheapest buyer."

As part of their bent toward diversification, the Glaizes grow York and Ida Red for processing, but their focus is on the wholesale fresh-pack market. Growing fresh-pack apples requires different orchard practices than a processing orchard. Pristine fruit that meets the strin-

Apple packing line at Glaize Apples, Winchester, VA. Photograph courtesy of Glaize Apples.

gent requirements of outlets like Safeway and Walmart requires careful management of orchard pests and disease and thinning to increase fruit size. "We were one of the first in the state to start growing apples on trellises twenty-five years ago. It has helped tremendously to grow more apples on the same acreage." Capital investment in the orchard and the packhouse has been essential to a fresh-pack orchard like Glaize.

Behind the Fred L Glaize facade, the eight-lane packing line snakes through a 16,600-square-foot workspace. The twenty-year-old line includes a computerized weight sizer and color sorter. "Color sorting was a game changer for us. We were able to offer a consistent product to the chain stores," said Phil. Apples travel down a conveyor through the computer sorter that sorts fruit into twenty-one different packs by grade and packaging, from Extra Fancy tray packs to five-pound bags. Forklift drivers maneuver pallets of apples around the busy factory floor. Workers adjust dials and levers and transfer boxes and bags. I was reminded of a busy high-end restaurant with a cadre of skilled servers who all know their roles and who dance a complex quadrille every night.

Like Diane Kearns, Phil Glaize gains psychic income from his family orchards. "What's kept me going for forty years is wanting to preserve the land and pass it on to the next generation. I want to be ecologically minded and keep at least the same amount in production that I started with," he related. At Fruit Hill, Robert Solenberger started a profit-sharing plan for his employees so they would have something to rely on as they got older. Providing good jobs also motivates Phil Glaize: "We've had generations of people work at Glaize. I want to keep these jobs going."

Twentieth-century southern orchards have had to navigate a complex environment as they changed from farm orchards to commercial orchards. The question, "What is a modern southern orchard?" has generated specialized solutions. Fruit Hill pursued processing fruit, while Glaize built a fresh-pack wholesale apple business. Diane Kearns grows organic fruit, and the young Glaize brothers concentrate on cider apples and their cidery. The twenty-first-century iterations of these multigenerational southern orchards face more obstacles, some seemingly insurmountable.

The southern growers who have persisted are smart, nimble business owners who take risks and incorporate new information. Many have the generational privilege of long tenure on the same land and access to capital to fuel growth and diversification. The growers who have endured possess the same curiosity that drove Prosper Berckmans to experiment with hundreds of apple varieties at Fruitland Nurseries and the same question mark that fueled Lee Calhoun's apple quest. They bring courage to their orchards, the daring to attempt uncertain ventures. They gain emotional income from keeping land productive, passing it on to the next generation, and providing jobs for a community.

Winchester orchards have survived European import tariffs, rising production costs, and changing consumer tastes. Today they face competition from Washington and China, even higher production costs, and market changes beyond their control. In downtown Winchester the vacant ZeroPak cold-storage building covers a full city block, but orchards still embrace this Shenandoah town.

On our farm, deer hunker down every night near the old Spence barn along our driveway, nestling among the ironweed and goldenrod the same as they've done for a century. They browse the blooms on my lobelias in summer and search for tiny *Iris crestata* in early spring. I think of our land as their landscape, not mine. That ancient barn with the chestnut sills has a forever home at Foggy Ridge. I don't know if global market forces will allow apples to have a forever home in the upper Shenandoah Valley. But thanks to a far-thinking generation with the courage to explore new directions, they have a robust start in the twenty-first century.

EVOLVED

Early March in Charleston, South Carolina, could mean flowering trees and tourists in shorts, or cold, driving rain off the harbor. Over my three years of participating in the Charleston Food and Wine Festival I had experienced both. In March 2015, I was happy to be with a group of Virginia fruit growers and beverage makers in a sunny room at an elegant hotel off East Bay Street. At my urging, the Virginia Wine Marketing office had sponsored a group of winemakers, plus Foggy Ridge Cider, in an event for media representatives and the many beverage professionals who attended the festival.

Ours was a convivial group, with no hint of competition. At that time only a few Virginia wineries distributed wine outside the state. I had seen the reputation-building benefits plus increased sales from selling Foggy Ridge Cider up and down the East Coast. The Charleston festival offered an opportunity for Virginia wineries to meet some of the chefs and sommeliers who supported our cider and might be interested in adding a well-made wine or two from Virginia. This event included Virginia food specialties made by friends from across the state—Travis Croxton's Rappahannock oysters from the coast, Sam Edwards's ham from Southside Virginia, and lamb from Craig Rogers's Border Springs Farm near Foggy Ridge.

The expensive boutique hotel was a dramatic change from the previous night's after-party. After joining a panel discussion and then leading a workshop on cider styles, I had grabbed a nap and headed to a dinner featuring Virginia wine and our cider. The after-party cranked up about midnight in a restaurant parking lot, complete with a pizza oven that traveled on a flatbed from Floyd, Virginia; a whole lamb cooked over a pit; and table after table of wine, beer, and spirits made in the South. Plus a very loud band. Three years of Charleston Food and Wine after-parties educated me that a nap and throat lozenges were essential to pouring cider until 3:00 a.m.

We were all a bit bleary-eyed the next morning, but we smiled, poured, and tasted with an engaging group of beverage pros. As the event wrapped up, we gathered around Claude Thibaut's table to enjoy his lovely Virginia sparkling wine. Cappie Peete, the beverage director for McCrady's restaurant, ran up to me with her phone outstretched. "Have you seen this?" she shouted. "You made the list and we did too!" Everybody in the room knew Cappie was referring to the James Beard Foundation Awards, the holy grail for anyone in the food and beverage business.

McCrady's was nominated for Outstanding Wine Program, and Foggy Ridge Cider for Outstanding Beverage Professional. My phone started pinging and didn't stop for days.

The James Beard Awards are like the Augusta National Golf Club: you don't apply. You find out that you are a member when you see the list or get the call. Only one cidermaker had ever been on the list, Steve Wood, a close friend from Farnum Hill Cider in New Hampshire. I was thrilled that cider was again on this influential list. The James Beard Awards are an industry endorsement of reputation and influence, and I felt honored to be recognized by my peers. The next few weeks were a blur of congratulatory messages—plus more than a few requests from restaurants and shops to carry Foggy Ridge.

For me, Steve's James Beard nomination and now mine meant that cider had a voice in the American beverage discussion. I strongly believed that cider—the kind made from cider-worthy apples, fermented with care, and crafted to reflect fruit and place—offered a point of view deserving of a seat at the table. In every market visit I had made over the last few years, I stressed the value of cider made to reflect apple varieties and a specific terroir, in my case a southern site. "Finally," I thought, "we've arrived." And by "we," I meant both cider and Foggy Ridge.

With Sue Carter's encouragement and support, I had embraced my nearly full-time sales role at Foggy Ridge. I had thrown myself into educating colleagues and customers about apples and cider. I wanted people to know that cider can taste austere with a steely edge or smell like tropical fruit. I proselytized about Foggy Ridge Serious Cider, a delicate cider that tasted the way ripe peach skins smell. I shared ciders made by talented cidermakers with different apples and cellar practices, like Eve's Cider from the Finger Lakes, where Autumn Stoscheck makes complex cider with layered flavors. I wanted the beverage world to be as excited as I was about well-made cider from any region.

When Cappie held out her phone in that Charleston hotel, the warmth of this professional accomplishment enveloped me. Here I was, surrounded by colleagues from my home state, hugged by customers who had become friends. I was in a joy-filled room, far from the orchard or the tank room.

In the midst of that celebratory announcement, I also knew a door had closed for me. I was no longer primarily a grower and maker. I was a business owner. I was a brand ambassador. And this realization carried a mixture of pride and sadness. A small voice inside me said, "This isn't necessarily what I wanted apples to be for me."

In the weeks after our first James Beard nomination, I desperately needed to ground myself. Each afternoon I walked down the long mowed avenue through a hayfield to the big oak tree in our north pasture. Twenty years earlier, when we sited our home exactly perpendicular to this tree, I mowed a Bush Hog–wide path straight across the field to its wide canopy. I once read that the architect Le Corbusier planted lawns around his buildings and waited for people to create walking paths. He called these "lines of desire." The path to my old tree was my line of desire.

Throughout my life I've planted my feet more firmly in the present by looking at the past. When I page through years of personal journals I see myself circling the same issues again and again. Every decade I vacillate between creativity and achievement. I toggle between acts that resonate with meaning and those that signify a single-minded drive for accomplishment.

Reading these old journals was like spiraling through a labyrinth—again and again, I saw myself skirting things that threatened me and moving toward those that brought comfort. I took small steps to quell fears and celebrated moments of joy. Again and again I learned the risks of turning away from uncomfortable truths. I saw that there are things I cannot lose and remain whole.

A week or so after news of the Beard nomination, I walked down the mowed path to a seat under that old oak. I read a journal entry about a dream I had around the time Sue and I reimagined my role at Foggy Ridge. I was struggling with work and vowed in this journal entry to focus more on how I should *be* rather than on what I should *do*.

In the dream I was flying, using a cloth over my head to catch the wind. Even though it seemed unlikely, I soared and dipped gracefully.

When I came back to earth, everyone around me wanted to know the secret. I said, "There are no secrets. It doesn't take a special cloth. It's all in the way you hold it."

Maybe, just maybe, I could find a way to hold a special cloth in my changed world.

Orchards deep in the north Georgia mountains, less than a dozen miles from the Tennessee and North Carolina border, have traveled a surprising path to the twentieth century. The 1832 and 1833 Georgia land lotteries distributed Cherokee land to white southerners, including lots in what is now Fannin County, home to the town of Blue Ridge and Mercier Orchards. Today the Blue Ridge Scenic Railroad, a historic narrow-gauge railroad, bisects the town's main street and transports tourists on a four-hour tour of the region. River sports outfitters, souvenir shops, and restaurants vie for the tourist dollars that drive this small town's economy. From the downtown depot, farming seems far away. But less than three miles northwest of town, a multigenerational southern orchard has evolved to thrive in the twenty-first century.

My first visit to Mercier Orchards was on the heels of visiting Jim Lawson. From Ball Ground I wound forty miles north through the Cherokee National Forest. Here Native names are powerful markers of the region's long Indigenous history, like the White Path community, named for the Cherokee leader White Path and Cherry Log, supposedly a corrupted Cherokee name.[1] Jim Lawson had ties to southern apples so historic they seem preserved in amber. I was driving toward a twenty-first-century commercial orchard making its future through constant reinvention.

While almost every nineteenth-century Georgia farmer had apples, significant commercial apple production began in the northern part of the state in 1910 centered in Fannin, Gilmer, Rabun, and Habersham Counties.[2] Like those in Tidewater Virginia in the early 1800s, Georgia orchardists first found a market exporting apples that ripened earlier than fruit from other states.

In 1943, Bill Mercier purchased a twenty-five-acre apple orchard in the rolling hills outside Blue Ridge as a side business to his position as the county extension agent. His wife, Adell, and later his son Tim expanded the orchard, at first selling mostly to local consumers.

One early summer day still crisp with a hint of spring, Tim and his son-in-law, David Lillard, took me on a tour through the Mercier Orchards retail store, a rambling 25,000 square feet of market space containing a bakery, a café, and a cider tasting room. The upstairs conference room, where we met to talk about his family's orchard legacy, seemed too small for Tim's enthusiasm, his booming voice, and the complex tale of Mercier Orchards. Over several hours, Tim and David walked me through the evolution of eighty years of growing apples commercially in north Georgia.

When Tim's father developed the orchard in the 1940s and 1950s, Mercier Orchards mostly sold old southern varieties like those found at Lawson's Nursery: Blacktwig, Arkansas Black, Virginia Winesap, Williams Early Red, and Kinnaird's Choice. Tim explained, "People in those early days canned apples and made applesauce. The same customers came every year to buy apples for their own use."[3]

Detroit Red changed the apple mix. "Detroit Red is where Georgia got started shipping apples," Tim said. "It was one of the first fresh apples of the season. At that time, the only other option for consumers was year-old apples out of storage, which were not in great shape."

Georgia was not the first southern state to plant this distinctive early-ripening apple. Thomas Jefferson planted "Detroit large red" at Monticello in 1805 with cuttings from an Ohio orchard.[4] Andrew Jackson Downing described Detroit Red in 1845 as "being brought to the neighborhood of Detroit by early French settlers, and these disseminated."[5] Detroit Red was a popular southern apple widely grown in Virginia's Shenandoah Valley and Tidewater region in the 1800s.

The Marietta and North Georgia Railroad arrived in Blue Ridge in 1886 and expanded markets for north Georgia's agricultural products, timber, marble, and copper. Georgia apples traveled to Chicago, Pennsylvania, New York, and New Jersey.

Tim talked about his family orchard's early days of shipping Georgia apples to northern markets: "Dad would start everybody out in the morning before he went to work, but my mother was the one actually running the orchard and selling the apples. She ring-packed apples in baskets and sent them to the Blue Ridge rail station." Ring-packing consisted of loading apples in tight concentric circles from the bottom to the top of a container.

Bill Mercier was an agricultural leader with great foresight. He spearheaded the formation of a cooperative packinghouse in the early 1960s, allowing north Georgia growers to pack and market their fruit under the Georgia Mountain brand. While Jim Lawson was sitting in his cinder block nursery in nearby Ball Ground grafting a thousand trees a day by hand, the Merciers were among those launching modern commercial orcharding in the South.

Detroit Red powered the Georgia apple industry and Mercier Orchards' growth until a technological intervention put an end to the need

for early southern apples. Controlled atmosphere storage altered the southern apple landscape.

Apples are a climacteric fruit, which means they continue to ripen after harvest by converting starch to sugar and releasing ethylene gas. CA storage controls temperature, humidity, and gas levels to inhibit the natural ripening process of apples by reducing the oxygen level in storage and replacing it with nitrogen and carbon dioxide. British scientists developed the first controlled atmosphere apple storage in 1929. By the 1950s, Cornell researchers adapted this technology for apple storage in the United States. Today, workers in every apple region enter CA storage facilities clad in moon suits with breathing support.

Pomologists describe the low-oxygen environment of CA storage as a way to "put apples to sleep" and reduce their natural ripening abilities. But CA storage changed more than the ripening of individual apples. It altered the seasonal nature of apple production. Once an apple variety could be stored for twelve months or longer, orchards no longer needed to produce early, mid-season, and late fruit. If consumers wanted Golden Delicious in May, no problem. Just pull that variety out of CA storage and send it to market.

Controlled atmosphere storage shuttered what was left of southerners' need for seasonally ripening apples. When anyone could buy a good-tasting apple from the previous year's harvest at the nearest grocery store, why look forward to Carolina Red June, the first ripe apple of choice for southerners for over two centuries? With the same apple on the shelf all year, nostalgia faded for the faint tropical aroma of a Summer Banana apple in August. There was no urgent need to wait for Terry Winter or White Winter Pearmain to ripen in October. The pleasant anticipation of an Albemarle Pippin stored until February waned.

Mercier Orchards saw the effect of CA storage on its wholesale markets in the early 1980s. "All the big growers in the West and Midwest started using CA storage. Apples were coming into southern markets in great shape all year long," Tim explained. The wholesale market for early apple varieties from north Georgia vanished.

When Tim left a military career to return to his family's orchard in 1972 he had two strengths that powered the orchard's survival: a strong scientific grounding with degrees in horticulture and plant pathology from the University of Georgia and Clemson and an expanded view of marketing fruit from his time in Europe with the army. Tim began to change things on the farm.

"When I came to the business we were strictly apples," he said. "We didn't grow any other fruit, and we didn't have a farm market with other

◄ Fried apple pies at Mercier Orchards (*top left*); Fresh pressed apple juice at Mercier Orchards, Blue Ridge, GA (*top right*); High density orchard planting at Silver Creek Orchards, Tyro, VA (*bottom*).

products. We didn't even have cold storage. We'd pour the apples on the floor in the old apple barn and open the bottom and the top of the barn. At night the cold air would fill the space, and in the morning we'd close it up. There would be Arkansas Black in one pile and Blacktwig in another." The farm stand closed every year on December 23 and didn't open until harvest began again in early summer.

Tim diversified the orchard business and began selling jams, jellies, and baked goods. Son-in-law David Lillard joined the business in 1997, bringing additional horticultural and marketing knowledge. In the early aughts, Mercier Orchards was still packing and selling 70 percent of its fruit in an increasingly difficult wholesale market. In an effort to gain more direct-to-consumer business, the family began opening the farm store as a year-round retail operation. In my time with the Merciers, I learned that in this farm family, agricultural adversity spurs innovation.

On Easter weekend in 2007, a relentless cold front slammed into southern orchards and triggered another dramatic change at Mercier.

Record low temperatures tore through the eastern and central United States causing almost complete fruit crop destruction in the South. Crop losses totaled over $2 billion.[6] A warm spring with March temperatures two to six degrees Fahrenheit over normal had forced even high-elevation trees into early bloom, setting the stage for maximum damage.[7]

Charlottesville, Virginia, reported twenty-five degrees and thirteen-mile-per-hour winds. Asheville, North Carolina, recorded lows of twenty-one degrees; Blackville, South Carolina, twenty-five. Gadsden, Alabama, clocked twenty-four degrees and fifteen-mile-per-hour winds. Over 1,500 weather stations reported record-breaking or record-matching low temperatures.[8]

In the Foggy Ridge Cider orchards, sleet blew sideways and cold wind bent red clover to the ground. Hewe's Crab, my most valuable cider apple, was in bloom, and many varieties were at the most vulnerable pink bud stage for three nights below twenty-five degrees.

North Georgia growers lost almost their entire apple and peach crop. North Carolina's 2007 harvest was 71 percent lower than in the previous year. In the ten-state area affected by the freeze, apple production declined by 67 percent. A few cold days destroyed over 318 million pounds of apples.[9] At Foggy Ridge we harvested a few hundred bushes of late-blooming apples that escaped the freeze but lost over 80 percent of our crop.

For the first time in the history of Mercier Orchards, there were no apples. The expanded product lines of apple juice, jams, and fried pies depended on fruit. Tim remembered thinking, "Are we going to close our business, or are we going to get out there and find apples somewhere and hold on to our customer base?"

What became known as the Big Freeze of 2007 prompted Tim to once again shift his business model. He began working his contacts in the apple industry. He called growers in central Virginia, Pennsylvania, and states not as hard-hit as Georgia. He developed relationships with other southern growers and bought apples from those who still had fruit. "That was the smartest thing we ever did," he said.

The same gleam of discovery that I saw in Jim Lawson's eyes when he talked about hunting old apples appeared when Tim talked about the evolution of his family orchard.

The American apple story has been one of lost diversity, of thousands of apples enjoyed for centuries reduced today to a half-dozen familiar, not-so-tasty varieties like Red Delicious and Granny Smith. The Mercier story moves in the opposite direction. The Big Freeze pushed Tim toward an increased emphasis on direct-to-consumer sales. To keep customers interested in returning to the orchard, he accelerated his father's practice of adding apple varieties to the family orchards.

In the 1970s, Mercier Orchards sold six or seven varieties; the most common were Detroit Red, Rome Beauty, Red Delicious, and Golden Delicious. This would change through Bill Mercier's enthusiasm for learning about and growing the newest varieties. Tim remembered, "Dad and two other Georgia growers traveled all over the country learning everything they could about apples. They were members of horticultural societies in Virginia, New York, Michigan, and Washington. Those three did more than anyone to bring varieties with customer appeal to our part of the country."

Mercier Orchards was one of the first in the South to plant Gala, an apple Bill Mercier learned about in New Zealand. He was an early fan of Pink Lady. "We're now growing EverCrisp, Honeycrisp, Crimson Crisp, Fuji, and Gold Rush. Pink Lady and Gala are our most popular apples." Today Mercier Orchards grows over fifty apple varieties, almost all destined for fresh eating.

Jim Lawson discovered, collected, and sold old southern apple varieties, apples steeped in legend that offered a wide variety of flavors and uses from June to May. But most of Mercier Orchards' twenty-first-century customers care only about eating fresh apples with flavors designed for modern palates.

The desire for variety introduced another problem.

A direct-to-consumer business demands a nimble product line that shifts quickly with customer trends, a pivot that is not easy in the tree fruit business. Modern high-density orchards planted with closely spaced dwarf trees provide fruit growers with greater flexibility to meet consumer desires. Today, consumers always desire the next new thing, including new apple varieties.

Apple trees grown on their own rootstock, called "standard trees," are typically planted thirty feet apart, resulting in about forty trees per acre. Early southern seedling orchards consisted of standard trees that could grow as tall as forty feet. These dramatic orchards held trees that could live over a century, but the trees also took up to ten years to produce a substantial crop of fruit. In my first orchard at Foggy Ridge Cider I planted semidwarf trees, twenty feet apart with about 108 trees per acre. Today, these trees are a quarter of a century old, over twenty feet tall with thick trunks and lichen-covered limbs. They yield prodigious amounts of fruit but required years to reach full production. Pruning these big trees requires climbing with loppers in hand, not an easy task.

Rootstocks offer a reduction in size from the size the tree would attain when grown on its own roots. Since the fifteenth century, orchardists have had access to dwarfing rootstocks designed to create smaller trees. Beginning in the mid-1800s, American nurseries offered apples grown on dwarfing rootstocks, though they were, as Andrew Jackson Downing stated, "the domain of the gardener not the orchardist."[10]

After World War II, consumer demand for high-quality fruit collided with rising production costs and increased price pressure due to competition. Costs related to insect and disease control, weed control, and soil improvement are about the same per acre regardless of the per-acre fruit production. The solution to this monetary squeeze was to gain more bushels of apples per acre. And the vehicle to achieve this was the apple tree itself.

Though dwarfing rootstocks had been available for centuries, it was not until England's East Malling Horticultural Research Station began researching them in 1912 that dwarf rootstocks were standardized. East Malling developed the first well-documented commercial rootstocks, identified by the prefix "MM." I grafted the original Foggy Ridge test orchard using MM111 rootstock, which creates a tree that is 80 percent of the size each variety would reach on its own roots. The two production orchards were grafted on MM7, which creates a tree that is 60 percent of the size of a standard tree. By 1937, American nurseries began offering dwarf apple trees grown on East Malling rootstocks.[11]

Apples are a long game—apple trees produce fruit for decades. Even today many growers I know resist removing bearing trees, even if the variety is not profitable. Growing apples on dwarf rootstock was risky and required new pruning and maintenance practices. Some rootstocks turned out to be incompatible with certain varieties.

Harold B. Tukey shifted the rootstock paradigm with his 1964 book, *Dwarfed Fruit Trees for Orchard, Garden, and Home*. A Cornell horticulture professor and former president of the American Society for Horticultural Science, Tukey made a cogent case for dwarf fruit trees and educated growers on how to plant and grow what came to be called a "high density orchard." Drawing on four decades of research, he advocated planting dwarf trees to achieve harvestable apples in just a few years rather than in six or seven. A dwarf orchard, he asserted, would produce fruit annually and cost less to spray, prune, and harvest. Better light penetration meant better color and bigger apples.[12]

Tukey also emphasized a fact that Tim Mercier seized upon: dwarf rootstocks allowed growers to more quickly meet consumers' demand for new apple varieties.

Today, high density orchards are the new normal. Using rootstocks, people tame apple trees to a shape that fits our twenty-first-century requirements. Corseted orchards filled with dwarf trees trained like vineyards have taken the place of tall trees swaying in the wind. A high-density orchard holds rows of fruit-bearing wood planted close together, displayed on a trellis system that splays the trees for good light distribution. Dr. Greg Peck, a Cornell pomologist and cider researcher, says that today's ideal apple tree is "a stick with lots of apples growing on it."[13] High-density orchards can consist of over 1,000 trees per acre, trees that will bear fruit in two to three years. Even with an installation cost of approximately $10,000 to $24,000 per acre, high-density is the direction for modern orchards.[14]

————————

Tim Mercier said, "High-density was a game changer."

High-density planting allowed growers to plant new apple varieties bred for modern consumer palates and get the apples to market more quickly. Even though the dwarf trees were ten feet rather than forty feet tall, a high-density planting yielded more fruit per acre and was easier to maintain than an orchard on semidwarf rootstock.

From consumers' standpoint, high-density meant variety. Tim put it like this: "Not everybody wants vanilla ice cream every time they go to the store." Today Mercier Orchards sells scores of apple varieties, and customers regularly ask for the latest.

There is a flip side of offering a wider range of apple varieties and flavors. Apple breeders and growers have created the expectation among consumers for "new and different" varieties in the apple aisle. Even with high-density planting, growing tree fruit does not allow for quick adjustment. New varieties might not perform well in Mercier's north

Georgia site, or they may experience disease or pest problems. David lamented, "Consumers only want what you tell them to want. I can spend the last fourteen years perfecting Jonagold and now I have to put in Cosmic Crisp because it's the latest offering."

Modern apples like Cosmic Crisp have Facebook pages, Twitter accounts, and public relations firms. Fruit growers in eastern Washington have invested $10.1 million over four years in marketing Cosmic Crisp.[15] Making the case for purchasing less-well-known but flavorful older apples adapted to Georgia orchards is a hard sell in the face of modern apple marketing campaigns.

It was this balance of old and new, tradition and innovation, that struck me most strongly in my time at Mercier Orchards. Tim and David were clear about the central value of their business. "We want to stay true to who we are, a family business growing fruit and finding a way to make a living off the orchard and our land," David asserted. And Tim backed him up by saying, "Instead of trying to be everything in the book, we want to do the things we are really good at and that make us a good return."

Tim's mother sold old southern varieties like Blacktwig and Kinnaird's Choice to customers who canned apples and applesauce for their families. The Merciers shipped early apples like Detroit Red to cities outside the South and then grew Red, Golden, and Rome for the wholesale market, which was 80 percent of their business.

Today, Mercier Orchards' more than fifty varieties of apples grow on 200 acres. The Merciers pack 20 to 30 percent of their fruit for wholesale and sell the rest direct-to-consumer in their expansive retail operation. Mercier Orchards Cider produces over 9,000 cases of cider and plans to expand. What was once a market stand selling fruit seven months a year now offers a café, a bakery, a gift shop, tractor tours, and a cider tasting room. The orchard is less than ninety miles from Atlanta. On a busy fall Saturday, over 5,000 customers might visit the U-Pick orchard. Over 600,000 people visit Mercier Orchards each year.

When I asked Tim what his parents would think if they saw Mercier Orchards today, he just laughed. "Dad would just look on in amazement. Mom would probably say, 'What in the world are you doing?'" A business doesn't always evolve in expected ways.

After our conversation, I walked around the Mercier retail space, packed with customers on an early summer Friday afternoon. I bought a fried apple pie made on-site. In 1965, Tim's mother began cooking fried pies in a cast iron frying pan in the original apple house. Now the bakery is the most profitable business unit for Mercier Orchards. All five locations of The Varsity, a storied Atlanta fast-food chain, sell Mercier fried apple pies, as do quite a few other Atlanta restaurants. The family business recently signed a contract for national distribution for its fried pies. I thought about David's desire to stay true to their family business roots and the complexities he will face with nationwide pie distribution.

The crust crackled as I took my first bite. The not-too-sweet apple filling tasted like ripe apples, with a subtle hint of added spice. I walked through two huge parking lots alongside customers loaded with apples, fried pies, and cider. I could only imagine what fall would look like.

The balancing act of Mercier Orchards' eighty-year evolution from a side business shipping early-season apples to northern markets, to a full-scale consumer-focused enterprise tells a tale of one family determined to constantly revive their orchard. Some modern growers scoff at this agritourism model of orcharding. Some think that in a business like Mercier, apples are merely the shill for a retail enterprise. I lament that marketing campaigns draw consumers to apples with Twitter accounts and simple flavor. I fear that we are in danger of abandoning the complex taste and history of old southern fruit.

But even though fried pies and fermented cider may seem to lie at the center of the Mercier model, each element of this business is aimed at keeping southern apple trees in the ground.

So far, this balancing act is working.

EXPLORED

The old barn by our driveway has been collapsing for fifty years. In the late nineteenth century the Spence family used this four-stall barn built with chestnut sills for livestock. Our ninety-year-old neighbor, Carrie Spence, told me about driving an ox-drawn wagon to the canning factory to sell produce and can vegetables for her family of nine children. When we bought our farm in 1996 I thought the barn would collapse in a year or two, but it's been a slow decay. We might repurpose the chestnut, but I hated to pull down a persistent barn.

Persistence is a strength I have leaned on all my life. But twenty years after planting my first orchard, this trait was not serving me. Sue's superb planning skills and my market work expanded Foggy Ridge's distribution to cover the East Coast, south to New Orleans, and most recently Chicago. Jocelyn and a rotating crew of interns and assistants created high-quality cider that reflected the fruit from our orchard. Ed Witt's Albemarle Pippins and Silver Creek Orchards' Old Virginia Winesaps contributed to our cider blends. My role on our three-woman management team was "national sales manager," with orchard and cellar work on the side.

National food and beverage publications praised our ciders, including one memorable month in which both *Martha Stewart Living* and *Penthouse* reviewed Foggy Ridge. I used our platform at conferences and festivals to preach the virtues of cider made from apples chosen for cidermaking. I extolled orchard terroir with journalists and beverage bloggers.

The skills and energy we all threw at this little business were paying off. At least it looked that way. Almost twenty years earlier, when I designed the cidery, I sized the space to make about 2,000 cases of cider a year. With production now over 5,200 cases, we were far from efficient. Tall stainless fermenters crowded the tank room. The cider staff joked that I was the only one narrow enough to squeeze between the tanks to pressure-wash the back walls. Our multipurpose crush pad hosted apple pressing in fall, fermenting in winter, and bottling in spring. Plus, nine months a year we did a quick changeover on weekends to use the same space for cider tastings.

My work life centered on building relationships in all our markets. Close connections with distributors and customers fueled me. Soulful conversations with talented chefs and beverage professionals in our many markets always sent me home inspired to try new things in the cellar and orchard. I had learned to say "no" to massive trade shows. I no longer called on chain stores or restaurants that really wanted a cheap version of "cider beer."

This persistent work filled my life to overflowing, but the scale was tilted more strongly toward accomplishment than meaning. And that was my lifelong conundrum: chasing a success that often lost its gloss.

But it was hard for me to reimagine success, especially success that led to the Chicago Lyric Theatre Opera.

In May 2018, Chuck and I traveled to Chicago as a finalist for the James Beard Award for Outstanding Beverage Professional. This was my fourth nomination and second trip to Chicago as a finalist. I was thrilled to be with chef friends from across the South who were also on the prestigious "short list." The morning of the ceremony, the Southern Foodways Alliance hosted an event at Chicago's Billy Reid clothing store to celebrate the "southern mafia," the many nominees from the region.

The crowd spilled onto West Randolph Street trailing aromas of spice and smoke. Chuck and I waded into a group of friends and new faces, all connected to the South's food and beverage community. It felt like a homecoming, but one with a tense undercurrent of high stakes. There were lots of masculine high-fives in the adrenaline-fueled room. Every other sentence was some version of "this must be your year." Newcomers jockeyed to get face time with the kingmakers. When introducing me to his staff, one multiple-Beard-winning chef referred to me as "new to the game," a statement that momentarily stunned me. I later discovered I had founded Foggy Ridge six years before he opened his first restaurant. Everyone seemed burdened with anxiety and agendas.

For restaurants, a Beard win is a very big deal. This recognition puts customers in seats. It attracts investors and can lead to more firm financial footing. In spite of the "I'm just honored to be here" comments, the event felt strained. "It's no wonder," I thought.

While I felt privileged to be among this group of professionals at the top of their game, I also knew that as much as I would enjoy the recognition, a Beard award would not change my business or my life. Our previous nominations and short listing had led to more sales and generated interest from distributors. But I knew even a win would not transform a niche endeavor of growing apples and making cider in a remote corner of the South.

At that southern breakfast with fiery Memphis Hot Chicken and overly strong cocktails, I began to feel as if I was circling again, revolving around pleasures and problems I had encountered in the past. I squeezed my way through crowds packed into rooms full of Alabama designer Billy Reid's casually elegant clothing. Even as I greeted friends I started to feel removed from the buzz of the room, uncomfortable in my skin. Too many eyes slid across my face in search of a more profitable conversation. I felt surrounded by people intent on performing. A vague regret crept into the day's satisfaction.

This feeling of remove, of being there yet not there, continued through a beautiful dinner with John and Karen Shields at Smyth restaurant, the chefs who endorsed our cider many years earlier at their first restaurant in Chilhowie, Virginia. This was an industry night—big-name chefs and wine writers filled every seat in the elegant dining room named for Smyth County, Virginia. I hugged friends and savored every bite, proud of my home state that inspired the Shieldses' cooking. But a change percolated inside me.

At the awards ceremony we sat in a long row filled with the owners and staff from The Dabney, one of Foggy Ridge Cider's first restaurant accounts in Washington, DC. We roared when Chef Jeremiah Langhorne won Best Chef Mid-Atlantic. Jeremiah's surprised grin and the excitement from the restaurant team pulled me into the moment, and I was, for a beat or two, entirely present.

As the night wore on, I knew that a shift was underway at my end of the row in the Lyric Theatre. In spite of the gratifying validation. In spite of friends around me. I knew my line of desire didn't live in this room.

We had one drink at one after-party, a beginner's dip into festivities that continued all night. I wanted to hold on to my favorite images from the day, unwilling to dilute them.

The next day we flew back to Virginia. By the time I turned onto our drive by the falling-down chestnut barn, my mind was clear. The time in Chicago was lovely, but the joy there would not persist. I needed to find a new path.

There is not an unattractive route from our farm to Silver Creek Orchards. For most trips to Ruth and John Saunderses' orchards in Nelson
County, Virginia, I liked to exit Interstate 81 at Steeles Tavern and travel
Crabtree Falls Highway over Big Spy Mountain. Driving the narrow
switchback road never failed to calm me. As I looped back and forth
over the South Fork of the Tye River, my mind emptied and I drank in
the shining water and dense green forest. Just before Tyro, where the
Appalachian Trail crosses the Tye River, Crabtree Falls Highway depos-
ited me in a wide valley carpeted with cow pastures bisected by trout
streams.

To the east, orchards lined the slopes of the Blue Ridge Mountains,
just as they have for over 200 years. I always felt at home when I first
saw that generous river valley with its soft views of gentle hillsides and
the rows on rows of apples snaking up the slopes. Dr. Rich Marini was
the pomologist at Virginia Tech when he wrote that "the best Virginia
apples are grown at elevations higher than 800 feet in the western
part of the state." Using this description, prime Virginia apple territory stretches from the north end of the Shenandoah Valley to the Blue
Ridge Plateau, home to Foggy Ridge's orchards. Nelson County sits
right in the middle, and this land "seems born to grow apples."[1]

Virginia nurseryman Tom Burford always described this region by
saying, "France has its Burgundy and Champagne, but we have the eastern slope of the Blue Ridge."[2]

Like so many Virginia counties, Nelson County is named for a white
slave-owner who once owned at least 400 individuals. Thomas Nelson
signed the Declaration of Independence, served as governor of Virginia,
and grew tobacco. I can't find a record of Nelson's orchards, but apples
likely grew on his plantations near Yorktown or in Hanover County,
where he spent his last years just a hundred miles from Nelson County's Tye River.

Apples have a long history in Nelson County. The Monacan people
grew corn, beans, and squash on this land for centuries and could have
cultivated fruit trees. In 1814, William Massie planted an Albemarle
Pippin orchard near Massie's Mill, one of the first commercial orchards
in the area.[3] Massie was a slave owner, so enslaved men and women
almost certainly performed the labor of clearing land and planting
apple trees. After first purchasing apple trees from the Prince Nursery
in Queens, New York, Massie abandoned non-southern apples, and enslaved field-workers performed the skilled work of grafting apple trees
from "old stock" growing on the farm.[4]

Today County Road 666 bisects this rich orchard land and likely follows a roadway built by enslaved people that connected Massie's three properties, Level Green, Pharsalia, and Tyro.[5] Though no longer planted in Pippin apples, the Saunderses' Silver Creek Orchards encompasses the old Massie orchard at Pharsalia.

Apple production lagged in the late 1800s, but railroads revived orchards in this part of Virginia. In 1901, 80 railcars each holding 160 barrels of apples left the Piney River depot. By 1924, 1,574 railcars transported over 90 percent of Nelson County apples outside the county.[6] Some suggest that during Prohibition, the remaining 10 percent ended up as cider and brandy.

In the 1950s, John Morton replanted orchards on the old Massie land and in nearby orchards. His daughter Perkins Morton Flippin partnered with another Nelson orchard family to form the produce company Flippin-Seaman, with a warehouse on Crabtree Falls Highway. This is the road that so captivated me when I first crossed the Blue Ridge in 2004 and drove into this valley strewn with apples to purchase Winesaps from her son Bill Flippin. My relationship with Bill led me to his daughter Ruth and son-in-law John and cemented my affection for the Tye River orchards and for this family

The eastern slope of the Blue Ridge mountains overlooking Silver Creek Orchards, Tyro, VA.

John Saunders and Ruth Flippin Saunders count generations of orchardists on both sides of their families who grew peaches and apples in this fruitful land. Today the Saunderses pilot their thoroughly modern orchard into an uncertain future with an explorer's mixture of courage and caution.

In 1997, John noticed someone surveying his land with a GPS device. He struck up a conversation with the Virginia Tech scientist who was scouting land for good vineyard sites. In the late 1990s, apple prices were depressed and there was a shortage of Virginia-grown grapes for the state's burgeoning wine industry. "He told me that land that's good for apples is also good for grapes," John remembered.[7]

John and Ruth planted their first wine grapes in 1999.

"One of the reasons we moved to planting grapes is we've had apples after apples for generations on this land. The land needed to rest and grow something else," said Ruth. "The block of land behind Pharsalia was in apples for generations, and now it's in grapes."

John and Ruth's Silver Creek Orchards, in addition to growing over 200 acres of apples, is now one of the state's most respected wine grape producers. This couple's spirit of exploration has not stopped with adding another fruit to their mix.

Ruth said, "You can't be conservative anymore in the apple business. Maybe [you could be] sixty years ago when you had a red apple, a green apple, and a yellow apple as the only three on the shelf. Now you have to risk change." John put a different spin on it: "Apple growers are professional gamblers."

In 1993, the Saunderses began planting high-density orchards. As was true for Tim Mercier in Georgia, faster-producing dwarf trees allowed Silver Creek Orchards to address competition.

John was eloquent on the effect of competition from Washington apples on his southern orchard. "It's very difficult for us to compete head-to-head with Washington State," he admitted. "They can grow apples a lot more cheaply, but they have to ship their fruit 3,000 miles. We are close to the people, and that's where we need to be in marketing." In addition, Washington apples gain color earlier, so growers there are able to harvest fruit when the apples turn red but are not yet ripe. "We pick ripe fruit," John says, "which makes our fruit taste better."

High-density orchards allow the Saunderses to pivot their fresh-pack and direct-to-consumer business as consumer tastes change. Ruth said, "We find varieties we know we can grow well and can market locally. We're always listening to our customers, and we concentrate on those varieties rather than trying to compete with Washington apples." Gold Rush and Pink Lady, two successful varieties in the Silver Creek Orchards, ripen late and perform well in the South's long growing season.

In addition to packing most of their apples for the wholesale market, the Saunders Brothers Farm Market sells directly to consumers. The market opens from June to September and sells apples like Jonagold, Mutsu, Arkansas Black, and Albemarle Pippin as well as blueberries and vegetables grown on the Silver Creek farm.

———————

From Crabtree Falls Highway, the long view over Silver Creek Orchards appears serene, even placid. Even to my eyes, someone who intimately knows the work of caring for trees, the neat rows of apples stretching up the slope of the Blue Ridge reveal no angst. The tidy landscape in this lovely valley obscures the immense labor required to tend, harvest, and sell a crop that has always been almost wholly managed with hand labor.

In the late nineteenth and early twentieth century, growing apples in Nelson County meant hard work, all by hand, assisted only by mule-drawn wagons and ground slides. Workers pruned apple trees with handsaws. They sprayed trees with manual pumps until gasoline-powered sprayers became available in the early 1900s. Apple trees grown on their own roots can grow twenty to forty feet tall. Workers climbed trees on handmade twenty-four-foot ladders constructed from split pine. They hooked galvanized metal picking buckets to ladder rungs or tree limbs and filled them with heavy fruit. When the pickers lowered the buckets on ropes, they yelled "Nipper!" The youngest workers, usually young boys called nippers, swapped the loaded buckets for empty ones. The nippers then tipped the heavy buckets into wooden barrels or onto a sorting table.

Apples traveled down steep slopes using ground slides, two-runner sleds loaded with barrels or boxes and pulled by a mule or horse. A one-horse box slide could hold about a dozen bushel crates in one layer, likely around 700 pounds of fruit. On flat ground, workers would double-load the slide.[8]

Photos from the early twentieth century show men and women, both white and African American, harvesting apples. Women did most of the work in the packhouse, where they sorted apples by size, sometimes using a wooden sizer, and then ring-packed the apples into wooden barrels. During World War II, prisoners of war at Camp Lyndhurst in nearby Augusta County harvested apples. Children often performed orchard work. In September 1943, Nelson County schools closed for two weeks so schoolchildren could help bring in the apple harvest.[9]

In 1945 Nelson County harvested 668,000 bushels of apples. In his and Darrell Laurant's book, *Packing Shed Memories*, John Saunders's father, Paul, writes that harvest crews in the 1950s and 1960s were racially mixed and from a mixed economic group.[10] There were few employment opportunities for young people in the summer. Entire families joined harvest. Some workers drove from nearby counties to pick fruit and lived in orchard bunkhouses during the week.

This system of local seasonal labor began to disintegrate in the 1970s. In *Packing Shed Memories*, Paul Saunders recalls the peach harvest of 1978 as the "tipping point" for labor: "Thousands of bushels of peaches weren't picked because there was nobody to pick them. Sweating in the August heat was beginning to be less attractive to young people who had air conditioned options, and most of the small farmers who once looked for extra work at picking time had stopped farming."[11]

In spite of improved equipment and dwarf rootstocks, apples today remain a high-labor agricultural endeavor. The variable labor cost for the agriculture sector is 17 percent. For apples it is 48 percent.[12]

Labor consumes Ruth Saunders more than any other task on her lengthy list.

Ruth defined her job description simply: "I'm in charge of acronyms. OSHA, GAP, H-2A"—worker safety, food safety, and finding workers.

The H-2A program allows employers to bring foreign workers to the United States to fill agricultural positions. Farmers using this program must demonstrate that there are insufficient US workers to fill the jobs and that H-2A workers will not suppress the wages or damage the working conditions of US workers employed in similar jobs. Employers must pay H-2A workers an adverse wage rate, a set amount above the state's minimum wage. In 2022, the Virginia minimum wage was $11.00 per hour and the adverse wage rate was $14.16 per hour. Additional piecework incentives can raise the per-hour rate to around $20.00.

Technology has helped some labor issues. Nelson County native Warren Mays worked at Silver Creek for forty-nine years and remembered cutting grass under trees with a hand scythe. "What you couldn't get to with the mower you'd have to cut with a hand scythe. I've pulled a hand scythe many a day. My daddy told me to always put the new guy in the front of the line to cut the heavy grass."[13]

Tractors with enclosed cabs and offset mowers are ubiquitous in today's orchards. High-density orchards reduce the amount of labor and the skill needed to prune trees. John stated, "The labor cost to prune a high-density orchard is about half, but even better, I can teach someone to prune in a few minutes."

For now the H-2A program provides a workable solution for large orchard operations like Silver Creek. "I don't love it, but it works. The H-2A program gives us a source of labor. The quality of people is very good. They are motivated and want to do a good job," Ruth said.

But can orchards continue to afford labor costs on the thin margins from each apple harvest? And will those thin margins attract the next generation to the complex work of growing apples?

John and Ruth's children work off the farm. "They never work on Saturday or Sunday," John said. "It's hard to encourage them to think about returning to the orchard because they make so much more money working off the farm. They can work fewer hours and deal with less stress."

Bill Flippin remembered when "you'd get off Highway 29 and it would be orchards all the way to Afton." Abandoned packinghouses still line the road that winds through the gentle landscape along the Tye River. The picturesque view still masks the labor required to bring fruit to market and the risk behind every harvest.

———————

Cider, an old beverage with a new life, may provide a twenty-first-century path for forward-thinking southern orchards like Silver Creek. When I opened Foggy Ridge Cider in the early aughts, my first orchard

◄
(*Top*) Blacktwig apples at Silver Creek Orchards reserved for fermented cider.

(*Bottom*) Apple barrels on sled in Rockfish Mountain Orchards, Afton, VA.
Courtesy of The Design Group, Lynchburg, VA.

had just begun producing apples, and my two newest orchards were not yet yielding fruit. I was thrilled that my first cider vintage sold out in a few months, but it was clear that I needed more apples, lots more apples. I knew I would not find English bittersweet apples in Virginia, but I wanted to purchase apples with distinctive flavors that could supplement the cider-specific apples I harvested at Foggy Ridge. My search led me to Silver Creek Orchards.

For my second cider vintage I purchased a few bins of Old Virginia Winesap apples from John and Ruth. Blended with apples from the Foggy Ridge orchards, Silver Creek's Winesaps created a rich, gold-colored cider with a hint of caramel balanced with bright acidity. I suggested that since the Saunderses were already experimenting with new apple varieties, why not plant old ones too, including traditional English cider apples and southern apples historically used for cider?

Fifteen years later, Silver Creek Orchards has the largest commercial planting of Harrison and Hewe's Crabapples in the South. They grow Ashmead's Kernel, an excellent high-acid English cider apple that grows well at Foggy Ridge. John grafted Blacktwigs from an old tree that grew behind their house. Their modern British-made cider press, purchased in 2016, sends juice to cideries from Maryland to Tennessee.

Adam Cooke manages the press room at Silver Creek. "Our press was held up in Norfolk customs for ninety days because the inspectors thought it was a bomb," Adam remembered. "Once we got it up and running, it's been nonstop. I press juice from our apples every week of the year."[14]

Silver Creek's Bucher XPlus 22 bladder press presses 2,200 liters in every run. An internal air compressor pushes a bladder against the crushed apple pomace, extracting the juice in incremental press cycles. The juice then passes through socks that separate the clear juice from the apple pomace. This modern press extracts about three and a half gallons of juice for each bushel of fresh apples.

Cidery customers who make a mass-market-style cider purchase Silver Creek juice from common dessert apples like Granny Smith and Red and Golden Delicious. "These cideries are almost always adding flavors over the actual apple taste," said Adam. "Cidermakers that work with cider-specific apples want Harrisons and other highly flavored cider apples. One cidermaker likes Blacktwig apples after they have been aged for months, so we press for him in January or February."

These two types of cideries, one making an inexpensive mass-appeal beer-style cider, and the other crafting a high-end cider made much like a fine wine, have very different economic models. The economies of each dictate the price the cideries can pay for juice from Silver Creek's

Bucher press. Cider business models determine the future of southern cider apple orchards.

Cideries that aim for mass-market customers interested in drinking an inexpensive cider on draft or in cans ferment cider all year from the most commonly available low-priced apples. Some cideries skip the apples and ferment apple juice concentrate mixed with water. These ciders complete fermentation and are ready for sale in as little as four to five weeks and are packaged and sold like beer.

Ciders that aim for more complex flavors are typically made from apples chosen for specific characteristics—cider-worthy varieties— that provide a balance of acid, tannin, sugar, and complex flavors, the same balance that winemakers seek for fine wine. Apples for this style of fine cider are pressed seasonally, in fall or early winter. This cider, often called "vintage cider," ferments for weeks, often months, and then ages in tanks or barrels before being bottled six months or more after fermentation.

Vintage cider, cider made from specific apples that reflect an orchard site and the time and attention of a long ferment, clearly carries high production costs and demands a higher market price. The majority of cider sold in the United States falls into the former category—cider either made from concentrate or made from dessert apples stored after harvest, pressed all year, fermented in a couple of weeks, and bottled, canned, or kegged without aging.

Fruit costs separate mass-market cider from vintage cider. Red Delicious, still a widely planted apple in the South, costs about $7.00 per bushel, or about $3.25 per gallon of juice. Silver Creek Orchards' Hewe's Crab, one of my favorite cider apples, can cost up to $45.00 per bushel, or $13.90 per gallon. Hewe's Crabs are rarer than Red Delicious; the apples are tiny and each bushel weighs much more than a bushel of medium-sized Red or Golden Delicious. Cider-specific apples are not as juicy as dessert apples and often yield less juice per bushel.

But there is more to cider economics than fruit cost. Eleanor Leger, founder of Eden Cider in Vermont, describes the economic realities of making vintage cider in her blog, *Cidernomics*.[15]

Asset allocation is different for vintage cider compared with a cider fermented and sold in a four- to five-week production. Cidermakers crafting cider from a single vintage harvest—let's call this "slow cider"— ferment batches of cider in expensive stainless steel tanks in fall and early winter. Cideries that produce "fast cider" use their tanks every month of the year. Slow cider remains in inventory longer, both in the fermentation tank but also during aging in tanks, barrels, or bottles. Fast cider heads out the door in kegs or cans and generates income in four to five weeks. Because their price is lower, cideries making fast cider need volume. They produce and sell more cider, so reaching economies of scale is easier. High-volume cidermakers can purchase a more efficient bottling line or larger tanks because they are spreading costs over a higher number of units.

Sales channels also differ for these two cider styles. Cideries that grow at least some of their fruit and produce cider by vintage are often located in rural areas that provide fewer opportunities for selling directly to customers, the highest margin sales channel. Fast cidermakers are often in urban areas or operate taprooms in high-traffic tourist locations, which increases their opportunity for high-margin sales.

Any apple can produce juice to ferment into cider: the cheapest grocery store apples, tiny starch-filled apples culled on the sorting line, foraged wild apples, organic or biodynamic apples, English bittersweet apples, and heirloom regional cider apples. Cider is often made from apple juice concentrate. The most common sources of apple juice concentrate used in cider production are countries such as Poland, Argentina, Italy, France, China, or Turkey.

Juice costs vary widely. Leger estimates that the cost of a gallon of juice from frozen apple juice concentrate reconstituted with water is about $0.70. Common grocery store apples pressed out of cold storage will cost around $1.80 per gallon. High-quality, fresh-pressed dessert apple juice will cost about $4.00 per gallon. Cider apples pressed in a small-scale cidery will have a juice cost of over $10.00 per gallon.[16]

As Leger writes in her excellent blog, "At one end of the spectrum: low cost, predictable supply, juice consistency, low flavor. At the other end: scarcity, biennial-ism, high cost, variability of sugar/acid/tannin levels, more flavor."[17]

Slow cider, made from a single apple harvest year, needs a value claim for cidermakers to pay for more costly raw ingredients and for consumers to purchase higher-priced cider. Highly flavored apples, like Hewe's Crab and Blacktwig, can produce elegant ciders full of complexity and nuance that offer a tasting experience similar to well-made wine. These ciders are often packaged like fine wine, in 750 mL bottles, and sold in a range of restaurants and wine shops rather than in package stores and chain restaurants. Cider made slowly from expensive, flavorful fruit usually costs from fifteen to twenty-five dollars per wine-sized bottle. A typical six-pack cider price for cider made quickly from inexpensive ingredients—apples or concentrate—is around eleven dollars A six-pack of twelve-ounce bottles is the same volume of cider as 2.8 wine-sized bottles of cider, which means the price of slow cider is about five times as expensive as fast cider.

In order to plant cider-worthy apples and potentially revive old southern varieties, orchards like Silver Creek require at least some cidery customers who can afford high-priced fruit.

Even with rootstocks that speed production, apple growers play a protracted game. Investing in an expensive apple press or a new high-density planting of cider apples carries risk with potential reward many years in the future. Market customers might covet the latest Washington State apple. More cidermakers may decide they would rather make a six-pack cider flavored with hops and pomegranate than a vintage cider made from a centuries-old southern cider apple. Navigating uncertainty and change requires courage and what John and Ruth Saunders might characterize as trust.

"If you don't invest in the future, your land won't survive as agriculture," Ruth asserted.

As it has for over 200 years, this Nelson County apple land embraces the twisting Tye River and climbs the gentle slopes of the Blue Ridge Mountains. Today John Saunders often heads to the Piney River to fish for trout. When they weren't growing or selling fruit, John's father and mother relished fishing the same waters. Decades ago, families that loaded metal buckets with apples and called out for the nippers fished for brown trout in these same streams. Two hundred years ago, the enslaved men and women who harvested Massie's orchards likely caught fish in the peaceful-looking Tye River, as did the Monacans, the first farmers.

Those who performed the labor of apple growing even a half-dozen decades ago would find the short, closely spaced trees at Silver Creek Orchards unrecognizable. There are no metal buckets, no mule-drawn ground slides, no nippers. But the unrelenting hand labor of apples remains.

When I drove away from Silver Creek Orchards, I thought about the trajectory of apple growing; the generations of laborers who cleared land, grafted, and planted trees; and the men, women, and children who pruned and harvested fruit in the valley and on the steep slopes. This region's apple history is not tied as neatly as the gentle landscape suggests. The labor of fruit growing doesn't lend itself to a tidy narrative, all wrapped up with a bow. Nonetheless, apples are tied hard and fast to this prime corner of southern apple country.

STUDIED

Light streamed through the tall windows in Lee Calhoun's living room. Since his cancer diagnosis I had driven to Pittsboro, North Carolina, as often as I could. Lee and I began with an update on his health and my orchard but quickly moved to our favorite plants, books we were reading, and dishes we were cooking. A bowl full of produce from Lee's garden sat on the kitchen counter with Carolina Red June apples, ripe persimmons, or Lee's favorite rattlesnake beans, depending on the season. An eye-catching vase from North Carolina ceramic artist Mark Hewitt held center stage on the sideboard. Signs of Lee's rich life surrounded him.

When Lee retired from the army in 1976, he and Edith built their Japanese-style house at Saralyn, a community founded to safeguard the environment and ecology. Their low-slung home with sliding glass doors embraced a koi pond framed by Japanese maples. Trees hugged every corner of the house. Lee was singularly focused on the natural world and the community around him. But his world emanated balance. Even after his cancer diagnosis, Lee radiated a centered calmness, one I envied.

Lee always thanked me for visiting him, but I was the one who left our conversations enriched. In the months since his diagnosis, Lee kept living. He worked with the University of North Carolina's Southern Historical Collection to archive the research materials for his book, *Old Southern Apples*. He taught a session with UNC students who were using his materials for their research projects. Lee and I led a panel at a Chapel Hill food festival and a cider workshop at Horne Creek Living Historical Farm. Lee *created* until the end of his life. He built new friendships. He shared knowledge. I admired his balanced, full life.

My life was full, but it was far from balanced.

The realization that had begun percolating at the Chicago Lyric Theatre grew into a conviction: I was rowing into a strong current of my own making. The blend of work I had created for myself was skewed far too strongly toward achievement. I missed the sense of possibility that comes with creating something new. Foggy Ridge Cider's successes on the national and regional stage, even the joy of the Lyric Theatre, didn't outweigh the grind of maintaining a business. The tasks that fueled me—time in the orchard, planting, creating—were corralled into slivers of my life. Regret tinged even this energy-giving work.

I was sixty-five years old and determined to find a fresh path. My long trips back to the farm from Pittsboro gave me plenty of time to ponder what this path might look like.

Sue and I began studying ways to reconfigure the cidery into one that brought more satisfaction and remained a viable business. We examined models that shrank production to levels in our early years. We considered expanding and building a more efficient facility in nearby Floyd. To lessen my not-so-gratifying travel, we evaluated reducing our distribution footprint. Chuck and I talked to cideries and one winery about purchasing the Foggy Ridge Cider brand, keeping the farm and the orchard in our hands.

I thought, "Whatever it is, my next path must include creativity, learning, and a sense of possibility." I was determined to recapture the joy at the top of the swing.

A few years earlier I attended a Southern Foodways Alliance event that honored Ben and Karen Barker. This chef couple founded Magnolia Grill in Durham, North Carolina, in the mid-1980s, one of the first in the South to serve inspired southern dishes made with local ingredients. Chuck and I had courted at their farm-to-fork restaurant, before anyone even used that term. When the Barkers decided to retire, they retired Magnolia Grill but remained active in the culinary world. I knew I never wanted to leave the farm. I didn't want to abandon orcharding or eliminate cider from my life. Maybe I could use Ben and Karen's model to find a path for Foggy Ridge.

On one of those long drives back from Pittsboro to Virginia, I decided on retirement. Not *my* retirement. Not an end to the farm or the orchards. But retirement for Foggy Ridge Cider and a new beginning for me.

The first thing I did was chop the tops out of a fourth of the trees in the Old Orchard.

The high-pitched whine of the chainsaw startled bluebirds from their nests and sent them swooping through Foggy Ridge's Old Orchard. Early April was far too late for pruning, but here I was, cutting the tops out of twenty-year-old apple trees. I climbed each one and sawed off the biggest limbs. In less than a minute I cut through trunks that I had watched grow inch by inch over my entire farming life. In less than an hour, two-thirds of each tree lay on the orchard grass. What had been a long row of mature Northern Spy apple trees with graceful limbs now looked like decapitated skeletons with a stump cut off four feet from the ground and only a few low limbs remaining.

I remembered the long, cold days I spent planting this orchard and the frustration I felt from my inexperience. Over two decades later, on a sunny early spring day in 2018, I was once again a novice. But this time I had an expert teacher.

By the time Raul and Mary Godinez arrived in their big Chevy Silverado, sun had warmed the orchard rows and I was standing in a tangle of downed limbs. Northern Spy makes extraordinary cider when grown in New York's Finger Lakes district, but this apple struggled in our hot, humid summers. On my site, Northern Spy lacked the sharp edge of acidity that balances its syrupy-sweet flavor.

Raul and Mary were here to topwork, a specialized grafting technique in which a skilled grafter inserts a new apple variety onto existing apple limbs or the trunk of the tree. Home gardeners often use topworking to create a "single tree orchard," a tree with different apple varieties grown on each limb. I wanted to use the twenty-year-old roots of my Northern Spy trees to get a head start on a special cider apple—Redfield, a red-fleshed apple I had first tasted over two decades earlier with Terry Maloney at West County Cider in Massachusetts. West County still makes a delicate, red-tinged cider, and Terry's son, Field, had shared grafting wood from his orchard with me.

Over thirty years spent closely observing fruit trees has equipped Raul with the intimate knowledge of the perfect moment to topwork an apple tree. "The sap needs to rise enough that the bark slips easily to slide in the graft, but not so much that the new graft rushes too quickly into growth," he said as he inserted three-inch-long sections of Redfield apple wood onto the big round stumps of my Northern Spy trees.[1]

With Raul's expert topworking, I expected the twenty-year-old root systems to send up to four feet of new growth from each short stick of Redfield apples in just the first year. Raul taught me to leave a few nurse limbs below the cut to provide photosynthesis. He showed me how to braid and tie the fresh growth into a bundle that would eventually fuse into a new trunk and side limbs, creating an entirely new tree grown on an established root system. In two years I would have a few Redfield apples and in three years perhaps a full crop.

Topworking seemed like magic to me. Magic as practiced by a master magician.

Raul grew up in the Washington State fruit tree industry. Beginning at age eighteen, he worked for large nurseries grafting apples, pears, plums, and ornamentals. He managed hundreds of acres of nursery stock and honed his grafting skills before moving east in 2003 with the goal of starting his own nursery.

"In Washington I was the main guy for budding, grafting, digging, and grading trees and shipping them out," Raul recalled. "One night it was almost midnight. We were loading a tractor trailer and I'm going through the order list, and I realized we were putting a half a million dollars on that truck. I thought, 'What am I doing here?' That's when it clicked and I knew I needed my own nursery."

Raul and Mary met in Winchester, Virginia, where Mary used her landscape and horticulture degrees as director of a historic garden, which included a small orchard. When she planned a grafting workshop at the garden, she searched out Raul, who was known locally as "the guy who knows everything about grafting." As Raul put it, "Right away, we became a couple and a business."

Mary described their union more graphically: "The first trip we took together we went to Washington State and budded 48,000 Aztec Fujis. If I hadn't learned by then, I quickly figured out this was the plan. We didn't graft trees on our honeymoon, but it was close."

In 2011, the Godinezes leased land and started a fruit tree nursery. In 2014, they purchased their first farm and founded Countryside Farm and Nurseries. A few years later, they bought Cross Keys, a family property that had been in Mary's family since the 1800s. Since their first meeting, a blend of risk taking and hope for the future has fueled their relationship and fruit ventures.

When I picture Raul walking through his carefully tended rows of nursery trees, observing new buds, noticing signs of struggle and healthy growth, I think about Prosper Berckmans stalking his Fruitland Nurseries, small notebook in hand. Almost 150 years apart, both men noticed apples in the South. They took note and pursued knowledge. They both held three-inch sticks of grafting wood in skilled hands; they both wielded sharp knives and inserted genetic material onto rootstocks or tree trunks. They worked magic in their orchards and nurseries.

On that spring day in the Foggy Ridge orchard, Raul said, "I've always liked to ask questions. I've always wanted to do it right. The beauty

of grafting is you never stop learning." That day I saw Raul as someone who studied fruit, another in a long line of orchardists born with question marks in their brains.

———————

Raul and Mary study trees every day. Their quotidian research is practical, tied to the realities of each season's growing conditions in their nursery and each apple's predilections. In universities and research centers around the world, pomologists, food scientists, and fermentation specialists study apples with scientific rigor from all angles, beginning with the most basic, the apple genome.

In 2010 an Italian-led team of eighty-five scientists sequenced the genome of the Golden Delicious apple.[2] They learned that the apple genome is large and unique, befitting a plant that reproduces sexually and has adapted to all temperate zones in the world. It consists of 800 million base pairs (Mb), compared to 230 Mb for peaches and 480 Mb for grapes. The apple genome for *Malus domestica* encodes 57,386 predictive genes, the highest for any plant sequenced to date.[3] Of these, nearly 20 percent are apple-specific, which means they do not show meaningful similarities with other plants.

Knowing the apple's genetic code is heady stuff, seemingly far removed from a row of trees topworked by hand. Scientists studying the apple genome engage with the fundamental building blocks of life. So far they have learned that several gene families are over-represented in apples: genes related to sorbitol (a type of sugar), disease resistance, antioxidants, and the biosynthesis of volatiles and aromatics. Scientists are using these data to prepare this ancient fruit for a risk-filled future.

University-based apple breeding programs bring study straight to the orchard. Apple breeding programs at Cornell, the University of Minnesota, and Washington State University aim to produce improved apple varieties suited to the growing conditions of New York, Minnesota, and the Pacific Northwest. Since the University of Minnesota first introduced Minnehaha in 1920, these three breeding programs have introduced over 100 apple varieties.

In the late 1970s, apple varieties from other countries began to capture American palates. New Zealand introduced Braeburn and Gala. Granny Smith, an old Australian apple, and Fuji from Japan gained popularity with consumers. By the late 1980s, growers began replacing varieties that were falling out of favor, like Red Delicious, with new varieties grown on dwarf rootstock.[4] Southern growers, many with or-

◄
Raul Godinez cutting budwood at Countryside Farm and Nurseries, Crimora, VA. A single grafted bud creates a tree in one year.

chards dedicated to processing apples, were slow to adopt new varieties and planting schemes.

Raul remembered this period: "When I came to the Southeast from Washington, this area was twenty years behind Washington on every-thing—ladders, bins, planting, rootstocks. But the South is catching up."

A University of Minnesota apple introduced in 1991 and bred for that state's cold climate sparked a change in southern orchards. Cornell pomologist Dr. Greg Peck described this apple flavor revolution: "Honeycrisp totally changed what consumers thought an apple could be. You get a more balanced flavor in Honeycrisp than Red Delicious. Consumers learned that an apple didn't have to be only sweet, mealy, and have a bitter peel."[5]

Even conservative southern orchardists with long roots in processing fruit jumped at the chance to grow an apple that captured customers' palates and pocketbooks.

In 2006, Honeycrisp was named one of the "25 Innovations That Changed the World."[6] Until its US patent expired in 2008, Honeycrisp earned over $14 million for the University of Minnesota. This apple still earns foreign royalties under the name Honeycrunch.

Georgia orchardist Tim Mercier called it "Moneycrisp" and said this apple's success with consumers spurred him to plant new varieties.

Honeycrisp turned out to be a fussy apple to grow outside Minnesota, prone to a flaw called bitter pit and a challenge to prune due to vigorous growth. Once harvested, Honeycrisp required tender treatment. The apple's skin is so thin that stems can scratch and scar the flesh. But high prices and consumer demand drove even risk-averse southern growers to plant this moneymaker. More important, Honeycrisp prompted southerners to experiment with other new varieties.

Kenny Barnwell, a third-generation apple grower in Henderson County, North Carolina, pivoted to new varieties to help navigate his region's decline in apple processing. In 1980, when Kenny graduated from college and returned to his family farm, the county had 10,000 acres of apples and thirty-three packinghouses. Global food processors like Gerber, National Fruit, and Seneca Foods paid prices that allowed growers to keep orchards in the ground. When the processing market shifted to lower-priced apples from outside the United States, the processors left Henderson County. Growers like Barnwell had to change or abandon their orchards.

"In 2005 we gambled the farm on new varieties. We put in Pink Lady and other new apples on dwarfing rootstock. I used to plant 100 trees to the acre, and now it's 1,000 to 1,200. That's when we really turned the corner."[7] Barnwell now wholesales almost all his fruit to regional grocery chains and markets. Today, apples like EverCrisp, Aztec Fuji, Honeycrisp, and a red Gala strain dominate his Henderson County orchards.

New varieties and high-density planting accelerated the South's abandonment of apples with deep regional history. Apples named for individuals, like Captain Davis, a fragrant apple from Mississippi, disappeared from southern orchards. Junaluska, grown in North Carolina since the 1800s, and Tennessee's Kinnaird's Choice faded from nurseries and orchards. New apples celebrated modernity—Jazz, Snap Dragon, SweeTango, and Cosmic Crisp—with names that stressed crisp, sweet fruit. Altered southern orchards replaced old varieties with modern fruit.

University of Minnesota apple breeders took thirty years to develop Honeycrisp.[8] They cross-pollinated hundreds of apple blossoms by hand. They grafted seedlings onto rootstocks and waited years for young trees to bear fruit. Out of 5,000 seedlings, university researchers might choose 25 to clone, and then they repeated the cycle. With Honeycrisp, this laborious process resulted in a sea change in apple flavor. Once consumers tasted Honeycrisp, they demanded more varieties that provided what marketers called "a crisp eating experience" and more complex flavors. Breeding programs saw an opportunity for profit.

Today most of the apples developed by the three university breeding programs are "club apples," apples licensed to growers who pay for the right to grow the new variety. When SweeTango was launched in 2009, only forty-five orchardists were certified to sell this apple.[9] When Washington State University introduced Cosmic Crisp in 2017, only thirty-five Washington growers gained permission to plant this widely anticipated apple in the first year.[10]

With no university-based breeding program in the region, the South has not been a member of the club.

The USDA Agricultural Research Station in Kearneysville, West Virginia, hopes to speed the process of developing new apple varieties through genetic research. The genetic sequencing of apples that began in 2010 means that researchers now know the specific genes responsible for many desirable and disadvantageous apple traits. When combined with a process called "rapid cycle breeding," apple breeders can now produce new varieties in half the time it took to develop Honeycrisp.

In rapid cycle breeding, apple geneticists manipulate a gene responsible for early flowering to stimulate early and continuous flowering in a test apple. The test apple is then grown in a nursery setting, where it flowers all year. Scientists can then use this continually flowering apple as a resource to create genetic crosses all year, rather than only in an annual flowering cycle. Researchers select for desirable traits like sweetness, a lower chill period, or resistance to disease. Once scientists select the desired new combination of apple traits, they then breed out the trans-genetic material that led to increased flowering.

This process allows breeders to create new varieties in half the time of the type of breeding used to create apples like Honeycrisp.[11]

Research geneticist Dr. Christopher Gottschalk came to West Virginia's Agricultural Research Station from Michigan State, where he was instrumental in creating the Great Lakes Cider Apple Collection with over 100 varieties used for cider trials. The Michigan State collection includes Hewe's Virginia Crab and Paragon/Blacktwig, a southern apple with a convoluted origin involving Virginia, Tennessee, and Alabama. In addition to adding southern varieties to the West Virginia apple collection, Dr. Gottschalk hopes to equip modern apples to respond to climate change using genetic material from an apple that is native to the southeastern United States.

Scientists have sequenced the genome for *Malus angustifolia*, the southern crabapple. This apple species exhibits resistance to abiotic, or nonliving, parts of the environment, factors like temperature, humidity, and precipitation. "We want this apple to inform and empower us to breed their abiotic resistance into modern apples," Dr. Gottschalk said.[12]

Using genetic technologies, a southern native apple holds the potential for modern apples to withstand climate change.

———————

Wise Bird Cider occupies a corner ground-floor space in Lexington, Kentucky's Distillery District. A sleek concrete-topped bar dominates the tasting room. When I first visited this urban cidery on an early June afternoon in 2021, customers spilled onto an outdoor patio, glasses of cider in hand. I sat with owners Tim and Greta Wright under a row of cider apple trees. I smiled to see the same roll-up garage doors I had installed on the Foggy Ridge Cider crush pad almost twenty years earlier. The fruity aroma of fermenting apple juice made me feel right at home.

At Wise Bird, the Wrights pioneer orchard-centric cider in the midst of bourbon and beer country. Many of the state's storied distilleries like Buffalo Trace and Woodford Reserve are nearby. Kentucky has over forty craft breweries, many clustered in Lexington, home to the University of Kentucky. Wise Bird opened in 2019 and has grown rapidly.

"We're selling cider in a strong beer market," Tim said as we stood in the parking lot outside Wise Bird in sight of the James E. Pepper Distillery and next door to Fusion Brewing. "We pour eight ounces in a twelve-ounce stemless wine glass, and some customers complain about the pour size." He lamented that the Wise Bird tasting room staff often hear the question, "Do you have any of that cider beer my girlfriend likes?"[13] Even though Kentucky may not be on cider's cutting edge—cider is made like wine, not beer, and men do drink cider—the state has an abundant apple history.

Early orchards centered on the Kentucky side of the Ohio River and along the Mississippi. Apples, cider, vinegar, and dried apples traveled south by barge to markets in New Orleans.[14] To hedge their risk in the state's severe winters and hot summers, most orchardists grew a combination of tobacco, grain, corn, and livestock in addition to apples. As late as the early 1980s, the state's Cooperative Extension Service still recommended varieties that originated or were widely grown in this part of the South like Polly Eades, Summer Champion, Grimes Golden, and Rome Beauty.[15]

Polly Eades apple from Henderson, KY, by Mary D. Arnold. US Department of Agriculture Pomological Watercolor Collection, Rare and Special Collections, National Agricultural Library, Beltsville, MD.

Over a dozen popular southern varieties originated in Kentucky, like Henry Clay from Hopkins County. Stark Brothers Nurseries and Orchards Company trademarked this apple in 1910 and distributed it nationally. Forest Nursery in Todd County, Kentucky, listed over 370 apple varieties in its 1870 catalog.[16] Short Core, a dark-red apple from Berea, Kentucky, stored well through winter. Jake's Seedling was a perennial county fair winner; Green River, from Dunnville, Kentucky, ripened in August. Polly Eades was resistant to fire blight. For a state with challenging growing conditions, Kentucky produced a host of apples with names that reflected people and places.

The book *Old Southern Apples* includes over a page of now-extinct Kentucky apples. Kentucky Cream, Kentucky Sweet, and Kentucky Longstem are long gone from southern orchards. Modern cidermakers should mourn losing Kentucky Red. This cider apple was purported to have "the same quality as Hewe's Crab but is four times larger. The cider is rich and will keep without any reducing."[17]

Today Kentucky grows less than 1,000 acres of apples.

Twenty-five growers grow the majority of the state's apples and sell most on site or at farmers' markets. Gala, Golden Delicious, and Honeycrisp make up 32 percent of apple production.[18] Many Kentucky apple growers base their orchards on an agritourism model featuring corn mazes, festivals, and apple doughnuts.

Cider and cider apples may offer a path forward for some Kentucky orchardists.

Tim and Greta Wright have inspired one orchard's operation to include fermented cider. Evans Orchard, a fifth-generation farm located twelve miles outside Lexington, began as a diverse farm with tobacco, corn, cattle, and a few fruit trees. In the early 1990s, Kevan Evans added twenty acres of apples to supply the farm's market and gift store. Kevan's daughter, Jenny, explained, "The tobacco settlement funds allowed Kentucky to invest in farmers. We got a grant to turn our tobacco barn into a farm market with an apple press. Then we added a play area for kids, then a kitchen. This was successful, so we've now expanded the market."[19]

Kentucky's tourism-based orchards contribute $10 billion per year to the state's economy. Tourism has helped keep Kentucky orchards in the ground.[20]

This southern farming family created early and close ties with the University of Kentucky. Kevan remembered, "My father was good friends with the ag department at UK. If they needed a test plot, he was always game for anything. He was always willing to open a door and walk through."

In 2019, Evans Orchard partnered with Wise Bird Cider to offer fermented cider in a tasting room on the farm during the market season from May 1 through the end of November.

"I was apprehensive in the beginning because we are an agritourism site with lots of families visiting. But the Wise Bird tasting room was a real success right away. We're already talking about expanding," Kevan said.

Evans Orchard sells juice to Wise Bird and has also planted apples like Brushy Mountain Limbertwig, Arkansas Black, and Razor Russet for cidermakers. But Wise Bird and other Kentucky cideries have to purchase apples or juice from out of state. There aren't enough apples in Kentucky, and even fewer cider-specific apples, to supply the growing industry.

At the University of Kentucky, Dr. Jeff Wheeler studies cider and cider apples with the goal of expanding the state's cider and apple production through regionally identifiable cider styles. The university's 100-acre experimental farm has six acres of vineyards and orchards, including a cider apple cultivar trial. "We're growing eleven cider apple varieties to see what performs best in this climate and which varieties produce distinctive cider. We want to learn how little input we can put in the orchard and the ideal crop load," he said. "We're trying to find out if growing cider apples can be a viable enterprise for apple growers in Kentucky."[21]

Dr. Wheeler believes that beverage makers, both cider and wine, can inspire apple and grape plantings in the state. "Cidermakers and wine-makers have a higher net profit than farmers and typically have more capital to invest. They are the ones working to develop the trust and relationships with growers that will enable them to take planting risks. The main driver of apples going into the ground in Kentucky will be cidermakers," he said.

The university operates a licensed winery that produces ten wines and several ciders for sale to students and faculty. This facility allows Dr. Wheeler to test with fermenting apples from his experimental planting, including Blacktwig, Brushy Mountain Limbertwig, King David, and Arkansas Black. "What we are doing in the cellar will have even more impact than the orchard," he stated. "The goal is to have regionally iden-tifiable styles—this means little or no additions, including yeast."

The fertile exchange of information and enthusiasm among univer-sity researchers, cidermakers, and growers seems to be bearing fruit. "We take our cider over to Jeff. We taste his from the university and he tastes ours," Tim Wright said. "We just sit together and learn." Tim wants this learning to extend to orchards. Wise Bird offers grafting workshops to the community and shares grafting wood from the Uni-versity of Kentucky's experimental orchards.

In our conversations, both Tim and Jeff were clear that Kentucky apple growers are still cautious about cider and cider fruit. They agree, as Jeff states, that "growers are feeling out cidermakers to see what kind of legs they have. They are afraid to plant something they can't sell to consumers." Tim reminds me that Wise Bird is currently the only cidery in Kentucky with a pricing structure that supports growers adding new orchards for cider apples.

For Kentucky orchardists, the path forward is murky. Orchards in Georgia, Virginia, and North Carolina have proven that cider aids or-chard diversification and profitability. Experiments and trials at the University of Kentucky plus cideries' experience building a consumer market will provide direction. Perhaps even more important, as Cornell pomologist Greg Peck stated, "Cider helps consumers connect with the cultural history of apples in a way you don't see in wholesale operations."

Perhaps present-day cider in Kentucky can connect consumers with southern apple history.

University researchers are studying more than apple cultivars and fermentation techniques. Dr. Jacob Lahne at Virginia Tech studies how production changes lead to different flavors in cider and how consumers perceive these flavors. "The idea of where flavor lives is not well understood. Our sensory organs respond to external stimuli, and these are integrated in the brain into flavor. But this integration is culturally and socially conditioned," Dr. Lahne explained. Understanding consumer perceptions will help cidermakers describe and frame the products of their ferments.[22]

More research at Virginia Tech addresses how plant chemistry in apples drives flavor in cider. Dr. Susan Whitehead studies the evolutionary ecology of plant interactions and the role of phytochemicals in plant defense. Her work with Dr. Amanda Stewart examines how the microbiome on the surface of apples affects fermentation and the sensory properties of cider. "I want to understand connections," she said. "Orchard and fermentation practices can shift one factor; then [there] is a cascading effect. If we understand these interactions we can better predict outcomes."[23]

Drs. Stewart and Whitehead are working with researchers at Cornell University to compare the same variety of apples from New York and Virginia under different fermentation techniques. "We have a grand total of 160 fermentations in the walk-in right now," Dr. Whitehead reported.[24]

At Foggy Ridge Cider, we experimented with cider ferments every year to test new yeast strains or try out modifying fermentation temperatures or sulfite additions. Virginia Tech and Cornell research multiplies the knowledge available to cidermakers.

Southern orchards have long abandoned thirty-foot-tall trees, forty to an acre. Most now segregate old varieties with antiquated uses to fall festivals offering spicy apple butter and dried slices on strings. Uniform blocks of trees, all blooming at the same time with the same color flower, have replaced the vibrant sequence of pink, carmine, and white in an orchard filled with diverse varieties. Many southern orchards now look more like a vineyard, with corseted trees trained on wire to tall, flat apple walls.

Following the nineteenth-century flowering of southern apples, change gestated under the surface of orchards in the South. Circumstances nudged and then shoved growers and their orchards into transformation. The South lost apples with evocative names and history.

Southern orchards gained apples with Twitter accounts, violently crisp flesh, and sugary flavor. Through this change, some southerners have found ways to keep southern apple trees in the ground.

Agriculture never stands still. Southern orchards still lack a clear path forward. Study—in the nursery, at the lab, planted in soil at university experiment stations—can illuminate the next chapter. Old southern apples may yet have a homecoming in new orchards.

I've always believed that beauty is at hand in my orchard every day. When I walk through my orchard rows, I inhabit a space as alive as I am, full of rich and varied life. Like Lee Calhoun, I feel a sense of wonder in my orchard, and this wonder takes me to science, commerce, and communion with people.

I see this fellowship in conversations around glasses of cider in Lexington, Kentucky. I hear a sense of possibility from researchers all over the South when they talk about apples that can better resist disease, or about cider that reflects a specific terroir. Varied life thrives every day in the long rows of hundreds of apple varieties at Raul and Mary Godinez's nursery.

Like other southern growers, I need to grow trees that bear annual fruit, resist disease, and produce apples that someone wants to purchase. But I regret our wholesale disregard for less-than-perfect fruit, fruit that holds history but not the flavor of the moment. By letting go of this deep past, the future becomes more shallow.

Science and practical research may tell us that old varieties are not just evocative of the past but relevant to today's changing climate and the desires of modern cidermakers. I say they are not just relevant but necessary.

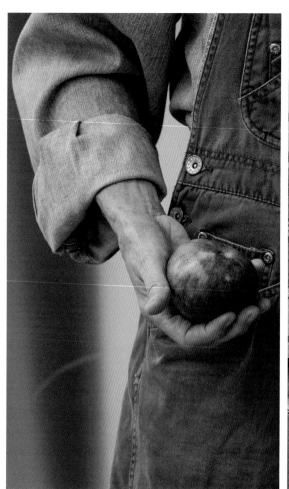

Coda

In the years before she died in 2015, my mother told the same stories, over and over. I always heard about the German shepherd she loved as a child, about picking apples as a teenager in the 1930s at a North Carolina boarding school, and about attending college as a northerner in a small southern town. Dementia dimmed her sharp brain, but her stories were a well she could still visit to remind her of who she was.

In today's commerce, stories are often used as a means, a vehicle for selling a product or promoting a lifestyle. But Lee Calhoun reminded me that apple stories exist in the service of something deeper and more urgent. They evoke the people behind the fruit. They relate complex cultural histories.

On one of our last visits, Lee described hearing about an old southern apple called Sally Gray while waiting for a haircut at his local barbershop. He "fell to talking about apples" with a customer who pointed Lee toward Wake County, North Carolina, and the owner of a Sally Gray tree. This apple was first described in the *Virginia Gazette* in 1763, and nurseries from Georgia to Tennessee sold Sally Gray for over a hundred years.[1] Lee grafted the tree and sold it through Calhoun Nursery. Today Sally Gray lives in the Southern Heritage Apple Orchard at Horne Creek Living Historical Farm and in a few southern orchards.

It's fair to ask if the world could survive without Sally Gray apples. Of course. And do we really need to preserve another late-summer yellow apple with red stripes and a sweet flavor? I think so. The world is richer with Sally Gray in it. But, perhaps, it is more important how Sally Gray came back to us. Lee's memory of Sally Gray, an apple that bounced around the South for over 250 years, reverberates with meaning and shows us how this humble fruit connects us all. After all, it was happenstance that the man in the barbershop remembered a rare apple, that the grower recalled how a relative grafted his tree in 1900, and that a Tennessee woman remembered her family drying Sally Gray apples in eastern North Carolina. The flavor of leathery fruit lingered in her memory for decades. This result—

▲ (*Overleaf*)
(*Top left*)
Photograph by
Fábio Câmara,
Fábio Câmara
Studios.

249

a saved apple, something from our shared history—was salvaged from small talk and memories.

Like Lee, I believe that southern apples are a vector that transports much more than flavor. And like my mother's last stories, southern apples hold history, culture, and desire. Their influence extends far from their canopy. Southern apples remind us of not only who we are but the people we come from.

––––––––––––––

At the most basic level, I think most people are disconnected from the natural world that surrounds them. And writing about old southern apples can feel like writing in the sand against an incoming tide. Customers visiting Foggy Ridge Cider in April often asked, "Where are the apples on the trees?" Children can recognize over a thousand corporate logos but fewer than ten plants native to their region. Apples are ubiquitous but unnoticed.

University-based research understandably centers on apples as economic engines. Washington State University introduced Cosmic Crisp in 2019 with a $10.1 million consumer marketing campaign. Cosmic Crisp is a tasty apple, but I would wager if faced with a choice between the complex flavor of Magnum Bonum and this mild one-note apple, people would favor the distinctive apple grown in the South for almost 200 years. There is no vanity in the old varieties, no posturing on Facebook. Magnum Bonum was a seedling apple until John Kinney noticed this fruit on his Davidson County, North Carolina, farm in 1828. A Davidson College professor christened it with a fancy name, one that accurately describes this "great good" apple.

Apples like Magnum Bonum are an act of worship, not commerce.

But growing tree fruit is a challenging economic equation. Cosmic Crisp stores well in controlled atmosphere storage, bears heavy crops, and ripens uniformly. Modern orchardists have trained Americans to reach for fire-engine-red apples, not Magnum Bonum's subtly striped light-red skin. Cosmic Crisp has the shattering crispness of one of its parents, Honeycrisp, a trait consumers have come to value. The Washington apple industry contributes $6 billion in economic impact to the state—the stakes are high for apples and apple growers.

When I began writing about southern apples, I felt trapped between the comforting blanket of nostalgia and the realities of commerce. Reducing apples to simple flavors that store well and appeal to modern palates seems a hollow representation of a complex fruit, one that has been linked to humans for thousands of years. But having access to old varieties shouldn't mean that growers struggle to make a living. Southern apples are more complex than a lament, more nuanced than an ex-ultation. You could say the same about the South.

The three-mile-long rows of apples in an irrigated Washington State orchard bred for sweetness, crunch, and a long shelf life aren't evil. But they aren't enough. The commerce-filled life that Foggy Ridge Cider became wasn't enough for me. I had to learn that my farming life holds precious gifts I should not squander. Southern apples hold gifts beyond price, too, and we must find a way to honor and savor these.

Southern apples speak of resistance, sometimes through commerce, like the long-keeping Pippin apples that Johnny, an enslaved man at Monticello, grew and sold to Jefferson's daughter in May.[2] Rachel Naomi Remen said that "sometimes we need a story more than food in order to live."[3] Apples offer both.

Drawing closer to our food, to this fruit, also has societal benefits. Apples offer the chance for a deeper understanding of our region's foun-dation in violence toward Indigenous people and of the lived experience of enslaved people in the South. Looking at our history as closely as a farmer examines his crops doesn't *destroy*. Close attention *enriches*. The moment I found I could no longer look away from the contradic-tions and stresses in my farming life was the moment I began to move toward closer connection to my orchard and creativity.

Science can take us only so far. Our vision of apples, and agriculture, has narrowed from richness and flavor to a marketplace vision. I believe this narrow vision is a poor place to live. Grafting and planting apple trees means planting dreams. And we should share our dreams.

———————

At six o'clock on a cold November night in 2018, a festive crowd streamed into the Parkway Grille in downtown Floyd, Virginia. Tracey Love, a friend and owner of Hill & Holler in Charlottesville, had transformed the restaurant into a celebration of cider and apples. I stood beside ta-bles covered with bowls of fruit greeting every guest. This eclectic group of friends and colleagues traveled to southwest Virginia to celebrate a retirement—Foggy Ridge Cider's, not mine.

Craig Rogers, lamb grower and dear friend, had wrangled chefs to cook everything from smoked rabbit to leg of lamb. Sean Wilson manned the Full Steam Brewery taps. A crew from the Virginia Wine Marketing Office poured our favorite Virginia wines. The soon-to-be-retired Foggy Ridge tasting room staff, all teachers who had shared cider with customers in our weekend tasting room, took turns filling glasses with our final cider, Foggy Ridge Final Call.

Sue and I debated for weeks over the label for this last vintage. I wanted our last cider to express the sense of possibility that I felt about cider's future and my own. Years earlier photographer Kate Medley had captured an image of me in silhouette walking up the long mowed path away from the old oak tree in our front pasture, the path I thought of as my "line of desire." I suggested, "Let's flip the image. I should face the tree. By retiring Foggy Ridge Cider I'm moving toward my trees, not away from them."

This was a final call for producing cider but the beginning of a new path for me.

A long list of customers was waiting to purchase future harvests that I planned to sell to cidermakers rather than make into my own blends. Raul and Mary Godinez topworked the Old Orchard with Redfield and Winter Jon, cider apples that I hoped would excite a new generation of producers. My work with Lee Calhoun to archive his research at the University of North Carolina brought the opportunity to write about the South through the lens of apples. I wanted to tell stories, ones we were growing away from. Now I had the chance to reclaim the core of my own story, to explore new lines of desire.

Two months earlier, while cycling with Craig on a gravel road, I fell and broke the femoral neck in my right hip, a painful injury that required surgery. Even though I was on crutches and dosed on Extra Strength Tylenol, I felt I was at the top of the swing.

Years later, guests still talk about that retirement party. Cidermakers mixed with winemakers. Bartenders with extensive tats chatted up farmers. Our elegant city friends in leather pants and cashmere sweaters danced with the Carhartt crowd from Floyd, while Nicole Lang and Marty Key spun tunes on vinyl.

And we ate. When Chef Ian Boden from The Shack in Staunton greets you with a dish described as Pork Heart Yakitori, Sorghum Cider, Sumac, and Benne Togarashi, you know you are in for an experience. Chef Jeff Farmer from Fortunato in Roanoke served Smoked Rabbit Gumbo z'Herbes. We ate Rappahannock River oysters doused with ramp mignonette. Tracey's husband, Bridge Cox, brought his lovely cheeses from Twenty Paces. Everyone downed lamb sliders as fast as Craig could assemble them.

I piled bushels of Albemarle Pippins from the Witt Orchard by the door for guests to take home. I had been rowing hard against a current of my own making, and I was finally pointing my bow downstream. That night I wanted everyone to leave buoyed by the joy inside the room.

A few months later, I hobbled out to the Old Orchard on a slowly healing hip to prune a short row of White Winter Pearmain trees. For over a decade I had grown this seventeenth-century apple to make a cider that smelled like peach skins. This season a younger cidermaker would ferment and blend and create an entirely new cider.

As always, time slowed in the orchard along with my heartbeat. A few seed heads swayed in the grass. The world seeped through my boot soles into my skin. Wind in the trees sounded like the orchard whispering to me.

When I committed to my cider path, I wanted to work my agency in the world. I wanted to grow fruit never grown in the South and pioneer a beverage. I didn't know that this path would change me in ways I never expected. Building the orchard and cidery situated me in the vise of creativity and achievement. I flourished for a while, and then I didn't.

Back in the orchard, I could again home in on the natural world, on gratitude and hope. I began as a pioneer and became a pilgrim. The orchard was an invitation to dream, and in dreaming, apples remade my world and my place in it. Now I was ready to set my feet more firmly in my wide place.

On my last visit to Lee, he was bedridden. Hospice care managed his pain, and he knew his time was near. I told him how much our visits meant to me, how he shaped my life and ambitions. I cut open an Albemarle Pippin and held it for him to inhale.

One night not long after Lee's death, I stared at the twisted apple tree outside my office window, fingers resting on my laptop keyboard. I wondered how to begin writing about apples. I had signed a contract with the University of North Carolina Press to write about the history of apples in the South. I was a beginner again, and happy to be one.

A nine-foot-tall deer fence kept deer out of the orchard, but I liked to watch them visit the old tree outside my office. I measured seasons by the color of their coats and saw them shed in spring. When I watched them eat windfall apples all winter, I felt awake to the world around me.

Looking out my window, daydreaming about the rich history contained in this particular fruit, I saw a flash of color. A gray fox slipped under the old tree and crouched near the overripe fruit. I stayed as still as I could and allowed the image of his salt-and-pepper coat and brilliant red ruff to flow into me, just like the orchard seeps through my boot soles. He cocked his head to gnaw on an apple and seemed to look straight in my eyes. I thought, "I'm happy my future holds as many surprises as that wild windfall fruit."

ACKNOWLEDGMENTS

The rich harvest of colleagues, counselors, and friends who made this book possible could fill many apple bins. My editor at the University of North Carolina Press, Lucas Church, suggested I pursue a book about apples in the South and then supported me in writing what became a larger look at the region and agriculture. I am thankful for his enthusiastic sponsorship and expert pruning.

Lee Calhoun's meticulous research and questioning mind set my writing in motion. The time we shared in the last years of his life inspired me to look more closely and live more fully.

I am grateful for the advice provided by Elizabeth Engelhardt and Marcie Ferris, stellar authors who sat, one on each shoulder, and whispered in my ears as I pounded away on my laptop. I hope I have been an attentive student.

Angie Mosier—photographer, stylist, and friend—immediately grasped my vision of a book about apples full of deeply felt images that reflect the reality of southern orchards. She captured the beauty and spirit of every site we visited.

Learning is my highest value, and writing this book brought daily lessons. I benefited from more formal education in Matt and Ted Lee's excellent Cookbook Boot Camp. John T. Edge and Sara Camp Milam coached and encouraged me in the Southern Foodways Alliance nonfiction writing workshop, where I shared rooms with Brian Noyes, owner of Red Truck Bakery, accomplished writer, dear friend, and on-call book tutor. Barry Yeoman showed me ways to cultivate the craft of writing in his workshop on narrative nonfiction, my first Zoom experience of the pandemic. I am grateful for the gifts from these experienced authors.

Scholars galore influenced my work. I read and reread Marcie Ferris's books, especially her introduction to *Edible North Carolina: A Journey across a State of Flavor*, in hopes a modicum of her elegant style and rigorous research might rub off. Ronni Lundy's book *Victuals* was never far from my side. Her insights about the South and agriculture, shared across cups of tea in her living room, encouraged me early in my research. A far-ranging conversation with Gary Nabhan shaped my direction, and I am thankful for his insights. Conversations with Tom Oakie, Claudio Saunt, Peter Hatch, David Shields, David Diamond, Jim Kibler, Daniel Cobb, and Staci Catron, as well as their writing, provided valuable perspectives on key figures and events in the South's orchard history. I benefited from not only the work of these writers, but in having nourishing conversations with them, for which I am grateful. Tom Oakie generously provided a translation by his colleague Gerrit Voogt of young Prosper Berckmans's journal. Elizabeth Engelhardt coached me through the tough bits of writing and publishing with her always wise, balanced advice.

Archivists across the South helped me navigate valuable holdings on southern agriculture and, especially during the pandemic, provided documents I could not review in person. I gained insights at the University of North Carolina's Wilson Library, the South Caroliniana Library at the University of South Carolina, the Virginia Museum of History and Culture, the Hargrett Rare Book and Manuscript Library at the University of Georgia, the University of Virginia's Albert and Shirley Small Special Collections Library, the Quaker Archives at Guilford College, the Cherokee Garden Library, the Reece Library at Augusta University, the South Carolina Historical Society Archives at the College of Charleston, and the W. L. Eury Appalachian Collection at Appalachian State. The Museum of the Cherokee Indian provided useful information on the location of apple orchards in Cherokee Georgia. Cornell's Carl A. Kroch Library's cache of material on Liberty Hyde Bailey and the National Agricultural Library's collection of nursery catalogs and pomological watercolors were invaluable.

I found regional libraries and historic societies across the South filled with orchard treasures, including the Haywood County Library, Virginia, the Augusta County Historic Society, Georgia, the Berkeley County Historic Society, West Virginia, and the Greensboro History Museum, North Carolina. The Handley Regional Library in Winchester, Virginia, and the Patrick County Historic Society in Stuart, Virginia, were especially rich in images, history, and helpful staff.

Michael Aday shared abundant information from the Great Smoky Mountains National Park Archives, and Jackie Holt helped me navigate the Blue Ridge Parkway Archives.

I could not have completed this book without the support of my local library, the Jessie Peterman Library in Floyd, Virginia, and the librarians there who hunted down scores of obscure texts through interlibrary loan. (I owe you!)

Apple scholars and growers Dan Bussey, John Bunker, Josh Fuder, Jason Bowen, David Anderson, Larry Stevenson and, best of all, ninety-six-year-old Jim Lawson graciously offered their time and extensive knowledge. Greg Peck from Cornell advised me at critical points in my writing. Amanda Stewart and Jacob Lahne's research at Virginia Tech into cider fermentation and sensory evaluation inspires me and countless cidermakers. The Saunders family in Tyro, Virginia, and Raul and Mary Godinez at Countryside Nursery in Crimora, Virginia, dispensed expert advice on everything having to do with orchards.

Cidermakers continue to inspire me at every turn, especially those who make cider with fruit from Foggy Ridge: Will and Cornelia Hodges at Troddenvale Cider, Kate Arscott-Mills of Molley Chomper Cider, and Anne Marie and David Thornton from James Creek Cider House. I continue to learn from cidermakers at Eve's Cider, Eden Cider, Farnum Hill Cider, Wise Bird Cider, Albemarle Ciderworks, Cider From Mars, and Botanist and Barrel, plus far too many more to mention.

Though this is a book about an ingredient, not about cuisine, chefs whom I count as friends kept me going with pep talks and fine meals—Ian Boden, Sean Brock, Brian Noyes, John Fleer, and Tyler Brown chief among them.

Orchards and farms don't take care of themselves. I would not have had the time to research and write this book without the smart people who keep the tractor running and our farm healthy: Antonio Alocer-Castillo, Phillip Marshall, and Dale Robbins. Bethany Hill Schaepler and Courtney Schaepler are valued colleagues in growing cider apples and making sure our Foggy Ridge fruit ends up in the hands of cidermakers across the region.

And though we no longer bottle 70,000 bottles of our own cider (by hand), I am forever grateful to the team at Foggy Ridge Cider: Jocelyn Kuzelka, Sue Carter, Amy Baldwin, Irena Childress, Liz Schearer, Melissa Kile, Wayne Marshall, Zack Burgess, and Nora Mabry.

My talented team at the UNC Press, including Kim Bryant, Valerie Burton, and Peter Perez, shepherded this work through production and launch, polishing at every step.

My husband, Chuck, is my greatest supporter, my best friend, and my greatest love. Thank you, Chuck, for your support and endorsement for a farm and writing life.

NOTES

Preface

1. Juniper and Mabberley, *Extraordinary Story of the Apple*, 224.

WILD
Seeds

1. Crosby, *Ecological Imperialism*, 188.
2. Wilson and Carril, *Bees in Your Backyard*, 163.
3. Juniper and Mabberley, *Extraordinary Story of the Apple*, 105.

Blooms

1. Nabhan, "Place-Based Foods of Appalachia," 2.
2. Okie, *Georgia Peach*, 13.
3. Hedrick, *History of Horticulture in America*, 4.
4. Juniper and Mabberley, *Extraordinary Story of the Apple*, 197.
5. Bunker, *Not Far from the Tree*, 21; Hedrick, *History of Horticulture in America*, 297, 346, 350.
6. Juniper and Mabberley, *Extraordinary Story of the Apple*, 199.
7. US Department of Agriculture, *Survey of Commercial Apple and Peach Orchards*, 6.
8. Beverley, *History and Present State of Virginia*, 251.
9. Hatch, *Fruits and Fruit Trees of Monticello*, 62.
10. Calhoun, *Old Southern Apples*, 117.
11. Juniper and Mabberley, *Extraordinary Story of the Apple*, 165.

Roots

1. Fitzhugh, "Letters of William Fitzhugh," 176.
2. R. Davis, "Chesapeake Pattern and Pole-Star," 526.
3. Rice, *Nature and History in the Potomac Country*, 12.
4. P. Martin, *Pleasure Gardens of Virginia*, 5.
5. C. Purcell McCue, "The Virginia Apple Industry," Old Time Apple Growers Collections, 239 WFCHS, Handley Regional Library, Winchester, VA.
6. Holbert, "William Fitzhugh," 121.
7. Bruce, *Economic History of Virginia*, 1:486.
8. Hedrick, *History of Horticulture in America*, 104.
9. Fitzhugh, "Letters of William Fitzhugh," 176.
10. Bruce, *Economic History of Virginia*, 2:224.
11. Fitzhugh, "Letters of William Fitzhugh (continued)," 396.
12. Bruce, *Economic History of Virginia*, 2:214.
13. Beverley, *History and Present State of Virginia*, 259.
14. Quoted in Davis, 526.

Limbs

1. Doolittle, *Cultivated Landscapes*, vii.
2. Kirby, *Mockingbird Song*, 59.
3. Doolittle, *Cultivated Landscapes*, 58.
4. Rice, *Nature and History in the Potomac Country*, 112.
5. Hedrick, *History of Horticulture in America*, 20.
6. Calhoun, *Old Southern Apples*, 7.
7. Kerrigan, "Apples on the Border," 39.
8. Page, "Christie Cain Site," 238.
9. Riggs, "Removal Period Cherokee Households," 153.
10. Hamalainen, *Indigenous Continent*, 390.
11. Riggs, "Removal Period Cherokee Households," 152.

12. Saunt, *Unworthy Republic*, 260.

13. Rozema, *Coveted Lands*, 47.

14. Riggs, "Removal Period Cherokee Households," 152.

15. Saunt, *Unworthy Republic*, 13.

16. Saunt, *Unworthy Republic*, 276.

17. Saunt, *Unworthy Republic*, 277–78.

Juice

1. "Thomas Jefferson to James Mease, June 29, 1814," Founders Online, National Archives, https://founders.archives.gov /documents/Jefferson/03-07-02-0331.

2. Hedrick, *History of Horticulture in America*, 38.

3. Dolan, *Fruitful Legacy*, 17.

4. Quoted in Hedrick, *History of Horticulture in America*, 97.

5. Hedrick, *History of Horticulture in America*, 105.

6. Dolan, *Fruitful Legacy*, 14.

7. Bruce, *Economic History of Virginia*, 2:214.

8. Hatch, *Fruits and Fruit Trees of Monticello*, 17.

9. Records of Elizabeth City County, vol. 1684–99, 144, Virginia State Library, Richmond.

10. Records of York County, vol. 1687–91, 64, Virginia State Library.

11. Bruce, *Economic History of Virginia*, 2:228.

12. Hedrick, *History of Horticulture in America*, 113.

13. Quoted in Hedrick, *History of Horticulture in America*, 105.

14. Bruce, *Economic History of Virginia*, 2:231.

15. Records of York County, vol. 1671–94, 165.

16. Johnson, "On Cider," 32–33.

17. Lawson, *New Voyage*, 109.

18. "[March 1760]," Founders Online, National Archives, https://founders .archives.gov/documents/Washington /01-01-02-0005-0003.

19. "Observations–in–August [1768]," Founders Online, National Archives, https://founders.archives.gov/documents /Washington/01-02-02-0003-0024.

20. Fitz, *Southern Apple and Peach Culturist*, 213–14.

21. *Yazoo Democrat* (Yazoo City, MS), October 28, 1846, Chronicling America: Historic American Newspapers, https://chroniclingamerica.loc.gov/lccn /sn87065704/1846-10-28/ed-1/seq-6/.

22. Johnson, "On Cider," 31.

23. Johnson, "On Cider," 35.

24. Gosse, *Letters from Alabama*, 253.

25. Hedrick, *History of Horticulture in America*, 337.

26. Ferris, *Edible South*, 12.

27. Ferris, *Edible South*, 12.

28. "From Thomas Jefferson to Ellen Wayles Randolph Coolidge, 19 March 1826," Founders Online, National Archives, https://founders.archives.gov /documents/Jefferson/98-01-02-5969.

29. "Featured Letter: Thomas Jefferson Requests a Sampling of Cider," Monticello. org, December 2017, www.monticello.org /site/research-and-collections/featured -letter-thomas-jefferson-requests -sampling-cider.

30. "Thomas Jefferson to Thomas Newton, 20 November 1802," Founders Online, National Archives, https:// founders.archives.gov/documents /Jefferson/01-39-02-0037.

31. "Thomas Jefferson to Edmund Bacon, [15 November 1817]," Founders Online, National Archives, https://founders .archives.gov/documents/Jefferson/03-12 -0-0153.

32. "Jupiter Evans: 1743–1800, an Enslaved Coachman, Hostler, Stonecutter, and Valet," Monticello.org., accessed February 28, 2022, www.monticello.org /slavery/landscape-of-slavery-mulberry -row-at-monticello/meet-people/jupiter -evans/.

33. "From Thomas Jefferson to Thomas Mann Randolph, 4 February

1800," Founders Online, National Archives, https://founders.archives.gov /documents/Jefferson/01-31-02-0304.

Fruit

1. "Thomas Jefferson to James Mease, 29 June 1814," Founders Online, National Archives, https://founders.archives.gov /documents/Jefferson/03-07-02-0331.

2. Walker, "Of Lost Letters and Forgotten Fruit," 70.

3. "Thomas Jefferson to James Mease, 29 June 1814."

4. "Thomas Jefferson to James Mease, 29 June 1814."

5. Hatch, *Fruits and Fruit Trees of Monticello*, 78.

6. Byrd, *Westover Manuscripts*, n.p.

7. Hatch, *Fruits and Fruit Trees of Monticello*, 17.

8. Hatch, *Fruits and Fruit Trees of Monticello*, 49.

9. Calhoun, *Old Southern Apples*, 83.

10. Quoted in Calhoun, *Old Southern Apples*, 127.

11. *Farmer and Planter* 9, no. 2 (February 1858): 40.

12. Fitz, *Southern Apple and Peach Culturist*, 153.

13. William Coxe to Timothy Pickering, December 13, 1809, Timothy Pickering Papers, Massachusetts Historical Society, Boston.

14. Walker, "Of Lost Letters and Forgotten Fruit," 47.

15. Hatch, *Fruits and Fruit Trees of Monticello*, 74.

16. *Virginia Gazette* (Williamsburg), November 6, 1766.

17. *Pomaria Nurseries, Descriptive Catalogue of Southern and Acclimated Fruit Trees, Evergreens, Roses, Grape Vines, Rare Trees, Shrubs, Etc.*, 1862, n.p., South Caroliniana Library, University of South Carolina, Columbia.

18. *Fruitland Nurseries, Descriptive Catalogue of Fruit and Ornamental Trees, Shrubs, Vines, Roses, Evergreens, Hedge Plants, Etc.*, 1868–69, Henry G. Gilbert Nursery and Seed Trade Catalog Collection, National Agricultural Library, US Department of Agriculture, Beltsville, MD.

19. Downing, *Fruits and Fruit Trees of America*, 226.

20. Coxe, *View of the Cultivation of Fruit Trees*, 151.

21. Calhoun, *Old Southern Apples*, 215.

22. Calhoun, *Old Southern Apples*, 218.

Leaves

1. Catron-Sullivan, "Jarvis Van Buren," 1.

2. Hedrick, *History of Horticulture in America*, 53.

3. Humphreys, *Ghost Orchard*, 13.

4. Humphreys, *Ghost Orchard*, 22.

5. Hedrick, *History of Horticulture in America*, 67.

6. Hedrick, *History of Horticulture in America*, 212.

7. Catron-Sullivan, "Jarvis Van Buren," 3.

8. Kollock, *These Gentle Hills*, 32.

9. William Prince, "To be Sosd, By William Prince, at Flushing-Landing on Long-Island, Near New York, A Large Collection of Fruit Trees . . ., 1771," Nursery and Seed Trade Catalogues Collection, Special Collections and Archives Research Center, Oregon State University, Corvallis.

10. *Southern Nurseries, Catalogue of Fruit and Ornamental Trees and Plants*, 1851–52, 7–9, James R. Cothran Papers, Kenan Research Center, Atlanta History Center.

11. Meyers, "Fruitland Nursery," 53.

12. *Gloaming Nursery Catalogue*, 1859–60, 1, James R. Cothran Papers, Kenan Research Center, Atlanta History Center.

13. Bonner, *History of Georgia Agriculture*, 156.

14. Calhoun, *Old Southern Apples*, 234.

15. *Gloaming Nursery Catalogue*, 1859–60, 3–6, James R. Cothran Papers,

Kenan Research Center, Atlanta History Center.

16. *Gloaming Nursery Catalogue*, 1859–60, 3–6, James R. Cothran Papers, Kenan Research Center, Atlanta History Center.

17. Frances Tufts (descendant of Jarvis Van Buren) interview by the author, September 1, 2020.

18. Coleman and Gurr, *Dictionary of Georgia Biography*, 2:1014.

19. Tufts interview.

20. Census of 1850, James C. Bonner Papers, 483, Ina Dillard Russell Library, Special Collections, Georgia College, Milledgeville.

21. *Southern Cultivator*, 17, no. 10 (October 1859): 304.

TAMED
Planted

1. Silas McDowell to Moses Ashely Curtis, 1810, Silas McDowell Papers, 1827–1968, no. 01554, box 1, folder 8, series 1: 1885–95, Southern Historical Collection, Wilson Library, University of North Carolina at Chapel Hill.

2. Quoted in Fletcher, *History of Fruit Growing in Virginia*, 27–28.

3. Upshall, *History of Fruit Growing and Handling*, 140.

4. Polk County Agricultural Agent to Gary S. Dunbar, January 22, 1962, Silas McDowell Papers, 1827–1968, no. 01554, box 1, folder 14, series 3: 1959–68.

5. Auchter, *Apple Orchard Survey*, 4–5.

6. Auchter, *Apple Orchard Survey*, 36.

7. Auchter, *Apple Orchard Survey*, 6.

8. Ryan, *Life in Rock Castle*, 115.

9. Upshall, *History of Fruit Growing and Handling*, 154.

10. Hedrick, *History of Horticulture in America*, 350.

11. Upshall, *History of Fruit Growing and Handling*, 139.

Tasted

1. McGee, *On Food and Cooking*, 246, 248.

2. McGee, *On Food and Cooking*, 353.

3. Hatch, *Fruits and Fruit Trees of Monticello*, 71.

4. George Washington, Memorandoms [*sic*], Founders Archive, March 21, 1763, https://founders.archives.gov/?q=Author%3A%22Washington%2C%20George%22%20Dates-From%3A1763-03-21&s=1111311111&r=1&sr=.

5. Quoted in Hatch, *Fruits and Fruit Trees of Monticello*, 70.

6. Fletcher, *History of Fruit Growing in Virginia*, 16.

7. Hatch, *Fruits and Fruit Trees of Monticello*, 73.

8. *Southern Planter* 3 (1843): 22.

9. Hench, "Name 'Albemarle Pippin,'" 21.

10. *Wm. C. Geraty, Catalogue of Cabbage, Sweet Potato & Strawberry Plants, Fruit Trees, Grape Vines and All Kinds of Nursery Stock, Young's Island, South Carolina*, 1907, n.p., Henry G. Gilbert Nursery and Seed Trade Catalog Collection, National Agricultural Library, US Department of Agriculture, Beltsville, MD.

11. Hench, "Name 'Albemarle Pippin,'" 23.

12. Quoted in Fitz, *Southern Apple and Peach Culturist*, 155.

Cultivated

1. Conlogue, *Working the Garden*, 3.

2. Calhoun, *Old Southern Apples*, xvi.

3. Meacham, *Every Home A Distillery*, 19.

4. Fitzhugh, "Letters of William Fitzhugh (continued)."

5. Stafford County, Virginia, Will Books, 1669–1709, 97–102, Records of Stafford County, State Records Center, Library of Virginia, Richmond.

6. "Thomas Jefferson's Notes on Household Consumption, 3 June 1809–23 October 1811," Founders Online, National

Archives, https://founders.archives.gov /documents/Jefferson/03-04-02-0192.

7. "Observations–in–August [1768]," Founders Online, National Archives, https://founders.archives.gov/documents /Washington/01-02-02-0003-0024.

8. Hatch, *Fruits and Fruit Trees of Monticello*, 19.

9. Catron-Sullivan, "Jarvis Van Buren."

10. Howard, "William Summer," 6.

11. Quoted in letter from Gary S. Dunbar to Mrs. Albert Skaggs, in Silas McDowell Papers, 1827–1968, no. 01554, box 1, #14, series 3, 1959–68, Southern Historical Collection, Wilson Library, University of North Carolina at Chapel Hill.

12. Nelson, *Pharsalia*, 143.

13. Berlin, *Many Thousands Gone*, 134.

14. Hatch, "African American Gardens."

15. Gawalt, "Jefferson's Slaves," n.p.

16. Nelson, *Pharsalia*, 212.

17. Calhoun, *Old Southern Apples*, 39–40.

18. Jori Finkel, "The Enslaved Artist Whose Pottery Was an Actor of Resistance," *New York Times*, June 17, 2021.

Shared

1. *Southern Agriculturist*, March 1853, 85.

2. Jarvis Van Buren to Silas McDowell, December 3, 1856, Silas McDowell Papers, 1827–1968, no. 01554, Southern Historical Collection, Wilson Library, University of North Carolina at Chapel Hill.

3. Van Buren to McDowell, December 30, 1856, in Silas McDowell Papers.

4. Walter L. Steele, Account Book, Walter L. Steele Papers, no. 3681, Southern Historical Collection, Wilson Library.

5. Howard, "William Summer," 8.

6. Howard, "William Summer," 14.

7. Calhoun, *Old Southern Apples*, 40.

8. Calhoun, *Old Southern Apples*, 64, 159.

9. Creighton Lee Calhoun Papers on Southern Apples, Apple Binder A–C, 9,

Southern Historical Collection, Wilson Library.

10. David Vernon (nursery owner), interview by the author, February 15, 2021. Subsequent quotes from Vernon in this chapter are from this interview.

11. Hatch, *Fruits and Fruit Trees of Monticello*, 64.

Grafted

1. Kibler, *Taking Root*, xxv.

2. *Southern Agriculturist* 1 (January 1853): 17–18.

3. Kibler, *Taking Root*, 1.

4. Summer, "Character of the Pomologist."

5. South Carolina Department of Archives and History, accessed August 19, 2022, https://scdah.sc.gov/historic -preservation/resources/native-american -heritagem.

6. Howard, "William Summer," 5.

7. "The First People of South Carolina Lowcountry," Charleston County Public Library, accessed February 26, 2023, www .ccpl.org/charleston-time-machine/first -people-south-carolina-lowcountry.

8. Kibler, "Every Garden," 31.

9. Howard, "William Summer," 6, 12.

10. Kibler, "Every Garden," 31.

11. Calhoun, *Old Southern Apples*, 57.

12. Quoted in Calhoun, *Old Southern Apples*, 91.

13. Calhoun, *Old Southern Apples*, 87.

14. Downing, *Fruits and Fruit Trees of America*, 114.

15. William Summer to George Adam Fike, May 22, 1832, Summer Family Papers, South Caroliniana Library, University of South Carolina, Columbia.

16. *Farmer and Planter* 1 (December 1859): 377.

17. William Summer to George Adam Fike, May 14, 1850, Summer Family Papers.

18. Summer family ledger, Collection 8796, MS vol. bd., 1859–61, Summer Family Papers.

19. William Summer to George Adam Fike, April 12, 1860, Summer Family Papers.

20. Kibler, "On Reclaiming a Southern Antebellum Garden Heritage," 2.

21. Howard, "William Summer," 18.

22. Howard, "William Summer," 12; William Summer to George Adam Fike, May 14, 1850, Summer Family Papers.

23. Kibler, "On Reclaiming a Southern Antebellum Garden Heritage," 2.

24. Kibler, *Taking Root*, xxxii.

25. *Farmer and Planter* 2 (June 1860): 161.

26. Kibler, *Taking Root*, xxix.

27. Bernard E. Powers Jr., "Free Persons of Color, 1670–1863," South Carolina Encyclopedia, last modified August 3, 2022, www.scencyclopedia.org/sce /entries/free-persons-of-color/.

28. Howard, "William Summer," chap. 3, p. 10.

29. William Summer to George Adam Fike, April 8, 1867, Summer Family Papers.

30. Summer to Fike, April 8, 1867.

31. *Pomaria Nurseries, Descriptive Catalogue of Southern and Acclimated Fruit Trees, Evergreens, Roses, Grape Vines, Rare Trees, Shrubs, Etc.*, 1872, p. 8, South Caroliniana Library, University of South Carolina, Columbia.

32. Equal Justice Initiative, "Racial Terror and Reconstruction: A State Snapshot," Reconstruction in America: Racial Violence after the Civil War, 1865–76, 2020, https://eji.org/report /reconstruction-in-america/.

33. Kibler, "On Reclaiming a Southern Antebellum Garden Heritage," 8.

34. Howard, "William Summer," 18.

Celebrated

1. *Southern Cultivator* 17, no. 10 (October 1859): 312.

2. Bellamy and Walker, "Slaveholding," 167.

3. Prosper Alphonse Berckmans, "Voyage en Amérique," 1850, 14 (translated by Gerrit Voogt, 2014), Berckmans Family Papers, MS 122, Hargrett Rare Book and Manuscript Library, University of Georgia Libraries, Athens.

4. Range, "P. J. Berckmans," 219.

5. Berckmans, "Voyage en Amérique," 15.

6. Berckmans, "Voyage en Amérique," 7.

7. Berckmans, "Voyage en Amérique," 11.

8. Range, *Century of Georgia Agriculture*, 16.

9. Reynolds, "History of Fruitland Nurseries," 4.

10. Reynolds, "History of Fruitland Nurseries," 4.

11. Barry, *Fruit Garden*, 279–97.

12. Barry, *Fruit Garden*, 293.

13. Hedrick, *History of Horticulture in America*, 277.

14. Hedrick, *History of Horticulture in America*, 425.

15. Van Buren, "Fruit Culture at the South," 111.

16. Norse, *"Southern Cultivator"* 2.

17. Reynolds, "History of Fruitland Nurseries," 1.

18. Meyers, "Fruitland Nursery," 57.

19. *Southern Cultivator* 15 (1857): 359.

20. *Southern Cultivator* 15, no. 8 (August 1857): 249.

21. *Southern Cultivator* 10, no. 10 (1852): 324.

22. *Southern Cultivator* 15, no. 8 (August 1857): 245.

23. Range, "P. J. Berckmans," 220.

24. *Fruitland Nurseries, Descriptive Catalogue of Fruit and Ornamental Trees, Shrubs, Vines, Roses, Evergreens, Hedge Plants, Etc.*, 1858, Henry G. Gilbert Nursery and Seed Trade Catalog Collection, National Agricultural Library, US Department of Agriculture, Beltsville, MD.

25. *Fruitland Nurseries Catalogue*, 1858.

26. Meyers, "Fruitland Nursery," 70.

27. *Fruitland Nurseries Catalogue*, 1861.

28. *Fruitland Nurseries Catalogue*, 1861, 3.

29. *Fruitland Nurseries Catalogue*, 1861, 4.

30. Caldwell, "Legacy of the Berckmans Family."

31. Reynolds, "History of Fruitland Nurseries," 6.

32. Meyers, "Fruitland Nursery," 78.

33. Meyers, "Fruitland Nursery," 78.

34. Reynolds, "History of Fruitland Nurseries," 6.

35. Range, "P. J. Berckmans," 221.

36. Quoted in Range, "P. J. Berckmans," 226.

37. Reynolds, "History of Fruitland Nurseries," 7–8.

38. Owen, *Making of the Masters*; Bill Fields, "Berckmans Family Planted Seeds of Augusta Beauty," Masters, April 4, 2017, www.masters.com/en_US/news/articles /2017-04-04/berckmans_family_planted _seeds_of_augusta_beauty.html.

Named

1. "Secretary's Column: 'The Peoples' Department: 150 Years of USDA,'" USDA, February 21, 2017, www.usda.gov/media /blog/2012/05/11/secretarys-column -peoples-department-150-years-usda.

2. Daniel, "Last Plantation," 69.

3. Calhoun, *Old Southern Apples*, 122.

4. Calhoun, *Old Southern Apples*, 90.

5. *Yearbook of the United States Department of Agriculture, 1901*, 594.

6. Dolan, *Fruitful Legacy*, 111.

7. Special Collections of the National Agricultural Library: Deborah Griscom Passmore Watercolors, accessed February 27, 2023, https://specialcollections .nal.usda.gov/guide-collections/deborah -griscom-passmore-watercolors.

8. Special Collections of the National Agricultural Library: Deborah Griscom Passmore Watercolors.

9. *Yearbook of the United States Department of Agriculture, 1901*, 596.

10. Quoted in Calhoun, *Old Southern Apples*, 245.

11. Calhoun, *Old Southern Apples*, 140.

LOST

Forfeited

1. Neighbors, *Apples*, 2.

2. Calhoun, *Old Southern Apples*, 148.

3. Neighbors, *Apples*, 1.

4. Agricultural Marketing Resource Center, s.v. "Apples," last modified September 2021, www.agmrc.org/commodities -products/fruits/apples.

5. *Albemarle Apple Nurseries Descriptive Catalogue*, 1871, Albert and Shirley Small Special Collections Library, University of Virginia, Charlottesville.

6. Puckett and Allen, *Rock Castle Gorge*, 106.

7. *Southern Cultivator* 17 (July 1859): 357.

8. *Richmond Nurseries, Descriptive Catalogue of Fruit Trees, Vines & Plants, Cultivated and For Sale by Franklin Davis & Co., Richmond, Virginia*, 1869, Henry G. Gilbert Nursery and Seed Trade Catalog Collection, National Agricultural Library, US Department of Agriculture, Beltsville, MD.

9. Neighbors, *Apples*, 17.

10. Neighbors, *Apples*, 9.

11. *Pomaria Nurseries, Descriptive Catalogue of Southern and Acclimated Fruit Trees, Evergreens, Roses, Grape Vines, Rare Trees, Shrubs, Etc.*, 1862, p. 13, South Caroliniana Library, University of South Carolina, Columbia.

12. Dunaway, *First American Frontier*, 153.

13. Meacham, *Every Home a Distillery*, 6.

14. *Virginia Gazette*, October 3, 1777, 4.

15. *Virginia Gazette*, November 14, 1777, 2.

16. Dabney, *Mountain Spirits*, 47.

17. Jim Lawson (nursery owner) interview by the author, June 11, 2021.

18. Fitz, *Southern Apple and Peach Culturist*, 144.

19. Calhoun, *Old Southern Apples*, 158.

20. A. B. Williams, "As to Apples: An Address by Col. A. B. Williams, Editor of the Roanoke Times," n.p., newspaper clippings, Patrick County Historical Society, Stuart, VA.

21. *History of Patrick County*, 296.

22. *History of Patrick County*, 359.

23. "Looking Back on Southside," *Martinsville Bulletin*, October 13, 2017, https://martinsvillebulletin.com/news /looking-back-on-southside-the-history -of-patrick-county-s-apples/article _9ffb9c3e-01c6-5583-a2fe-56ab3ea73ee1 .html.

24. Puckett and Allen, *Rock Castle Gorge*, 80.

25. Ryan, *Life in Rock Castle*, 119.

26. *History of Patrick County*, 386.

27. Ryan, *Life in Rock Castle*, 125.

28. *Fruitland Nurseries, Descriptive Catalogue of Fruit and Ornamental Trees, Shrubs, Vines, Roses, Evergreens, Hedge Plants, Etc.*, 1861, 10. Henry G. Gilbert Nursery and Seed Trade Catalog Collection, National Agricultural Library, US Department of Agriculture, Beltsville, MD.

29. Fruitland Nurseries, Originators and Growers since 1856, Season 1937, 38, Henry G. Gilbert Nursery and Seed Trade Catalog Collection.

30. Neighbors, *Apples*, 1.

Displaced

1. Olausen, Daly, and Kline, *Great Smoky Mountains*, 17.

2. D. Davis, *Where There Are Mountains*, 63.

3. Carroll, Pulley, and Great Smoky Mountains Natural History Association, *Historic Structures Report*, 15.

4. Carroll, Pulley, and Great Smoky Mountains Natural History Association, *Historic Structures Report*, 15.

5. Carroll, Pulley, and Great Smoky Mountains Natural History Association, *Historic Structures Report*, 15.

6. Olausen, Daly, and Kline, *Great Smoky Mountains*, 18.

7. Kibler, "On Reclaiming a Southern Antebellum Garden Heritage," 2.

8. Medford, *Early History of Haywood County*, 77.

9. *Pomona Hill Nurseries, Descriptive Catalogue of Fruit Trees, Vines, Etc. Pomona, North Carolina*, 1893, 8–10, Henry G. Gilbert Nursery and Seed Trade Catalog Collection, National Agricultural Library, US Department of Agriculture, Beltsville, MD.

10. Carroll, Pulley, and Great Smoky Mountains Natural History Association, *Historic Structures Report*, 26.

11. *Stark Bro's Nurseries & Orchards Co., Seeds and Fruit Trees Catalogue*, 1901, 39, Henry G. Gilbert Nursery and Seed Trade Catalog Collection.

12. Carroll, Pulley, and Great Smoky Mountains Natural History Association, *Historic Structures Report*, 26.

13. Carroll, Pulley, and Great Smoky Mountains Natural History Association, *Historic Structures Report*, 75.

14. Carroll, Pulley, and Great Smoky Mountains Natural History Association, *Historic Structures Report*, 24.

15. D. Davis, *Where There Are Mountains*, 165.

16. D. Davis, *Where There Are Mountains*, 166.

17. Forest History Society, accessed February 28, 2023, https://foresthistory .org/research-explore/us-forest-service -history/policy-and-law/the-weeks -act/.

18. D. Davis, *Where There Are Mountains*, 117.

19. Olausen, Daly, and Kline, *Great Smoky Mountains*, 62.

20. National Park Service website, accessed November 9, 2021, www.nps.gov /aboutus/index.htm.

21. Gatewood, "North Carolina's Role," 169.

22. Gatewood, "North Carolina's Role," 184.

23. Gatewood, "North Carolina's Role," 178.

24. "Park History: Great Smoky Mountains," National Parks Traveler, accessed November 14, 2021, www .nationalparktraveler.org/parks/great -smoky-mountains-national-park /park-history-great-smoky-mountains.

25. H. Davis, *Cataloochee Valley*, 188.

26. Carroll, Pulley, and Great Smoky Mountains Natural History Association, *Historic Structures Report*, 20.

27. "Shenandoah National Park," Virginia History, accessed November 15, 2021, www.vahistory.org/shenandoah .html.

28. Eisenfeld, *Shenandoah*, 43.

29. Eisenfeld, *Shenandoah*, 33.

30. Eisenfeld, *Shenandoah*, 33.

31. "Exploring Shenandoah National Park History," accessed February 27, 2023, https://nps.maps.arcgis.com/apps /webappviewer/index.html?id=81acffc694 a24f4692e704051526f61c&fbclid=IwAR 0wim41BmjjT2mK-M9MCUdmmm6 ybzhu0tdlN1-w31rWlEHFRcsd1DXfo0Y.

32. Kyle, "Dark Side of Skyline Drive."

33. Kyle, "Dark Side of Skyline Drive."

34. Kyle, "Dark Side of Skyline Drive."

35. Powell, "Time to Leave."

36. "Shenandoah National Park," Library of Virginia, accessed February 27, 2023, https://lva.omeka.net/exhibits/show /law_and_justice/eminent_domain /shenandoah.

37. Carroll, Pulley, and Great Smoky Mountains Natural History Association, *Historic Structures Report*, 28.

Transported

1. Diamond, "Migrations," 196. The procession included twenty-two people, four saddle horses, seventy-five head of cattle, and about forty-five oxen.

2. Diamond, "Migrations," 19.

3. Coffin, "Early Settlements," 31.

4. Diamond, "Origins of Pioneer Apple Orchards," 439.

5. Diamond, "Migrations," 133.

6. Diamond, "Migrations," 194.

7. McClintock, "Henderson Luelling," 156.

8. Coffin, "Early Settlements," 31.

9. Dolan, *Fruitful Legacy*, 44.

10. Dolan, *Fruitful Legacy*, 44.

11. Marrs, *Railroads in the Old South*, 5–6.

12. Griffin and Dixon, *Virginia Railroads*, 7.

13. Marrs, *Railroads in the Old South*, 114.

14. Fletcher, *History of Fruit Growing in Virginia*, 26.

15. Dixon, *West Virginia Railroads*, 11.

16. Marrs, *Railroads in the Old South*, 57.

17. Dolan, *Fruitful Legacy*, 70.

18. Fletcher, *History of Fruit Growing in Virginia*, 34.

19. Upshall, *History of Fruit Growing and Handling*, 114.

20. Jane Harriet Luelling, "Bringing the Traveling Nursery across the Plains in 1847," 4, Clackamas County General History, Biography XI, Historical Records Survey, Special Collections and University Archives, Knight Library, University of Oregon, Eugene.

21. Diamond, "Migrations," 226.

22. McClintock, "Henderson Luelling," 159.

23. Lake "Apple in Oregon." Virginia Greening, an apple grown in the South since the 1700s, was among Luelling's trees.

24. Cardwell, "First Fruits of the Land," 35.

Altered

1. *Pomaria Nurseries, Descriptive Catalogue of Southern and Acclimated Fruit Trees, Evergreens, Roses, Grape Vines,*

Rare Trees, Shrubs, Etc., 1862, p. 11, South Caroliniana Library, University of South Carolina, Columbia.

2. Conlogue, *Working the Garden*, 3.

3. Fite, *American Farmers*, 3.

4. Dolan, *Fruitful Legacy*, 32.

5. Upshall, *History of Fruit Growing and Handling*, 127.

6. Upshall, *History of Fruit Growing and Handling*, 142.

7. Waugh, *American Apple Orchard*, 199.

8. Upshall, *History of Fruit Growing and Handling*, 154.

9. Calhoun, *Old Southern Apples*, 44.

10. Taylor, *Fruit Industry*, 351.

11. Beach, *Apples of New York*, 69.

12. Upshall, *History of Fruit Growing and Handling*, 31.

13. Upshall, *History of Fruit Growing and Handling*, 55.

14. *Wm. C. Geraty, Catalogue of Cabbage, Sweet Potato & Strawberry Plants, Fruit Trees, Grape Vines and All Kinds of Nursery Stock, Young's Island, South Carolina*, 1906, 24; *Fruitland Nurseries, Descriptive Catalogue of Fruit and Ornamental Trees, Shrubs, Vines, Roses, Evergreens, Hedge Plants, Etc.*, no. 1, 1897, 6, both in Henry G. Gilbert Nursery and Seed Trade Catalog Collection, National Agricultural Library, US Department of Agriculture, Beltsville, MD.

15. Calhoun, *Old Southern Apples*, 44.

16. Proceedings of the Twenty-Ninth Session of the American Pomological Society, Kansas City, MO, September 19–20, 1905, 3–4.

17. Conlogue in *Working the Garden* uses the terms "old agriculture" and "new agriculture," 12–16.

18. David Ricardo defined the concept of comparative advantage in the early nineteenth century.

19. Auchter, "Apple Orchard Survey," 62.

20. Upshall, *History of Fruit Growing and Handling*, 154.

21. Upshall, *History of Fruit Growing and Handling*, 143.

22. Dolan, *Fruitful Legacy*, 74.

23. *Yearbook of the United States Department of Agriculture, 1907*, 306.

24. *Yearbook of the United States Department of Agriculture, 1907*, 306.

25. *Yearbook of the United States Department of Agriculture, 1907*, 306.

26. Dolan, *Fruitful Legacy*, 76.

27. Dolan, *Fruitful Legacy*, 77.

Abandoned

1. *Pomaria Nurseries, Descriptive Catalogue of Southern and Acclimated Fruit Trees, Evergreens, Roses, Grape Vines, Rare Trees, Shrubs, Etc.*, 1862, p. 11, South Caroliniana Library, University of South Carolina, Columbia.

2. Stempien and Linstrom, *Liberty Hyde Bailey Gardener's Companion*, 145.

3. Stempien and Linstrom, *Liberty Hyde Bailey Gardener's Companion*, 176.

4. Handwritten notes, 1857, n.p., Prosper J. Berckmans orchard notebook, MS 1261, Hargrett Rare Book and Manuscript Library, University of Georgia, Athens.

5. Fite, *American Farmers*, viii.

6. Fite, *American Farmers*, 3.

7. Fite, *American Farmers*, 15.

8. National Agricultural Library, accessed February 28, 2023, www.nal.usda.gov/legacy/topics/act-establish-department-agriculture (page discontinued).

9. Louisiana Agricultural Extension Bulletin, 1908, 5.

10. Dolan, *Fruitful Legacy*, 67.

11. March 1939 Extension Circular No. 208, 8, Extension Circulars, 1930–46, S544.3.NB, Special Collections Research Center, North Carolina State University Libraries, Raleigh.

12. March 1936 Extension Circular No. 210, 3.

13. Bill Best refers to being "literate" in the ways of the land in *From Existence to Essence*, 102.

REVIVED

Preserved

1. Lee Calhoun (nurseryman and author), interview by the author, February 23, 2019.

2. Calhoun interview, February 23, 2019.

3. Calhoun interview, October 17, 2019.

4. Calhoun interview, January 23, 2019.

5. Calhoun interview, January 23, 2019.

6. Jim Lawson (nursery owner), interview by the author, June 10, 2021.

7. Lawson interview, June 10, 2021.

8. *Gloaming Nursery Catalogue*, 1859–60, 4, James R. Cothran Papers, Kenan Research Center, Atlanta History Center.

9. Lawson interview, June 10, 2021.

10. Lawson interview, June 10, 2021.

11. Lawson interview, June 11, 2021.

12. Creighton Lee Calhoun Papers on Southern Apples, Apple Binder D–J, Southern Historical Collection, Wilson Library, University of North Carolina at Chapel Hill.

13. Calhoun, *Old Southern Apples*, 137.

14. Neighbors, *Collecting Old Southern Varieties*, 14.

15. Lisa Turney (site manager, Horne Creek Living Historical Farm), interview by the author, February 1, 2022.

16. Stephen Mihm (associate professor and director of undergraduate studies, University of Georgia), interview by the author, March 8, 2021.

17. Mihm interview.

18. Josh Fuder (agriculture and natural resources agent, Cherokee County, GA), interview by the author, February 26, 2021.

19. David Anderson (horticulture operations supervisor, Eastern Band of Cherokee Indians), interview by the author, January 14, 2022.

20. Calhoun, *Old Southern Apples*, 58.

Specialized

1. Auchter, "Apple Orchard Survey," 62.

2. Guttmann, "Agricultural Land-Use Change," 63.

3. US Department of Agriculture, *Survey of Commercial Apple and Peach Orchards*, 6.

4. Burton, "Apple Orchard's Demise."

5. Guttmann, "Agricultural Land-Use Change," 86.

6. Diane Kearns (owner, Fruit Hill Orchard), interview by the author, February 1, 2022.

7. Calhoun, *Old Southern Apples*, 169.

8. *Lawson's Nursery Catalogue, Specializing in Old Fashioned and Unusual Fruit Trees*, Fall 1982, Private collection of Jim Lawson. Ball Ground, GA.

9. Guttmann, "Agricultural Land-Use Change," 143.

10. Kearns interview, January 20, 2022. Subsequent quotes from Kearns in this chapter are from this interview.

11. CiderCon2022, Workshop on Organic Apple Production, Richmond, VA, February 5, 2022.

12. Futrell, *Good Apples*, 61.

13. David Glaize, interview by the author, January 19, 2022. Subsequent quotes from David Glaize in this chapter are from this interview.

14. Phil Glaize, interview by the author, January 31, 2022. Subsequent quotes from Phil Glaize in this chapter are from this interview.

15. Helm, Helm, and Markle, *Family Windows*, 92.

Evolved

1. Kenneth K. Krakow, *Georgia Place Names* (Macon, GA: Winship Press, 1975), www.kenkrakow.com/gpn/georgia_place-names.htm.

2. Upshall, *History of Fruit Growing and Handling*, 43.

3. Tim Mercier, interview by the author, February 18, 2021. Subsequent quotes from Mercier in this chapter are from this interview.

4. Hatch, *Fruits and Fruit Trees of Monticello*, 76.

5. Downing, *Fruits and Fruit Trees of America*, 134.

6. Wolf, "Easter Freeze of 2007," n.p.

7. Wolf, "Easter Freeze of 2007," 1.

8. Wolf, "Easter Freeze of 2007," 1.

9. Wolf, "Easter Freeze of 2007," 11.

10. Quoted in Dolan, *Fruitful Legacy*, 52.

11. Dolan, *Fruitful Legacy*, 118.

12. Dolan, *Fruitful Legacy*, 123.

13. Greg Peck (associate professor, Cornell University), interview by the author, July 13, 2021.

14. Peck and Knickerbocker, "Economic Case Studies," 7.

15. Baker, "Marketing Campaign."

Explored

1. Marini, "Growing Apples," 1; Laurant and Saunders, *Packing Shed Memories*, 34.

2. Tom Burford (nurseryman and author), interview by the author, April 22, 2009.

3. Pollard, *Under the Blue Ledge*, 157.

4. Nelson, *Pharsalia*, 143.

5. Nelson, *Pharsalia*, 230.

6. Pollard, *Under the Blue Ledge*, 159.

7. John Saunders and Ruth Saunders (owners, Silver Creek Orchards), interview by the author, January 23, 2020. Subsequent quotes from the Saunderses in this chapter are from this interview.

8. Laurant and Saunders, *Packing Shed Memories*, 238.

9. Laurant and Saunders, *Packing Shed Memories*, 248.

10. Laurant and Saunders, *Packing Shed Memories*, 135.

11. Laurant and Saunders, *Packing Shed Memories*, 187.

12. Seabrook, "Crunch."

13. Warren Mays (retired orchardist), interview by the author, February 22, 2022.

14. Adam Cooke, interview with the author, February 22, 2022. Subsequent quotes from Cooke in this chapter are from this interview.

15. Eleanor Leger, "Apple Choices: What's in YOUR Cider?," *Cidernomics: Life in the Underdog Economy* (blog), December 10, 2016, https://cidernomics .com/2016/12/10/apple-choices-whats -in-your-cider/.

16. Leger "Apple Choices."

17. Leger, "Apple Choices."

Studied

1. Raul Godinez and Mary Godinez (nursery owners), interview by the author, January 14, 2020. Subsequent quotes from the Godinezes in this chapter are from this interview.

2. Xu, "Apple Genome."

3. Xu, "Apple Genome."

4. Dolan, *Fruitful Legacy*, 130.

5. Greg Peck (associate professor, Cornell University), interview by the author, July 13, 2021. Subsequent quotes from Peck in this chapter are from this interview.

6. University of Minnesota, "Honeycrisp: The Apple of Minnesota's Eye," AUTM, 2018, https://autm.net/about -tech-transfer/better-world-project/bwp -stories/honeycrisp-apple.

7. Kenny Barnwell (orchardist) interview by the author, March 2, 2022.

8. Abad-Santos, "Honeycrisp Was Just the Beginning."

9. Abad-Santos, "Honeycrisp Was Just the Beginning."

10. Baker, "Next Celebrity Apple."

11. Yao, "Researchers 'FasTrack' Plum Breeding."

12. Christopher Gottschalk, interview with the author, March 8, 2022.

13. Tim Wright, interview with the author, March 7, 2022. Subsequent quotes from Wright in this chapter are from this interview.

14. Upshall, *History of Fruit Growing and Handling*, 62.

15. Upshall, *History of Fruit Growing and Handling*, 63.

16. "The Golden Age of Apples in the South," North Carolina Historic Sites, accessed February 28, 2023. https://historicsites.nc.gov/all-sites/horne-creek-farm/southern-heritage-apple-orchard/apples/apple-history/golden-age-apples-south.

17. Calhoun, *Old Southern Apples*, 232.

18. Gauthier et al., *Profile of Commercial Apple Production*, 1.

19. Kevan Evans, interview with the author, March 8, 2022. Subsequent quotes from Evans in this chapter are from this interview.

20. Gauthier et al., *Profile of Commercial Apple Production*, 2.

21. Jeff Wheeler (senior agricultural extension specialist), interview by the author, July 30, 2021. Subsequent quotes from Wheeler in this chapter are from this interview.

22. Jacob Lahne, interview with the author, March 14, 2022.

23. Susan Whitehead, interview with the author, January 31, 2022.

24. Whitehead interview.

CODA

1. Calhoun, *Old Southern Apples*, xiii.

2. Gawalt, "Jefferson's Slaves," 31.

3. Krista Tippett and Rachel Naomi Remen, "How We Live with Loss," August 11, 2005, *On Being* podcast, 50:51, https://onbeing.org/programs/rachel-naomi-remen-how-we-live-with-loss/.

BIBLIOGRAPHY

Manuscripts and Archival Collections

Asheville, NC
    Blue Ridge Parkway Archives
        Moses Cone Manuscripts
Athens, GA
    University of Georgia Libraries, Hargrett Rare Book and Manuscript Library
        Berckmans Family Papers, MS 122
        Prosper J. Berckmans orchard notebook, MS 1267
Atlanta, GA
    Atlanta History Center, Kenan Research Center
        Cherokee Garden Library
            James R. Cothran Papers
Augusta, GA
    Augusta University Reece Library Special Collections
        Berckmans/Fruitland Nurseries Records, 1835–1947
Beltsville, MD
    US Department of Agriculture, National Agricultural Library
        Henry G. Gilbert Nursery and Seed Trade Catalog Collection
        Prince Family Manuscript Collection
Boston, MA
    Massachusetts Historical Society
        Thomas Pickering Papers
Chapel Hill, NC
    University of North Carolina at Chapel Hill, Wilson Library
        Southern Historical Collection
            Creighton Lee Calhoun Papers on Southern Apples
            Silas McDowell Papers, 1827–1968, no. 01554
            Waler L. Steele Papers, no. 3681
Charleston, SC
    South Carolina History Society
        Charles T. McIntosh and Son Records, 1858–1913
Charlottesville, VA
    University of Virginia
        Albert and Shirley Small Special Collections Library
Columbia, SC
    University of South Carolina, South Caroliniana Library
        Summer Family Papers
Corvallis, OR
    Oregon State University, Special Collections and Archives Research Center
        Nursery and Seed Trade Catalogues Collection

Eugene, OR
  Knight Library, Special Collections and University Archives
    Historical Records Survey
Greensboro, NC
  Greensboro History Museum
    Lindley Nurseries Collection, 1839–1965, no. 120
  University of North Carolina Greensboro
    Martha Blakeney Hodges Specials and University Archives
      Rare Book Collection
Milledgeville, GA
  Georgia College and State University, Ina Dillard Russell Library
    Special Collections
      James C. Bonner Papers
Raleigh, NC
  North Carolina State University Libraries
    Special Collections Research Center
      Extension Circulars, 1930–46
Richmond, VA
  Library of Virginia, State Records Center
    Records of Elizabeth City County
    Records of Stafford County
    Records of York County
Stuart, VA
  Patrick County Historical Society
    Newspaper clippings
Winchester, VA
  Handley Regional Library
    Old Time Apple Growers Association Collection, 239 WFCHS
    Stuart Bell Jr. Archives

Journals

American Fruit Grower   *Southern Agriculturist*
Farmer and Planter   *Southern Cultivator*
Horticulturist   *Southern History*
North Carolina Planter   *Southern Planter*

Primary and Secondary Sources

Abad-Santos, Alex. "Honeycrisp Was Just the Beginning: Inside the Quest to Create the Perfect Apple." *Vox*, September 11, 2017.

Auchter, E. C. "An Apple Orchard Survey of Berkeley County." West Virginia University Agriculture Experiment Station, Bulletin 151, 1915.

Ayres, Edward. *Fruit Culture in Colonial Virginia*. Research report for Colonial Williamsburg, Williamsburg, VA, April 1973.

Baker, Sharon M. "Marketing Campaign for Cosmic Crisp Heats Up." *Seattle Business*, July 2019.

Baker, Sharon M. "The Next Celebrity Apple Is Washington's Cosmic Crisp." *Seattle Business*, November 2017.

Barry, P. *The Fruit Garden: A Treatise*. Rochester, NY: Published by the author, 1863.

Baszile, Natalie, ed. *We Are Each Other's Harvest: Celebrating African American Farmers, Land, and Legacy.* New York: Harper Collins, 2021.

Beach, S. A. *The Apples of New York, Vol. I & Vol. II.* Albany: J. B. Lyon Company, 1905.

Bellamy, Donnie D., and Diane E. Walker. "Slaveholding in Antebellum Augusta and Richmond County, Georgia." *Phylon* 48, no. 2 (1987): 165–77.

Berlin, Ira. *Many Thousands Gone: The First Two Centuries of Slavery in North America.* Cambridge, MA: Harvard University Press, 1998.

Best, Bill. *From Existence to Essence.* Lexington: Kentucky Imprints, 1999.

Beverley, Robert. *The History and Present State of Virginia.* A new edition with an introduction by Susan Scott Parrish. Chapel Hill: University of North Carolina Press, 2013.

Bonner, James C. "Genesis of Agricultural Reform in the Cotton Belt." *Journal of Southern History* 9, no. 4 (1943): 475–500.

———. *A History of Georgia Agriculture, 1732–1860.* Athens: University of Georgia Press. 1964.

Bruce, Philip Alexander. *Economic History of Virginia in the Seventeenth Century.* 2 vols. New York: Peter Smith, 1935.

Bunker, John P. *Not Far from the Tree: A Brief History of the Apples and Orchards of Palermo, Maine, 1804–2004.* Self-published, 2008.

Burton, Cynthia Cather. "Apple Orchard's Demise Marks the End of an Era." *Winchester Star*, January 31, 2019.

Byrd, William. *The Westover Manuscripts: Containing the History of the Dividing Line betwixt Virginia and North Carolina.* Petersburg, VA: Printed by E. and J. C. Ruffin, 1841.

Caldwell, Lee Ann. "The Legacy of the Berckmans Family." *Augusta Magazine*, April 2016.

Calhoun, Lee. *Old Southern Apples: A Comprehensive History and Description of Varieties for Collectors, Growers, and Fruit Enthusiasts.* Revised and expanded edition. White River Junction, VT: Chelsea Green Publishing, 2010.

Cardwell, J. R. "The First Fruits of the Land: A Brief History of Early Horticulture in Oregon, Part 1." *Oregon Historical Quarterly* 7 (March 1906): 28–51.

Carrier, Lyman. *The Beginnings of Agriculture in America.* New York: McGraw Hill, 1923.

Carroll, Roy, Raymond H. Pulley, and Great Smoky Mountains Natural History Association. *Historic Structures Report, Little Cataloochee, North Carolina: Jim Hannah Cabin, Will Messer Barn, Dan Cook Cabin and Apple House, Great Smoky Mountains National Park.* Boone, NC: Appalachian State University, 1976.

Catron-Sullivan, Staci. "Jarvis Van Buren: A Brief History of Georgia Horticulturist, Writer, Nurseryman, and Builder." *Magnolia* 16, no. 1 (Fall 2000): 1–9.

Coffin, Addison. "Early Settlements of Friends in North Carolina, Traditions and Reminiscences, II." *Southern Friend: Journal of the North Carolina Friends Historical Society*, Autumn 1883, 27–33.

Coleman, Kenneth, and Charles Stephen Gurr, eds. *Dictionary of Georgia Biography.* 2 vols. Athens: University of Georgia Press, 1983.

Conlogue, William. *Working the Garden: American Writers and the Industrialization of Agriculture.* Chapel Hill: University of North Carolina Press, 2001.

Coxe, William. *A View of the Cultivation of Fruit Trees.* Philadelphia: M. Carey and Son, 1817.

Crosby, Alfred W. *Ecological Imperialism: The Biological Expansion of Europe, 900–1900*. Cambridge: Cambridge University Press, 1986.

Dabney, Joseph Earl. *Mountain Spirits: A Chronicle of Corn Whiskey from King James' Ulster Plantation to America's Appalachians and the Moonshine Life*. Asheville, NC: Bright Mountain Books, 1974.

Daniel, Pete. "The Last Plantation: The USDA's Racist Operating System." In *We Are Each Other's Harvest: Celebrating African American Farmers, Land, and Legacy*, edited by Natalie Baszile, 69–87. New York: Harper Collins, 2021.

Davis, Donald Edward. *Where There Are Mountains: An Environmental History of the Southern Appalachians*. Athens: University of Georgia Press, 2000.

Davis, Hattie Caldwell. *Cataloochee Valley: Vanished Settlements of the Great Smoky Mountains*. Alexander, NC: Worldcom, 1997.

Davis, Richard Beale. "Chesapeake Pattern and Pole-Star: William Fitzhugh in His Plantation World, 1676–1701." *Proceedings of the American Philosophical Society* 105, no. 6 (1961): 525–29.

———, ed. *William Fitzhugh and His Chesapeake World, 1676–1701*. Chapel Hill: University of North Carolina Press, 1963.

Diamond, David H. "Migrations: Henderson Luelling and the Cultivated Apple, 1822–1854." PhD diss., Northern Arizona University, 2004.

———. "Origins of Pioneer Apple Orchards in the American West: Random Seeding versus Artisan Horticulture." *Agricultural History* 84, no. 4 (2010): 423–50.

Dixon, Thomas W., Jr. *West Virginia Railroads*. Forest, VA: TLC Publishing, 2009.

Dolan, Susan. *A Fruitful Legacy: A Historic Context of Orchards in the United States with Technical Information for Registering Orchards at the National Register of Historic Places*. Washington, DC: National Park Service, 2009.

Doolittle, William E. *Cultivated Landscapes of Native North America*. Oxford: Oxford University Press, 2000.

Downing, Andrew Jackson. *The Fruits and Fruit Trees of America, Revised*. New York: John Wiley and Son, 1865.

Dunaway, Wilma. *The First American Frontier: Transition to Capitalism in Southern Appalachia, 1700–1860*. Chapel Hill: University of North Carolina Press, 1996.

Dunbar, Gary S. "Thermal Belts in North Carolina." *Geographical Review* 56, no. 4 (October 1966): 516–26.

Eisenfeld, Sue. *Shenandoah: A Story of Conservation and Betrayal*. Lincoln: University of Nebraska Press, 2014.

Ferris, Marcie. *The Edible South*. Chapel Hill: University of North Carolina Press, 2014.

Fite, Gilbert C. *American Farmers: The New Minority*. Bloomington: Indiana University Press, 1981.

Fitz, James. *The Southern Apple and Peach Culturist, Adapted to the Soil and Climate of Maryland, Virginia, the Carolinas, Georgia, and Farther South Including Portions of the West and West Virginia, Containing Full and Practical Instructions . . . .* Richmond, VA: J. W. Randolph and English, 1872.

Fitzhugh, William. "Letters of William Fitzhugh (continued)." *Virginia Magazine of History and Biography* 1, no. 4 (April 1894): 391–410.

———. "Letters of William Fitzhugh." *Virginia Magazine of History and Biography* 4, no. 2 (October 1896): 176–84.

Fletcher, S.W. *A History of Fruit Growing in Virginia*. Reprinted from the Proceedings of the Thirty-Seventh Annual Meeting of the Virginia State Horticultural Society, December 6, 7 and 8, 1932.

Futrell, Susan. *Good Apples: Behind Every Bite*. Iowa City: University of Iowa Press, 2017.

Gatewood, Willard Badgette. "North Carolina's Role in the Establishment of the Great Smoky Mountains National Park." *North Carolina Historical Review* 37, no. 2 (1960): 165–84.

Gauthier, Nicole Ward, Kimberly Leonberger, Ricardo Bessin, Matthew Springer, John Strang and Shawn Wright. *A Profile of Commercial Apple Production in Kentucky in 2017*. Lexington, KY: Southern Integrated Pest Management Center, 2017.

Gawalt, Gerard W. "Jefferson's Slaves: Crop Accounts at Monticello, 1805–1808." *Journal of the Afro-American Historical and Genealogical Society* 13, no. 1–2 (Spring/Fall 1994):19–38.

Givens, Peter Shelburne. "Cataloochee and the Establishment of the Great Smoky Mountains National Park." Master's thesis, Western Carolina University, 1978.

Gosse, Philip Henry. *Letters from Alabama*. London: Morgan and Chase, 1859.

Griffin, William E., and Thomas W. Dixon Jr. *Virginia Railroads, Vol. 1*. Marceline, MO: Walsworth Publishing, 2010.

Guttmann, Joseph Paul. "Agricultural Land-Use Change and Local Context: The Shenandoah–Cumberland Valley Apple-Growing District in the Eastern United States." PhD diss., University of Tennessee, 2012.

Hamalainen, Pekka. *Indigenous Continent: The Epic Contest for North America*. New York: W. W. Norton, 2022.

Hatch, Peter. "African American Gardens at Monticello." *Twinleaf*, January 2001, n.p.

———. *The Fruits and Fruit Trees of Monticello*. Charlottesville: University Press of Virginia, 1998.

Hedrick, U. P. *A History of Horticulture in America to 1860*. New York: Oxford University Press. 1950.

Hedrick, U. P. *Systematic Pomology*. New York: Macmillan Company, 1925.

Helm, Elizabeth, Walter J. Helm, and Elaine Markle. *Family Windows*. Self-published, 2019.

Hench, Atcheson L. "The Name 'Albemarle Pippin.'" *Magazine of Albemarle County History* 14 (1954): 21–25.

History of Patrick County, Virginia. Stuart, VA: Patrick County Historical Society, 1999.

Holbert, Patricia Katherine. "William Fitzhugh: A Self-Made Aristocrat." Master's thesis, University of Virginia, 1942.

Howard, William Herbert. "William Summer: Nineteenth Century Horticulturist." Master's thesis, University of South Carolina, 1982. Collection Number: SoCar 378.757UO, H83w, 1985.

Humphreys, Helen. *The Ghost Orchard: The Hidden History of Apples in North America*. Toronto: Harper Collins, 2017.

Joachim, David, and Andres Schloss. *The Science of Good Food*. Toronto: Robert Rose, 2008.

Johnson, Rev. John B. "On Cider." In *Transactions of the Society for the Promotion of Agriculture, Arts and Manufactures, Instituted in the State of New York*, 31–37. Albany, NY: John Barber, 1807.

Juniper, Barrie E., and David J. Mabberley. *The Extraordinary Story of the Apple*. Royal Botanic Gardens, Kew: Kew Publishing, 2019.

Kerrigan, William. "Apples on the Border: Orchards and the Contest for the Great Lakes." *Michigan Historical Review* 34, no. 1 (2008): 25–41.

Kibler, James Everett. "Every Garden a Volume of Nature's Poetry: The Pomaria Nursery and the Summer Family Heritage." *Caroliniana Columns* 36 (Fall 2014): 29–35.

———. "On Reclaiming a Southern Antebellum Garden Heritage: An Introduction to Pomaria Nurseries, 1840–1879." *Magnolia* 10, no. 1 (Fall 1993): 1–16.

———. *Taking Root: The Nature Writing of William and Adam Summer of Pomaria.* Columbia: University of South Carolina Press, 2017.

Kirby, Jack Temple. *Mockingbird Song: Ecological Landscapes of the South.* Chapel Hill: University of North Carolina Press, 2006.

Kollock, John. *These Gentle Hills.* Clarkesville, GA: Habersham House, 1976.

Kyle, Robert. "The Dark Side of Skyline Drive." *Washington Post*, October 17, 1993. www.washingtonpost.com/archive/opinions/1993/10/17/the-dark-side-of-skyline -drive/d72e6151-6b96-483c-ab68-dea952288b6a/.

Lake, Edward Ralph. "The Apple in Oregon, Part I." In *Eighth Biennial Report of the Board of Horticulture of the State of Oregon*, 107–21. Salem, OR: J. R. Whitney, 1905.

Laurant, Darrell, and Paul Saunders. *Packing Shed Memories.* Piney River, VA: Saunders Publishing, 2018.

Lawson, John. *A New Voyage to Carolina.* London, 1709.

Lawson's Nursery Catalogue. Specializing in Old Fashioned and Unusual Fruit Trees, Fall 1982 & Spring 1983. Private collection of Jim Lawson. Ball Ground, GA.

Lundy, Ronni. *Victuals: An Appalachian Journey, with Recipes.* New York: Clarkson Potter, 2016.

Marini, Richard P. "Growing Apples in Virginia." Series 422–023, Virginia Cooperative Extension, Virginia Tech, Blacksburg, August 17, 2020.

Marrs, Aaron W. *Railroads in the Old South: Pursuing Progress in a Slave Society.* Baltimore: Johns Hopkins University Press, 2009.

Martin, Alice A. *All About Apples.* Boston: Houghton Mifflin, 1976.

Martin, Peter. *The Pleasure Gardens of Virginia: From Jamestown to Jefferson.* Princeton, NJ: Princeton University Press, 1991.

Martin, Toni Tipton-Martin. *The Jemima Code: Two Centuries of African American Cookbooks.* Austin: University of Texas Press, 2015.

McClintock, Thomas C. "Henderson Luelling, Seth Lewelling and the Birth of the Pacific Coast Fruit Industry." *Oregon Historical Quarterly* 68, no. 2 (1967): 153–74.

McGee, Harold. *On Food and Cooking: The Science and Lore of the Kitchen, Revised.* New York: Scribner, 2004.

McGregor, S. E. *Insect Pollination of Cultivated Crop Plants.* US Department of Agriculture, Agriculture Handbook No. 496. University of Virginia, 2008.

Meacham, Sarah Hand. *Every Home a Distillery: Alcohol, Gender, and Technology in the Colonial Chesapeake.* Baltimore: Johns Hopkins University Press, 2009.

Medford, W. Clark. *The Early History of Haywood County.* Waynesville, NC: Miller Printing Company, 1961.

Meyers, Christopher C. "Fruitland Nursery: A 'Horticultural Mecca.'" *Georgia Historical Quarterly* 99, no. 1/2 (Spring/Summer 2015): 48–80.

Nabhan, Gary Paul, ed. "Place-Based Foods of Appalachia: From Rarity to Community Restoration and Market Recovery." Renewing America's Food Traditions Alliance, University of Arizona Southwest Center, Tucson, 2015.

Neighbors, Joyce L. *Apples: Collecting Old Southern Varieties*. Gadsden, AL: Self-published, 1998.

Nelson, Lynn A. *Pharsalia: An Environmental Biography of a Southern Plantation, 1780–1880*. Athens: University of Georgia Press, 2007.

Newman, C. C. "Notes of Varieties of Apples." Southern Carolina Experiment Station of Clemson Agricultural College, Bulletin 109, 1905.

Norse, Clifford Carlton. "The *Southern Cultivator*, 1843–1861." PhD diss., Florida State University College of Arts and Sciences, 1969.

Okie, William Thomas. *The Georgia Peach: Culture, Agriculture, and Environment in the American South*. Cambridge: Cambridge University Press, 2016.

Olausen, Stephen, John Daly, and Laura Kline. *Great Smoky Mountains Park Historic Resource Study*. Prepared for the National Park Service by The Public Archaeology Laboratory, Inc., Pawtucket, RI, April 2016.

Owen, David. *Making of the Masters: Clifford Roberts, Augusta National, and Golf's Most Prestigious Tournament*. New York: Simon and Schuster, 2003.

Page, Brett. "The Christie Cain Site: Historical and Archaeological Evidence of the Life and Times of a Cherokee Metis Household (1835–1838)." In *May We Remember Well: A Journal of the History and Cultures of Western North Carolina, Vol. 1*, edited by Robert S. Brunk, 228–48. Asheville, NC: Robert S. Brunk Auction Services, 1997.

Peck, Gregory M., and Whitney Knickerbocker. "Economic Case Studies of Cider Apple Orchards in New York State." *Fruit Quarterly* 26, no. 3 (2018): 5–10.

Pollard, Oliver A. *Under the Blue Ledge: Nelson County, Virginia*. Richmond, VA: Dietz Press. 1997.

Powell, Katrina M. "Time to Leave." *Virginia Living*, November 22, 2010. www.virginialiving.com/culture/time-to-leave/.

Puckett, Anita, and Leslie Shelor Allen. *Rock Castle Gorge: Special History Study, Rocky Knob Recreation Area*. Prepared for the National Park Service, December 31, 2018.

Ragan, W. H. *Nomenclature of the Apple: A Catalogue of the Known Varieties Referred to in American Publications from 1804 to 1904*. Washington, DC: Government Printing Office, 1905.

Range, Willard. *A Century of Georgia Agriculture, 1850–1950*. Athens: University of Georgia Press, 1954.

———. "P. J. Berckmans: Georgia Horticulturist." *Georgia Review* 6, no. 2 (1952): 219–26.

Reynolds, Michael. "A History of Fruitland Nurseries, Augusta, Georgia and the Berckmans Family in America." *Magnolia* 18, no. 1 (Winter 2002–3): 1, 3–11.

Rice, James D. *Nature and History in the Potomac Country: From Hunter-Gatherers to the Age of Jefferson*. Baltimore: Johns Hopkins University Press, 2009.

Riggs, Brett High. "Removal Period Cherokee Households in Southwestern North Carolina: Material Perspectives on Ethnicity and Cultural Differentiation." PhD diss., University of Tennessee, 1999.

Rozema, Vicki Bell. "Coveted Lands: Agriculture, Timber, Mining, and Transportation in Cherokee Country before and after Removal." PhD diss., University of Tennessee, 2012.

Ryan, Michael. *Life in Rock Castle, Virginia in Their Own Words: A Blue Ridge Mountain History*. Blacksburg, VA: Castle on the Watch Publications, 2018.

Saunt, Claudio. *Unworthy Republic: The Dispossession of Native Americans and the Road to Indian Territory*. New York: W. W. Norton, 2020.

Seabrook, John. "Crunch." *New Yorker*, November 14, 2011.

Stempien, John A., and John Linstrom, eds. *The Liberty Hyde Bailey Gardener's Companion*. Ithaca, NY: Cornell University Press, 2019.

Summer, William. "The Character of the Pomologist." *Southern Agriculturist* 1 (January 1853): 17–18; reprinted in *Farmer and Planter* 2 (April 1860): 122. Page references are to the 1860 edition.

Taylor, William A. *The Fruit Industry*. US Department of Agriculture Division of Pomology, Bulletin No. 7, 1898.

Tukey, Harold B. *Dwarfed Fruit Trees for Orchard, Garden, and Home: With Special Reference to the Control of Tree Size and Fruiting in Commercial Orchards*. Ithaca, NY: Cornell University Press, 1979.

Upshall, W. H., ed. *History of Fruit Growing and Handling in United States of America and Canada, 1860–1972*. Kelowna, BC: Regatta City Press, 1976.

US Department of Agriculture. *Survey of Commercial Apple and Peach Orchards of Virginia, 1938*. Washington, DC: USDA, 1938.

Van Buren, Jarvis. "Fruit Culture at the South." *Farmer and Planter*, January 1850.

Walker, Susan Russ. "Of Lost Letters and Forgotten Fruit: Timothy Pickering, John Taliaferro, and the Mystery Apple of Monticello." Unpublished manuscript last modified February 29, 2020.

Waugh, F. A. *The American Apple Orchard: A Sketch of the Practice of Apple Growing in North America at the Beginning of the Twentieth Century*. New York: Orange Judd Company, 1911.

Wilson, Joseph S., and Olivia Messinger Carril. *The Bees in Your Backyard: A Guide to North America's Bees*. Princeton, NJ: Princeton University Press, 2016.

Wolf, Ray. "The Easter Freeze of April 2007: A Climatological Perspective and Assessment of Impacts and Services." In *NOAA/USDA Technical Report 2008-01*. Silver Spring, MD: National Weather Service, January 2008.

Woody, Robert H. "Cataloochee Homecoming." *South Atlantic Quarterly* 49, no. 1 (January 1950): 7–17.

Xu, Kenong. "The Apple Genome: A Delicious Promise." *New York Fruit Quarterly* 18, no. 4 (Winter 2010): 11–14.

Yao, Stephanie. "Researchers 'FasTrack' Plum Breeding." *Fruit Grower News*, April 29, 2011.

Yearbook of the United States Department of Agriculture, 1901. Washington, DC: Government Printing Office, 1902.

Yearbook of the United States Department of Agriculture, 1907. Washington, DC: Government Printing Office, 1908.

INDEX

Page numbers in italics refer to illustrations. Entries followed by an asterisk are apple varieties.